The Bruins in 25 Games

ALSO BY THE AUTHORS
AND FROM McFARLAND

*World Series '48: The Cleveland Indians
and Boston Braves in Six Games,*
by John G. Robertson and Carl T. Madden (2023)

*The Mustache Gang Battles
the Big Red Machine: The 1972 World Series,*
by John G. Robertson and Carl T. Madden (2022)

*Hockey's Wildest Season: The Changing of the Guard
in the NHL, 1969–1970,* by John G. Robertson (2021)

*Amazin' Upset: The Mets, the Orioles
and the 1969 World Series,* by John G. Robertson
and Carl T. Madden (2021)

*When the Heavyweight Title Mattered:
Five Championship Fights That Captivated the World,
1910–1971,* by John G. Robertson (2019)

*Too Many Men on the Ice: The 1978–1979 Boston Bruins and the Most
Famous Penalty in Hockey History,* by John G. Robertson (2018)

*The Games That Changed Baseball: Milestones in Major League
History,* by John G. Robertson and Andy Saunders (2016)

A's Bad as It Gets: Connie Mack's Pathetic Athletics of 1916,
by John G. Robertson and Andy Saunders (2014)

*The Babe Chases 60: That Fabulous 1927 Season, Home Run by
Home Run,* by John G. Robertson (1999; paperback 2014)

*Baseball's Greatest Controversies: Rhubarbs, Hoaxes, Blown
Calls, Ruthian Myths, Managers' Miscues and Front-Office
Flops,* by John G. Robertson (1995; paperback 2014)

The Bruins in 25 Games

*Boston's Most Unforgettable
Wins and Heartbreaking Losses*

JOHN G. ROBERTSON *and*
CARL T. MADDEN

McFarland & Company, Inc., Publishers
Jefferson, North Carolina

LIBRARY OF CONGRESS CATALOGUING-IN-PUBLICATION DATA

Names: Robertson, John G., 1964– author. | Madden, Carl T., author.
Title: The Bruins in 25 games : Boston's most unforgettable wins and heartbreaking losses / John G. Robertson and Carl T. Madden.
Other titles: Bruins in twenty-five games
Description: Jefferson, North Carolina : McFarland & Company, Inc., Publishers, 2023. | Includes bibliographical references and index.
Identifiers: LCCN 2022060935 | ISBN 9781476691039 (paperback : acid free paper) ∞
ISBN 9781476648989 (ebook)
Subjects: LCSH: Boston Bruins (Hockey team)—History.
Classification: LCC GV848.B6 R629 2023 | DDC 796.962/940974461—dc23/eng/20221222
LC record available at https://lccn.loc.gov/2022060935

BRITISH LIBRARY CATALOGUING DATA ARE AVAILABLE

ISBN (print) 978-1-4766-9103-9
ISBN (ebook) 978-1-4766-4898-9

© 2023 John G. Robertson and Carl T. Madden. All rights reserved

No part of this book may be reproduced or transmitted in any form or by any means, electronic or mechanical, including photocopying or recording, or by any information storage and retrieval system, without permission in writing from the publisher.

On the cover: Boston Bruins goaltender "Tiny" Thompson, circa 1930s (Alamy Historic Collection)

Printed in the United States of America

McFarland & Company, Inc., Publishers
 Box 611, Jefferson, North Carolina 28640
  www.mcfarlandpub.com

To the thousand or so players
who have proudly donned the uniform
of the Boston Bruins since the team's 1924 inception.
This salute obviously includes a long list of noteworthy stars,
the likes of Eddie Shore, Milt Schmidt, Johnny Bucyk,
Bobby Orr, Phil Esposito, Raymond Bourque and Patrice Bergeron.
It is also intended to applaud those lesser-known players
from A (George Abbott) to Z (Rick Zombo)
who ably filled roles, played their parts well,
and rightfully earned their places
in the grand tapestry of Boston Bruins hockey.
Without them, we have no book to write
and no stories to tell.

Acknowledgments

The authors gratefully acknowledge the following individuals for their assistance in helping this book reach fruition:

- Mr. Bob Cullum, the curator of the wonderful Leslie Jones Collection of photographs held by the Boston Public Library, for generously allowing us access to these images.
- Lise Vézeau of the Library and Archives of Canada and Jacqueline Vincent of its subsidiary, The Brechin Group, for their assistance in providing additional photos from the archives of *Weekend Magazine*.

Table of Contents

Acknowledgments vi

Preface: Which Games to Include or Exclude 1

Authors' Note 4

1. March 29, 1929: Bruins Capture Their First Stanley Cup — 5
2. March 14, 1933: Bruins Defeat Chicago by Forfeit — 13
3. December 12, 1933: The Eddie Shore–Ace Bailey Incident — 18
4. March 26, 1936: Eddie Shore Loses Cool; Bruins Lose Playoff Series — 28
5. April 2, 1939: Mel Hill Scores His Third Overtime Goal in One Series — 38
6. March 16, 1944: Bruins Score Nine Times—But Lose — 48
7. January 21, 1945: Bruins Rout Rangers, 14–3 — 55
8. March 18, 1952: Bobby Bauer Scores in One-Game Comeback — 63
9. April 8, 1952: The Rocket's Greatest Goal Sinks the Bruins — 70
10. January 18, 1964: The Ultimate Outlier—Boston 11, Toronto 0 — 80
11. April 2, 1969: Playoff Brawl and Blowout—Boston 10, Toronto 0 — 88
12. April 24, 1969: Bruins Fall to Habs in De Facto Cup Final — 96
13. April 26, 1970: The Afternoon the Bruins Really Won the 1970 Cup — 107

14.	March 11, 1971: Phil Esposito Sets Single-Season Scoring Record	115
15.	February 23, 1972: Bruins Rally from Five Goals Down to Defeat Seals	121
16.	April 30, 1972: The One That Nearly Got Away	127
17.	December 30, 1973: Chris Oddleifson's Four-Goal Game	136
18.	October 7, 1976: Rick Middleton's Debut Hattrick	141
19.	December 23, 1979: Bruins Battle Ranger Fans	148
20.	February 26, 1981: Boston's Biggest Brawl	156
21.	May 8, 1988: Doughnut-Gate	164
22.	October 16, 1988: Cam Neely's Seven-Point Game	170
23.	April 11, 1990: Four Goals in Third Period to Salvage Playoff Series	176
24.	April 10, 2010: Bruins Score Three Shorthanded Goals on One Penalty	184
25.	May 13, 2013: Bruins Erase a 4–1 Deficit to Oust Maple Leafs	190
26.	Games That Just Missed the Cut	198
27.	… And 12 Games That Are Best Forgotten	205
28.	A Brief History of the Boston Bruins, Decade by Decade	214

Chapter Notes	225
Bibliography	235
Index	237

Preface

Which Games to Include or Exclude

As of the time of this book's initial draft, the Boston Bruins—the first American-based team to be granted a franchise in the National Hockey League—had played a combined total of nearly 7,400 regular season and playoff games since debuting on December 1, 1924, at cozy Boston Arena versus their expansion brothers, the Montreal Maroons. Of course, the task of whittling that huge number of meaningful contests down to a manageable 25 for inclusion in this book took considerable research, reflection and thought. (Admittedly, personal biases were liberally applied too. In such an undertaking this pitfall can hardly be avoided.) Such a project inevitably leads readers to wonder why some famous Bruin games were excluded while other lesser-known ones somehow made the final cut. One might also wonder why Bruin losses are included among the chosen 25 games. Allow us to address these issues.

How can you possibly exclude May 10, 1970, and May 10, 1979, from the list of memorable Boston Bruin games?

That is a perfectly valid question for any knowledgeable Bruin fan to pose. It is certainly not due to the lack of star quality of either game. They were deliberately stroked off the list. Why?

It could be argued that the two most famous games in the long history of the Boston Bruins were played precisely nine years apart. The first one, Boston winning the Stanley Cup for the first time in 29 years on Bobby Orr's famous Mother's Day overtime goal, is perhaps the most glorious game of them all. The latter, a devastating, emotionally crushing defeat at the hands of the Montreal Canadiens in a Cup semifinal, is a sore spot that still upsets hardcore Bruin fans despite the passage of decades.

Let's drift back to the subject of why these two landmark games are conspicuously absent from this book. Their exclusion was for a very practical reason: One of the authors (John G. Robertson) previously wrote entire books that centered on both those games. They are covered in very great depth in *Hockey's Wildest Season: The Changing of the Guard in the NHL, 1969–1970* and *Too Many Men on the Ice: The 1978–1979 Boston Bruins and the Most Famous Penalty in Hockey History*. Both are available through the publisher of this book, McFarland.

Why did you include several Boston losses among the 25 games that were selected?

Just because a hockey game is memorable does not mean it had a desirable outcome to a certain fanbase. This book contains 19 chapters about games in which the Bruins emerged victorious and just six providing details about a Boston loss. We figure that is a fair ratio. Focusing entirely on Boston wins would paint an inaccurately rosy picture of the team's century-old history—a chronicle splattered with numerous famous and important games that did not end up in the Bruins' win column. To completely balance the book, the authors have also included a concluding chapter focused entirely of brief descriptions of 12 Boston losses. This "dirty dozen" would not likely merit inclusion in many histories of the Black and Gold—unless those reminiscences were cruelly penned by sadistic fans of the Bruins' longstanding rivals, particularly the Montreal Canadiens and Toronto Maple Leafs.

Why are obscure Bruin games included at the expense of more famous ones?

This is another fair question to ask. In perusing this book's table of contents, one will find a chapter about a Second World War–era 10–9 loss to the Detroit Red Wings; a triumphant one-game comeback by Bobby Bauer in 1952; and a wholly unexpected four-goal outburst by Chris Oddleifson in 1973, a player rarely recalled for his short stint as a Boston Bruin, but as a longtime Vancouver Canuck. Certainly, none of these three games would immediately jump off the page and grab the reader's attention anywhere as readily as more noteworthy candidates for inclusion. Yes, those obscure games were thoughtfully included

Equipment manager Vin Green attends to his duties at Boston Garden, circa 1931. Note the attractive, old-style bear logo. It adorned the team's jerseys from 1924 through 1932 (courtesy Boston Public Library, Leslie Jones Collection).

while more prominent games were pared from our list (for example, Game #7 versus Montreal in the 2011 playoffs and Boston's Stanley Cup–clinching victories of 1939, 1941, 1972 and 2011). Two of those four seasons have other games featured in full chapters rather than the championship finale. In many respects, the lesser-known games are quite telling about certain eras of Boston Bruins hockey and simply made for better stories—at least more so than some specific nights when the Bruins skated off the ice with Lord Stanley's silverware.

We are hopeful that you, dear readers, will final these tales about the Boston Bruins to be entertaining, enlightening, and perhaps even educational. That was our intention when we began this project in 2021. You will be the judge as to whether we succeeded.

Authors' Note

In writing this book we have diligently tried to achieve perfection regarding the spelling of players' names. This includes accents on letters not normally seen in English-language written accounts of games and NHL histories. In all likelihood we have failed to achieve 100 percent accuracy. Any omissions of accents, hyphens, and mid-name capitalizations are purely accidental.

The name of Chicago's NHL team is Blackhawks—written as one word, according to the deed of franchise awarded by the league in 1926. For many years, newspapers, periodicals and hockey historians wrote it as two words. (In fact, the two-word version appeared in the club's logo for quite a while.) However, for the sake of consistency, throughout this book we have used the correct one-word version—except for a few occasions when we directly quoted from a primary source where it was inaccurately written as "Black Hawks."

The names of the NHL's two divisions from 1926 through 1938 were American and Canadian. Some American newspapers preferred to use the terms American and International divisions in their accounts of games and in their league standings. This was done, presumably, because the now-defunct New York Americans and St. Louis Eagles both played in the Canadian Division. Certainly, it was geographically incorrect that New York- and Missouri-based teams were slotted into the NHL's Canadian Division. Yet it is indisputable that they were. There is no evidence that this division (that also featured the original Ottawa Senators, Montreal Maroons, Montreal Canadiens, and Toronto Maple Leafs) was ever officially known as anything but the Canadian Division. Accordingly, we have stuck with the term "Canadian Division" for this book.

Similarly, the two divisions the NHL split itself into from 1967 to 1974 were called East and West—not Eastern and Western, as appeared in print quite often. Again, we opted for the correct terminology.

1

March 29, 1929

Bruins Capture Their First Stanley Cup

March 29, 1929, was a red-letter day in the history of the Boston Bruins. The Stanley Cup—the silver chalice emblematic of professional hockey supremacy—came to Boston for the first time late that Friday. It arrived on the Bruins' train that had departed from New York City not long after the team had swept the defending Cup champion Rangers in a best-of three championship series.

Winning the coveted trophy was the culmination of nearly half a decade of toil for the Boston Bruins organization. Over that time, the Bruins became progressively better each season and reached the National Hockey League's lofty pinnacle in their fifth year of operations.

Boston was given the honor of being the first American-based franchise in the circuit, chosen ahead of applicants from New York, Philadelphia and Pittsburgh. Amateur hockey was already well established in the Hub, so the Bruins were stepping into a market with potential customers who were knowledgeable about the game. According to team lore, owner Charles Adams, a self-made Vermont grocery store magnate, became enamored by the NHL after watching a Montreal Canadiens home game—featuring the always exciting superstar Howie Morenz in action—and immediately sought to acquire a club for Boston. At the time, scandal-plagued amateur hockey in Boston had fallen into disrepute, so Adams figured professional hockey might be an appealing alternative. For the price of $15,000—about $250,000 in 2022 money—Adams got his wish on November 1, 1924, when the NHL granted him a franchise. Adams outfitted his club in brown and gold uniforms (the same color as the logo of his grocery chain). He wanted the team to have an animal-inspired nickname. After a public name-the-team contest failed to produce any suggestions to Adams' liking, he went along with "Bruins." It was a moniker suggested by his secretary who thought the brown hue in the team's jerseys matched the color of a bear's fur. Boston Bruins was also pleasantly alliterative.

The Bruins were one of two expansion teams that entered the NHL in the 1924–25 season, the other being the Montreal Maroons. The Maroons played in a sparkling new, spacious modern arena constructed especially for them—the Montreal Forum. On the other hand, the Bruins contested their home games at tiny Boston Arena. Plans were being made by Adams and others, however, for Boston's new NHL team to have a bigger and better home, but there was no immediate rush to build it.

Adams sagely hired Art Ross, a legendary figure in Canadian hockey circles, to be the club's coach and general manager. Even with someone possessing the hockey smarts of Ross, there was no way the Bruins would be immediately successful on the ice. In their first NHL season, the nascent club struggled to be competitive. They won just six of their 30 regular-season games in 1924–25 to finish firmly at the bottom of the six-team loop. (Two of those wins came in Boston's twenty-eighth and twenty-ninth matches of the campaign.) In one four-game stretch in December, the overmatched Bruins were outscored 33–6. Boston scored just 49 goals over the course of the short season—an average of 1.66 per game—while four different goaltenders surrendered 119 goals to opponents who seldom showed any mercy. Obviously, this was not a ratio for an NHL titlist or a Stanley Cup contender. Those feats were two separate entities in 1925. The history of the Stanley Cup can be confusing to modern-day fans. During the Bruins' first two years of existence, the Stanley Cup finals were contested between the champion of the Western Canada Hockey League (formerly called the Pacific Coast Hockey League) and the NHL and its forerunner (the National Hockey Association). An annual east-west battle for Lord Stanley's gift to hockey to conclude the season had been the case since 1911 when the Cup was first awarded to professional teams.

Things improved noticeably for the Bruins the following season. The NHL schedule increased to 36 games in 1925–26 to maintain its mathematical balance as the growing circuit added a seventh team, the Pittsburgh Pirates. Despite losing to Pittsburgh, 2–1, on Opening Night and having a dismal 4–12–3 record 19 games into the season, Boston rallied dramatically to finish a very respectable fourth in their second NHL campaign with a 17–15–4 record, just one spot—and one point—out of a playoff position. Somewhat irksome for Bruin fans was the team that finished in third place to gain the final NHL playoff berth was the expansion Pirates. (Boston's catastrophic 2–1 overtime loss in Pittsburgh in their penultimate game of 1925–26 was critical in derailing any postseason hopes.) Furthermore, Boston's 1924 expansion brothers, the Montreal Maroons, finished second, won the NHL championship by defeating Pittsburgh and Ottawa in the league's playoffs, and then captured the Stanley Cup in a final series versus the Victoria Cougars. That series went down in history as the last time a non–NHL team vied for Lord Stanley's chalice.

According to most hockey historians, the 1926–27 season is considered the first in the "modern era" of the NHL because the NHL took sole possession of the Stanley Cup. The league also welcomed the Chicago Blackhawks, Detroit Cougars, and New York Rangers to the fold, making it a 10-team loop split into two divisions. It also saw the emergence of the Boston Bruins as a club to be reckoned with. Art Ross had patiently created an excellent team, picking up suddenly unemployed players from the now-defunct Western League at bargain rates to augment his improving club. A fiery 24-year-old defenseman from the Edmonton Eskimos named Eddie Shore was Ross' most promising acquisition. The Bruins responded by finishing the season in second spot in the NHL's newly formed American Division, qualifying for the Stanley Cup playoffs for the first time.

In those 1927 playoffs, Boston quickly dispatched the Blackhawks and then the first-place Rangers, both in two-game, total-goals series. Suddenly, in their third year of operations, the Boston Bruins were competing in the Stanley Cup finals against the mighty Ottawa Senators. In a best-of-five series, dubbed the "World Series of Hockey" by sportswriters on both sides of the border, the Bruins were beaten but not disgraced. In four games they lost two and played two tie games that were each terminated due to bad ice conditions before a winner could be determined. Still, a scribe for the *Ottawa Citizen* was not impressed by the Boston club. He declared after the fourth game (won by Ottawa, 3–1, to clinch the Cup) that "the locals showed superiority in every department,"[1] Still, most fair-minded observers figured that Art Ross' team was certainly one to watch in the near future.

The Bruins continued their upward progress in 1927–28. They carried the momentum from the previous season to a first-place finish. That achievement got Boston a first-round bye in the playoffs, but the rest did them no good. In a two-game, total goals semifinal round versus the New York Rangers, the teams played to a 1–1 tie at Madison Square Garden in the opener. Three nights later, the Rangers shocked the Bruins 4–1 in the return match at Boston Arena, scoring three times in the third period to put the game—and series—out of reach. Bruin goaltender Hal Winker, who had been terrific in the regular season, looked bad on a couple of the goals. "The Bruins went to pieces,"[2] bluntly declared the *Ottawa Citizen*. Boston's lone goal came with just 30 seconds remaining in the game. It was the first of many disappointing playoff departures for favored Bruins teams. The Rangers proved their mettle and went on to win the Stanley Cup, thus becoming, in their second season of operations, the first American-based NHL team to win Lord Stanley's famous trophy. (The Seattle Metropolitans had done it as a Pacific Coast Hockey League team in 1917.)

The NHL unfurled a new playoff format for the 1928–29 season. It seems peculiar by today's standards: The two regular-season divisional champions would face each other in a best-of-five series with the winner earning a spot in the Stanley Cup finals. The purpose was to guarantee that one of the regular-season titans would be playing for the Cup. (In 1928 neither divisional champion had survived its semifinal playoff series.) The second- and third-place clubs would battle it out to provide an opponent.

As in 1927–28, the Bruins won the American Division title. The Montreal Canadiens had the best record in the Canadian loop, setting up the first of many springtime encounters between teams that would evolve into one of hockey's greatest rivalries. The Bruins had a new arena for their home games in 1928–29: Boston Garden, which was primarily built as a boxing venue. The team also had a new goaltender—Cecil (Tiny) Thompson. His nickname was supposed to be comical and temporary; standing 5'10", Thompson was the tallest player on one of his first amateur teams in Calgary. The moniker stuck with him throughout his career, however. Thompson was certainly a giant against Montreal, recording shutouts in Boston's pair of 1–0 home wins in the first two games. Boston won Game Three at the Forum, 3–2, rallying from two goals down, to sweep the Habs. John J. Hallahan declared, perhaps with a bit of hyperbole, in the *Boston Globe* that the Bruins' three-game sweep was a "shock to the hockey foundation of the Dominion of Canada."[3]

Interestingly, the Boston newspapers generally considered the Boston-Montreal series to have already decided the true NHL championship, and that the Stanley Cup finals were merely a secondary sideshow. In fact, Hallahan wrote that the Bruins' series versus New York provided them with little to gain. Be that as it may, the Bruins had five days off to wait to see whom their opponents would be in the Cup series. As in the previous year, the New York Rangers advanced to the finals, this time advancing past their inter-city rivals the New York Americans, and the Toronto Maple Leafs.

The Stanley Cup finals would be a best-of-three affair starting with the opener in Boston Garden on Thursday, March 28. Game Two

1. March 29, 1929

would be played in Madison Square Garden the next night. If a third game was necessary, the two teams would trek back to Boston for a winner-take-all encounter.

Tiny Thompson recorded his third shutout in four playoff games as Boston took Game One by a 2–0 count. (His best save may have been when he thwarted his brother, Paul Thompson, a Ranger forward who was three years his junior.) Both Boston goals occurred in the second period. Aubrey (Dit) Clapper beat Ranger goalie John Ross Roach with a backhander to break the 0–0 deadlock. "A shower of paper came down from the gallery boys,"[4] declared John J. Hallahan in the next day's *Boston Globe*. Dutch Gainor got the second Boston goal. His first shot at Roach was blocked by New York defenseman Taffy Abel. Gainor swiftly collected the rebound and beat the surprised Roach. Again, streamers and confetti liberally poured from the upper reaches of Boston Garden.

All in all, Hallahan figured the Bruins were full value for their win. "The Bruins outplayed the New York team with a better exhibition of all-around play than was shown against the Canadiens." Hallahan conveniently provided an excuse for the visitors. "In justice to the Rangers," the scribe noted, "it must be admitted that they were very weary after their four playoff games leading to last night's contest."[5]

The Bruins and several thousand of their optimistic supporters headed to Gotham for Game Two the next night. Many of the fans came prepared to wager heavily on their favorite team. One scribe noted that the local bookmakers were a busy bunch collecting cash from the optimistic Boston tourists.

Game Two was a thriller, but it took a while for the scoreboard operator to get into the action. More than half the game had elapsed before Boston assumed a 1–0 lead in the second period. It came on a goal by Harry Oliver at 14:01. The Boston right winger took a pass from Eddie Shore and advanced along the right boards into the New York zone. Oliver was jostled by Ranger defensemen Taffy Abel and Sparky Vail, but he was still able to get an off-balance shot on goal. It whizzed past goaltender Roach into the New York net. The Boston supporters at Madison Square Garden roared their approval. They could smell the Stanley Cup.

There was no further scoring in the second period. The game was dominated by fine goaltending by both Roach and Thompson and strong defensive play by both clubs. It appeared that Oliver's goal may stand up as the only marker the Bruins would need on the night.

That was not to be the case as the Rangers found an equalizer. It was scored by Butch Keeling in the third period on a scrambly play. Keeling fired a shot from the blue line that eluded goaltender Tiny Thompson at 6:48. This time it was the Ranger fans who gleefully dumped baskets of paper onto their home ice to celebrate a crucial score.

Momentum discernably shifted to the home team, but the score remained level at 1–1. At one critical point, Eddie Shore put his body on the line and made a fine defensive play to break up a New York rush, sliding in front of a loose puck to break up a threatening Ranger attack. *Boston Globe* reporter John J. Hallahan described the desperate play as "a lifesaver"[6] for the visitors.

With overtime looming, the winning Boston goal came from a Toronto dentist. Bill Carson—whom hockey writers across North America routinely called "Dr. Bill Carson" out of respect for his offseason dental profession—was the hero for the Bruins. It came during a two-on-two rush. Two Ranger defenseman converged on Harry Oliver just inside their blue line. Oliver deftly fed a pass to Carson who let fly with what Hallahan described as "a wicked drive."[7] It cleanly beat Roach, sailing past his hip into the Rangers' net. Boston had regained the lead, 2–1, There was just 1:58 remining in the third period.

In an interview nearly half a century later, Harry Oliver, well into his seventies, recalled the Bruins' key goal in Game Two and his part in it. "I was going down the right side," he said. "I saw Bill Carson loose on the left side. I passed him the puck … and wingo! It was in [the net]." Oliver also remembered the casual attitude of the players about it. "Today they make a big fuss about a goal, hugging each other, jumping up and down" he noted. "We gave a tap on the shoulder … nice going … and that was all."[8]

Pulling the goaltender for a sixth attacker was unheard of at the time, but Rangers coach Lester Patrick did the next best thing: He put five forwards on the ice in an attempt to tie the game. They failed to make a dent in the Boston defense. In fact, the best scoring chance in the game's dying moments went to Boston's Harry Oliver who was stopped by Roach. The final bell rang with Boston still in front, 2–1. The Stanley Cup was theirs.

The delightful and triumphant news of the milestone victory was featured prominently on the front page of the March 30 *Boston Globe*. It ran beneath a cartoon of a bear holding a hockey stick, wearing a crown, and sitting atop a globe. The accompanying caption read, "Well, what do you think about that?"[9]

Correspondent Hallahan gushed with glee in reporting the happy story which bore a March 29 dateline from New York City. He wrote,

> The Boston Bruins gained undisputed claim to the world hockey title tonight by beating the New York Rangers 2 to 1 in the second and final game of the Stanley Cup series, at Madison Square Garden.

1. March 29, 1929

As in all previous games, the Bruins were too smart for the Rangers, whom they have now beaten seven games out of eight. Only the second game of the regular season went to the Rangers.[10]

An unnamed reporter for Canadian Press agreed with Hallahan's assessment of the deciding game. He wrote, "Boston held a clear margin in territorial play." Seemingly forgetting that the game was tied 1–1

Posing with his brother Paul, Cecil (Tiny) Thompson (left) was actually a large man for his era, especially among NHL goalies. Thoroughly dependable, he assumed Boston's goaltending duties in 1928 and missed just five games over the next decade. Thompson held the club record for wins (252) for more than 80 years until Tuukka Rask surpassed it. He still possesses Boston's career shutout mark (74) by a substantial margin (courtesy Boston Public Library, Leslie Jones Collection).

with just two minutes to play in the third period, the scribe curiously claimed, "The Bruins won tonight almost as decisively as they won in the Hub [in Game One]."[11]

Harry Oliver was the recipient of the majority of Hallahan's plaudits. "The 155-pound right wing starred tonight," the *Globe*'s reporter declared. "He had several chances, and, in the second period, with the path filled with obstacles, he counted. In the final period, Harry sent a pass to Dr. Bill Carson for the winning goal."[12] The CP story made a point of mentioning that Carson was "a product of the Ontario Hockey Association."[13] Carson would spend much of his later life in Parry Sound, Ontario where another Boston Stanley Cup hero would be born in 1948.

Oliver recalled having a low-key team dinner the following night where the Boston players each got a surprise $500 bonus from the club. (They also got about $1,000 in Stanley Cup money from the NHL.) The Bruins then dispersed to their offseason homes that were located as far away as Calgary in the west and Ottawa in the east; the Rangers immediately embarked on a tour of western Canada to exploit their fame and pocket a few extra dollars as Stanley Cup runners-up. Boston supporters with plenty of disposable income and deep pockets made money in a more traditional manner among sports followers. It was estimated by one journalist that $50,000 in gambling winnings had left Grand Central Station with them after the Bruins' triumph at Madison Square Garden in Game Two.

Coach Art Ross credited togetherness for the Bruins' first Cup victory. "There has never been a professional team where there has been less bickering, fewer jealousies, and better spirit," he claimed. "All season long this has been the case."[14]

Since beginning NHL play in 1924, giddy Bruin fans had waited five years to see the Stanley Cup reside in Boston for the first time. Despite the Bruins generally having excellent teams throughout most of the 1930s, their supporters would have to patiently wait twice as long to see a repeat performance from their hockey heroes.

Scoring Summary

First Period
- No scoring

Second Period
- 14:01 BOS Harry Oliver (unassisted)

Third Period
- 6:48 NYR Butch Keeling (unassisted)
- 18:02 BOS Bill Carson (assist: Harry Oliver)

2

March 14, 1933
Bruins Defeat Chicago by Forfeit

"Boston Bruins 1, Chicago Blackhawks 0. That is the official score of the National Hockey League game at Boston Garden last night," reported the *Boston Globe* in its March 15, 1933, morning edition.

But it was not as simple as that. The story, written by a scribe who did not merit a byline, continued, "The score on the actual play with both teams in action was Bruins 3, Blackhawks 2. And with only the home team on the ice, Boston 4 Chicago 2. Sounds rather weird, and so it is, quite in keeping with the entire game."[1]

It all made perfect sense when one realized the unusual circumstances accompanying Boston's late-season victory over their divisional rivals. *The Globe* explained, "Boston won by forfeit in the decision of William Stewart, the referee, because the Blackhawks refused to continue play after their protest of a goal scored by the Bruins in the fourth minute of the overtime period [was rejected]."[2] The Canadian Press called it "one of the wildest NHL games ever staged."[3] It was undeniably that.

In the long history of the NHL, there have been just a handful of forfeits. In the league's very first season, in 1917–18, one of the four charter teams—the Montreal Wanderers—suffered the huge misfortune of having their home arena burn to the ground after playing just four games. While they pondered their limited options, they forfeited two games. Eventually the homeless Wanderers withdrew from the NHL, leaving the nascent league to struggle through its first campaign with just three teams still operating.

The next NHL forfeits were economically motivated by disenchanted players. During the 1925 Stanley Cup playoffs, the first-place Hamilton Tigers forfeited an entire postseason series. The players were irked that their salaries had not been raised that season even though the league's schedule had increased substantially from 24 to 30 games—a jump of 25 percent. Hamilton simply refused to play the Montreal Canadiens in the NHL championship series unless their financial gripes were addressed. Their complaints were ignored. NHL president Frank Calder, a no-nonsense type of leader to be sure, dissolved the Hamilton franchise! It re-emerged in New York City in 1925–26 as the New York Americans, the second American-based team in the league.

The Hamilton forfeits were the most recent before the Chicago-Boston game of March 14, 1933. Not only was the game awarded to the Bruins, but there was also a remarkable fight between referee Bill Stewart and Chicago coach Tommy Gorman at the visitors' bench.

The Blackhawks were a desperate team that night in Boston. They were likely in a foul mood going into the overtime period when the fireworks started as they had squandered a two-goal advantage late in regulation time. Chicago was a last-place club as the 1932–33 season wound down. They had not been mathematically eliminated from the postseason, but they pretty much needed to run the table if they were to

Bill Stewart had a varied and somewhat checkered career in major professional sports. He went from being an NHL referee, to coaching the Chicago Blackhawks to the 1938 Stanley Cup, and then back to refereeing again. In the summer months, Stewart was employed as a Major League Baseball umpire in the National League for many years (courtesy Boston Public Library, Leslie Jones Collection).

maintain any hope of qualifying for the Stanley Cup playoffs. A perceived bad decision by a goal judge was the catalyst for the forfeit.

Despite having a crippled roster due to injuries on this night at Boston Garden, the Blackhawks had played the favored Bruins well, holding a 2–0 lead deep into the third period based on goals by Bill MacKenzie and Johnny Gottselig. Boston's Eddie Shore then staged a one-man comeback for the home team, scoring one goal at 14:49 and another with just two seconds left on the clock to force overtime. (Boston coach Art Ross had lifted goaltender Tiny Thompson for a sixth attacker, a strategy that he had invented.) "Eddie saved the Bruins from defeat,"[4] the *Globe* accurately noted. The Bruins smelled blood and decided on an all-out offensive approach for the overtime period.

"The amazing rumpus started when the Bruins went ahead after three minutes of overtime play," said a Canadian Press report. Again, Eddie Shore propelled the Boston attack. Shore drove the puck at the Chicago goalie at which point every Bruin on the ice swarmed near the net. "Every [Boston] player was slashing at the puck. Marty Barry drove [it], and it appeared to go over the line."[5] The goal light flashed.

The Blackhawks begged to differ with the reporter's opinion. "As soon as the red light went on, all the Blackhawks rushed behind their net to protest to goal umpire Louis Revcroft,"[6] the CP report continued. Defenseman Johnny Gottselig rammed his stick through the protective netting, angrily poking at the minor official.

Regular-season overtimes in those days were not sudden death; a full ten-minute period was required to be played regardless of how many goals were scored, so the game was supposed to continue. However. Chicago coach Tommy Gorman believed the Bruins' goal was a dubious one at best. He thought the red light had gone on before Barry had even made contact with the puck. He then did something unseemly. When Stewart skated by the Chicago bench, Gorman, in a brazen act, impulsively grabbed Stewart by his sweater to debate the issue. Punches were thrown—although who let loose with the first haymaker was subject to debate. Gorman insisted to the press that Stewart had punched him first. *The Boston Globe* saw it differently, declaring that it was Gorman who began the discreditable punch-up. The newspaper further noted, "Only the strength of [Boston's] Alex Smith ... kept Stewart from climbing over the boards."[7]

With the assistance of Boston police officers, Stewart then banished Gorman to the Chicago dressing room for the remainder of the evening's activities. Gorman responded by telling his players to leave the bench and join him in exile. Judging by his body language, goaltender Charlie Gardiner did not wish to comply with such an odd order, but peer pressure apparently coaxed him off the ice with his teammates. Stewart then escalated matters. Going beyond the NHL rule book, the referee restarted the game without the Blackhawks present. Stewart dropped the puck at center ice. Two Bruins, Eddie Shore and Art Chapman, leisurely advanced it across the Chicago blue line. After exchanging a few passes for the sake of showmanship, Chapman fired the puck into the gaping net, making the score, apparently, 4–2 for Boston.

With the Blackhawks showing no interest in returning to complete the overtime period, Stewart did not prolong the fiasco. He properly forfeited the game to Boston. The *Globe* writer declared that the strange contest had been one of the season's most exciting. Thus, "It was most unfortunate that the game should have had such an ending."[8] The win elevated the Bruins into a first-place tie with Detroit in the NHL's highly competitive American Division. On the other hand, Chicago's forfeit loss sealed the Blackhawks' fate: Chicago would miss the playoffs in 1933.

Referee Stewart would not comment to reporters on the forfeit or his sordid physical tussle with Gorman, explaining that he would be filing a report with NHL president Frank Calder to formally state his observations about what had occurred. It was noted that the NHL's bylaws featured a stiff penalty if a team forfeited a league game: The substantial fine was $1,000.

According to NHL rules, a forfeited game is recorded as a 1–0 victory for the non-offending team. To this day, the result of the March 14, 1933, Chicago-Boston game causes occasional confusion. The question marks are somewhat understandable because this was the first NHL game ever to be forfeited after it had started. Some statisticians have fully followed the letter of the law, maintaining that the 1–0 score is the correct one, wiping out the individual scoring statistics for both teams, with no Bruin getting credit for the score. The *Boston Globe* certainly assumed that would be the case, opining that it was a shame that Eddie Shore's two third-period goals would have to be expunged from the league's official records.

However, the NHL (and the website Hockey-reference.com) lists the game as a 3–2 Boston win, ignoring the superfluous goal scored by Art Chapman when no opposition was on the ice to confront the Bruins. (Presumably, the logic is that the players—especially the Boston players—should not be penalized for the actions of their opponents.) Referee Stewart's maverick decision to restart the game while the Blackhawks were steaming in the visitors' dressing room did not follow the sport's protocols. Play in a hockey game cannot begin or resume unless both teams have a minimum of four players on the ice. The Blackhawks, of course, had zero.

In all the years since 1933, only one other NHL game has been started and then forfeited. That was the infamous "Richard Riot" game at the Montreal Forum on March 17, 1955, when violence broke out within the arena and spread to the streets. With public safety imperiled, NHL president Clarence Campbell, on the advice of Montreal police, stopped play after the first period with Detroit holding a 4–1 lead over the Canadiens. Those five goals were counted in the league stats and remain there today.

In a strange turn of events, referee Bill Stewart would temporarily put away his whistle and, five years later, became the coach of the Chicago Blackhawks for the 1937–38 season! The Hawks only won 14 regular-season games, but it was good enough to earn the team a playoff berth. In one of the most surprising playoff campaigns in NHL history, Stewart led the unfashionable Blackhawks to the Stanley Cup that spring, winning three postseason series, all of them upsets. A native of Fitchburg, Massachusetts, Stewart thus became the first American-born coach to guide a team to a Stanley Cup. In the boisterous Cup celebrations, Blackhawks management heaped tremendous praise on Stewart for his wholly unexpected achievement. The support turned out to be fleeting, however. Stewart was fired 21 games into the following season when the Blackhawks underperformed. Stewart was reinstated as an NHL referee in 1939 and would remain on the league's staff of officials until 1941.

Stewart was also an umpire in Major League Baseball. A onetime minor-league prospect, Stewart was employed by the National League from 1933 to 1954. He is most famous in that capacity for making one of the most controversial calls in World Series history during the 1948 Fall Classic. Late in Game One, Stewart was perhaps the only person at packed Braves Field who failed to see that Cleveland pitcher Bob Feller had picked off Boston's Phil Masi at second base. Masi scored the game's only run moments later.

Scoring Summary

First Period
- 6:26 CHI Bill MacKenzie (assist: Roger Jenkins)

Second Period
- No scoring

Third Period
- 5:53 CHI Johnny Gottselig (assist: Bill MacKenzie)
- 14:49 BOS Eddie Shore (unassisted)
- 19:58 BOS Eddie Shore (assists: Marty Barry, Dit Clapper)

Overtime
- 3:11 BOS Marty Barry (assists: Dit Clapper, Red Beattie)

3

December 12, 1933

The Eddie Shore–Ace Bailey Incident

The movement to remove violence from hockey is not new. Reformers have forever been asking for fighting and rough play to be abolished from the sport. Although the voices have been growing steadily louder in the past half century, the entire crusade to clean up hockey began with the events of Tuesday, December 12, 1933. That night a National Hockey League game at Boston Garden got out of hand. A visiting player in the prime of his career nearly died.

The Boston Bruins-Toronto Maple Leafs rivalry was among the NHL's greatest during the 1930s. Both teams were loaded with stars and usually could be found near the top of their respective divisions. The two clubs had engaged in a titanic, best-of-five playoff series the previous spring which was decided, in Toronto's favor, on Ken Doraty's tally in the sixth overtime of the fifth game. When the 1933–34 season opened, the Bruins uncharacteristically slumped, losing their first three games. By mid–December Boston was reposing near the cellar of the American Division and was clearly in trouble. Eddie Shore, the Bruins' rugged defenseman, believed his team was playing too passively. On December 12, Shore informed Boston's sports journalists that he would no longer refrain from engaging in rough play. That statement would haunt Shore for the rest of his life.

Shore was a late bloomer a far as hockey was concerned. The son of a Saskatchewan rancher, he never thought much about the sport as a youth. According to one tale about Shore, his attitude changed abruptly when an older brother, Aubrey, began to question his younger sibling's toughness. Eddie responded by joining the hockey team at the school they both attended: Manitoba Agricultural College. Aubrey was already on the squad. With almost zero experience, Eddie Shore won a spot on the team and got a place in the lineup for its final three games of the season. It was the beginning of a remarkable, albeit checkered, hockey career for the eventual Hall-of-Famer.

3. December 12, 1933

The Toronto Maple Leafs were the Bruins' opponents that Tuesday night at Boston Garden. They had begun the 1933–34 NHL season well, having lost just twice in 12 games. Both teams behaved as if the game were a war. J.W. Mooney of the *Boston Post* described the contest as the most vicious ever played in that city. Odie Cleghorn, a referee who had a reputation of being overly lenient, was in charge of the game. In the two-official system commonly used by the NHL at the time, he was accompanied by linesman Eusebe Daigneault.

Despite a rash of dirty checks and slashes by both clubs, Cleghorn whistled just one penalty in the first period. "With only one penalty called when a dozen were warranted," wrote Mooney, "the game completely got out of the grip of the referee. The players started to take things into their own hands."[1]

With the score tied 1–1 and seven minutes left in the second period, Toronto's Red Horner boarded the volatile Eddie Shore. When he realized that no penalty to Horner was forthcoming, Shore became incensed. In an interview decades later, Horner described what happened:

> Shore was having a frustrating night. He was playing great, but it wasn't getting the Bruins anywhere. They couldn't score on us. Dick Irvin sent out King Clancy, me, and Ace Bailey to kill off the penalties. Bailey was [an] expert stickhandler. He ragged the puck for a while. Eventually, Shore got the puck and made a rush deep into our end. Shore came down my side. I gave him a very good hip check.[2]

As play moved back into the Boston end, Shore, dazed by the hit and searching for revenge, skated aggressively towards Toronto's Irvine (Ace) Bailey, perhaps thinking that he was charging toward Horner—or just to take out a random Maple Leaf player. Only Shore will ever know the truth. As he skated toward his defensive position on the Boston blue line, Shore deliberately tripped Bailey from behind. Bailey was one of Toronto's talented offensive stars. As a rookie, he had surprisingly led a poor Maple Leafs team in scoring in 1926–27. By his third NHL season, 1928–29, Bailey topped the entire league in scoring. Upon impact, the unsuspecting Bailey awkwardly toppled over backwards. His head slammed heavily against the Boston Garden ice surface. "Bailey fell with a sickening thud,"[3] wrote Lou Marsh in the next day's edition of the *Toronto Star*. Over his long career covering the Maple Leafs, legendary broadcaster Foster Hewitt too immediately recalled the crack of Bailey's skull slamming onto the Boston Garden ice whenever he was asked about the infamous incident. Horner continued,

[Shore] wanted to get even for the check I'd just put on him. He thought Bailey was me. He charged into Bailey on an angle. He hit Bailey and flipped him in the air, just like a rag doll. Bailey landed on his head just a few feet from where I was standing. Bailey hit the ice and he went into some kind of convulsion. I thought, "That's the end of Ace!"[4]

Bailey lost consciousness and began bleeding heavily from a head wound. Horner was both infuriated and sickened by the sight of his injured teammate—and intended to promptly do something about it. "Shore skated away in a very nonchalant fashion," he recollected. "I wasn't going to let him get away with that, so I went after him."[5]

Horner immediately retaliated. In a brazen tit-for-tat act of malice, Horner evened the score in mayhem by blindsiding Shore with a sudden right-handed punch to the jaw, knocking him to the ice unconscious. Blood streamed from a three-inch gash on Shore's head that eventually required seven stitches to close. Interestingly, Horner got the worst of the penalties from referee Odie Cleghorn. It did not really matter much, but along with a match penalty, Horner was also handed a game misconduct. Shore received a match penalty only.

Predictably, both teams' benches cleared and a melee erupted, but no other penalties were called. Even Toronto general manager Conn Smythe became involved in a scrap, tossing a few punches at a fan named Leonard Kenworthy who loudly accused Bailey of faking his injury! Smythe struck the man solidly in the mouth with a haymaker and was later arrested on an assault charge. The following day, Smythe was presented with an arrest warrant by two special police agents while having lunch at the University Club. Smythe avoided a criminal record by agreeing to pay for Kenworthy's dental expenses.

Despite the peripheral goings-on, the attention of everyone in Boston Garden was soon focused on the 30-year-old Bailey who was sprawled grotesquely on the ice. A doctor in attendance was dispatched to the playing surface to take a look at the fallen Maple Leaf. The physician diagnosed a five-inch skull fracture extending from the back of Bailey's forehead. Both Bailey and Shore had to be carried off the ice by teammates.

When Shore was revived, he headed to the visitors' dressing room to apologize to Bailey who too had regained his senses. With a straight face Shore told Bailey, "I'm awfully sorry, Ace. I didn't mean to hurt you, only to body check you."[6] Reputedly, Bailey generously told Shore what had happened between them was just part of hockey. Later, while being interviewed by a police lieutenant, Shore came up with a highly fanciful version of what had happened: Shore claimed he was merely skating at high speed with his head down to get out of the Toronto zone to avoid an offside situation. He told the policeman that he did not see Bailey until it was too late to avoid a heavy collision. Few people gave that tale much credence. Even fewer people today remember that Toronto won the game that night rather handily, 4–1, with Hec Kilrea scoring twice for the visiting victors.

Not long afterward, however, Bailey drifted out of consciousness again. He was initially taken to nearby Audubon Hospital to recuperate. The next day's *Boston Globe* reported that both its office and the hospital were being deluged with telephone calls from well-wishers from far afield inquiring about the hockey player's health.

The violence at Boston Garden got solidly negative reviews in the press. In his coverage of the game for the *Boston Globe*, Melville K. Webb acerbically wrote in a front-page article,

> Thirteen thousand fans jammed into the Garden last night to see the long-awaited game between the Bruins and the Toronto Maple Leafs. They witnessed not only the most desperate hockey battle of the winter, but also some sideshows which ordinarily have no place in a regulation contest between two National Hockey League teams.[7]

Initially, the prognosis for the fallen Maple Leaf was quite good. The first Canadian Press report about the incident stated that Bailey was in serious but not dangerous condition. Bailey was alert and able to communicate normally. Shore was not allowed to visit Bailey, but Boston coach Art Ross could and did. Bailey reiterated to Ross that he held no animus toward Shore. The same could not be said about Conn Smythe. The December 15 edition of the *Boston Globe* noted, "Smythe, still very bitter about Tuesday's episode … holds his lifelong enemy, Art Ross, to blame."[8] Eddie Shore did not suffer any lasting cranial damage from the blow he absorbed, but he was reputedly still a bit dizzy two days after Horner had decked the Bruin with his sucker punch.

Not long afterward, however, the situation turned quite serious. Bailey began to fall in and out of consciousness. The impact of his unprotected head striking the ice had caused a cerebral hemorrhage. His brain was swelling. Bailey's wife was summoned from Toronto. The reason was grimly obvious: Her husband was not expected to live. Newspapers across the continent prepared to report on the NHL's first fatality in the league's seventeenth season of play. With a potential homicide charge looming, NHL president Frank Calder wisely ordered players on both teams—especially the Maple Leafs—to stop publicly discussing their views about the incident.

Passions were naturally running high. Conn Smythe told reporters that the Leafs might forfeit all future games versus Boston if Shore was allowed to continue his pro hockey career. Bailey's father angrily headed to Boston, armed with a handgun, aiming to take personal revenge on Shore. He was intercepted in the bar at the Maple Leafs' hotel and disarmed. (Boston police seized the firearm and later mailed it back to him.) Local homicide detectives had begun to take statements from the two teams' players and other witnesses in anticipation of laying a manslaughter charge against Shore if Bailey succumbed to his head injury. Victor O. Jones eloquently wrote a piece for the *Boston Globe* that began, "All the glamour which has characterized big league hockey under the bright lights and roaring crowds of the Garden evaporated yesterday when the scene of the action shifted into dark and pungent police courts and the white and sterilizing quiet of a death-emburdened [sic] hospital."[9]

"The whole town, the whole province, the whole country is today pulling for Ace Bailey," penned Lou Marsh in the *Toronto Star*, declaring that a hockey player's "'courageous fight' [had] roused the Canadian sporting world as no other tragedy."[10] Indeed, a special prayer service for Bailey was held at a Montreal church. It was well attended.

Fortunately for Bailey, one of America's leading brain surgeons, Donald Munro, was employed at Boston's City Hospital. Bailey was transported there. Munro twice performed delicate cranial surgery on Boston's most famous hospital patient. Although Bailey remained on the critical list for several days, and with Dr. Munro himself less than fully optimistic about the fallen player's chances to pull through, in the end the operations proved to be successful. By December 23 the press happily reported that Bailey was fully alert in his hospital bed and eating a regular diet. Still, Bailey was not well enough to return to Canada until the middle of January.

Eighteen days into the new year, Conn Smythe greeted Bailey, his wife and three-year-old daughter Joanne as they disembarked from a train at Toronto's Union Station. Smythe personally drove them to their home in the city's Swansea neighborhood. Bailey's return was a major feel-good news story. "Yesterday afternoon," wrote the Toronto *Globe*'s Bert Perry on January 19, "following a short sleep, Ace took a medium-cold bath and then came downstairs to pose for more pictures [for news photographers]."[11] Hap Day, King Clancy and Buzz Boll all arrived shortly thereafter for a visit—as did a *Globe* news photographer. Those three teammates were all pleased by Bailey's improved appearance since they had last seen him at City Hospital in Boston.

Of course, discipline had to be meted out by the NHL. President Frank Calder suspended Eddie Shore indefinitely for his leading role in the incident almost immediately upon hearing the initial reports coming from Boston. Red Horner was also barred from playing in any league games until New Year's Day, which amounted to a six-game banishment. When Bailey's survival was a certainty, Shore's suspension was ended by Calder on January 28. He had missed 16 of Boston's games—a significant chunk considering the NHL season was a mere 48 games for its eight teams in 1933–34. Shore spent some of his unexpected mid-season vacation convalescing in Bermuda, far away from the questions of Canadian and American newspaper men.

The Toronto press suggested that Shore's undeniable status as a hockey celebrity likely saved him from an even more severe punishment compared to if it had been an unheralded player who upended Bailey. An editorial in the *Mail and Empire* opined, "What a different yelp would have gone up in some quarters if it had been some punk, palooka, or has-been that had pulled the Shore trick."[12]

Oddly, the Bruins embarked on a brief hot streak after Shore's suspension began, losing just one of six games. However, they collapsed shortly thereafter and ended the season uncharacteristically at the bottom of the heap in the NHL's highly competitive American Division with a disappointing 18–25–5 record. On the other hand, the Leafs eventually finished first in the Canadian Division, but they lost their opening-round playoff series to Detroit.

Predictably, Bailey's remarkable and unexpected recovery did not placate Toronto's hockey fans. Many called for Shore's permanent expulsion from the sport. Boston coach Art Ross scoffed at the idea. "We think it was an absolute accident,"[13] he said of the sordid incident, ignoring overwhelming evidence that it was not. Shore refused to give up hockey even though some writers asked him to voluntarily retire. Fans in other NHL cities clearly missed seeing Boston's free-wheeling defenseman in action, however. During his absence, chants of "We want Shore!" were frequently heard throughout the league's buildings whenever the shorthanded Bruins arrived to play a game. Interestingly, Shore began wearing a helmet after he returned to the Boston lineup. Such safety equipment was rare among NHLers in 1933–34. Hockey helmets would not be widely worn at the professional levels of hockey for decades.

Shore, of course, was demonized in Toronto for the rest of his career. However, blame was also liberally aimed at Horner, referee Cleghorn, and Frank Patrick, the NHL's commissioner of officials. Patrick publicly stated that he could not find fault with the on-ice officials that evening, a statement that surprised several journalists who had covered the December 12 game. One was correspondent Victor O. Jones of the *Boston Globe*. He wrote, "Criticism of Shore is equaled or surpassed by the firing upon the two referees [sic] who handled the match last Tuesday night."[14]

Bailey never participated in another hockey game, but his injury had a lasting effect on the NHL. A famous benefit game in his honor was played in Maple Leaf Gardens on February 14, 1934. Major League Baseball's first All-Star Game had been played in 1933. Inspired by that contest, Montreal sportswriter Walter Gilhooley came up with the idea of the Leafs vying against a team wholly comprised of notable NHL stars with its proceeds earmarked for Bailey and his family. On the evening of the exhibition game, Bailey was on the ice to greet each player and present him with a special jacket and a commemorative medal to mark the occasion. Among Toronto's opponents chosen to participate was Eddie Shore who embraced Bailey in an emotional scene. It was, in effect, the first All-Star Game in NHL history—and it is often listed as such in hockey reference books. The event was promoted in Toronto newspapers as "the greatest hockey match ever staged," but the hype was unnecessary. Tickets sold out in less than an hour and raised nearly $21,000 to help offset Bailey's significant medical and rehabilitation expenses and to set up a trust fund. The Bruins sent a check for $8,000—the full gate receipts from their December 19 home game versus the Montreal Maroons—to sweeten the pot. Shore's suspension certainly affected the gate that night. Boston Garden was only about half-filled to see the struggling Bruins play without their most noteworthy star.

The Leafs won the contest, 7–3. Defense was conspicuously absent. Unofficially, the teams combined for 93 shots on goal. Surprisingly, Eddie Shore's frequent rushes up the ice with the puck were greeted with enthusiastic cheering by the Toronto crowd. "They sure warmed my heart," Shore admitted afterward to a local reporter. "Please thank the Toronto fans for those cheers. I appreciate them more than any I have ever received."[15]

Another noteworthy occurrence concluded the pregame presentation ceremony. Conn Smythe made a remarkable announcement: As a tribute to Bailey, his #6 jersey was presented to him at center ice by Smythe who decreed it would never be worn again by any other Maple Leaf. It was the first time a professional athlete's uniform number in any sport in North America had been retired by his club. (Some 30 years later, Toronto rookie Ron Ellis so impressed Bailey with both his playing skills and his gentlemanly off-ice demeanor that Bailey insisted the team "unretire" his #6 so Ellis could have it. The Leafs complied. "This came completely out of left field," Ellis remembered. "I was flabbergasted. It was the greatest honor of my career. I will always be grateful to Ace Bailey."[16] As per Bailey's stipulation, #6 was re-retired by the Leafs when Ellis retired from hockey in 1981.)

Aghast at what had happened to their teammate that awful night in Boston, several Maple Leafs began wearing football-type helmets as a precaution against head injuries. However, the players generally found the unfamiliar headgear to be an uncomfortable annoyance and, within a short time, discarded them. When Bill Masterton of the Minnesota North Stars died of an injury similar to Bailey's in January 1968, an increasing number of NHL players gradually opted for the protective headgear. By the 1979–80 NHL season, helmets became mandatory for all rookies entering the league. Players whose NHL careers began prior to October 1979 retained the option of going helmetless. Craig MacTavish, who retired following the 1996–97 season, was the last NHLer to fall under the league's grandfather rule and chose to play without a protective helmet.

His playing career having been terminated in an instant, Bailey asked the NHL to hire him as a linesman, but the league turned down his request. Bailey then pursued another avenue and turned his interest in hockey to coaching. He did well in that capacity. At the University of Toronto, Bailey led the Varsity Blues to three Canadian national championships in a decade-long career that was interrupted by the Second World War.

Bailey was not forgotten by Toronto management. Beginning in 1938 he was employed as a penalty timekeeper at Maple Leaf Gardens. His tenure in that position lasted until 1984 when he was 81 years old. Six years later, in a 1990 interview, Bailey told Milt Dunnell of the *Toronto Star* that he still followed the NHL closely and watched many games on television. He found the violent aspects of the professional sport off-putting, however. "Sometimes I wonder if these guys are getting paid to play hockey or fight," he noted. "Maybe the owners think they need these brawls to fill their buildings, but I don't think they do."[17]

In 1964, Bailey seemingly cheated death for a second time. This time there was a comical aspect to it. It was widely reported in the Toronto area that Bailey had suddenly died of a heart attack after being involved in a minor traffic mishap. Based on that unsubstantiated news, more than a few people were surprised to see Bailey arrive at Maple Leaf Gardens for a Montreal-Toronto game, apparently in excellent health, and occupy his usual timekeeper's spot. It turned out the misinformation was caused because a longtime Toronto Parks employee named Harold Baillie (who was known to his co-workers as "Ace") was the man who had suddenly died of cardiac arrest—not the famed ex-hockey player. The Leafs had not properly confirmed Bailey's death and had

An on-the-mend Irvine (Ace) Bailey poses with his wife for a news photograph probably taken in January 1934. Bailey's life had tenuously hung by a thread after he suffered a major head injury in a game in Boston. His hockey career was over, but Bailey remained part of the Toronto organization for decades as a penalty timekeeper at Maple Leaf Gardens (courtesy Boston Public Library, Leslie Jones Collection).

planned a pregame posthumous tribute to honor Bailey. It was happily scrapped, of course, when the truth about Bailey's alleged demise was learned.

Eddie Shore continued his fierce play in the NHL until 1940 when advancing age forced him out of the league. He continued to play in the minors for a while, finally hanging up his skates in his early forties. (Shore's post-playing career as one of minor-professional hockey's most terrifying coaches and parsimonious owners is the stuff of legend.) Before Doug Harvey entered the NHL in the late 1940s, Shore was unquestionably the best defenseman in the league's history. Shore passed away on March 16, 1985, at the age of 82. Two nights later, the Bruins honored Shore with a moment of silence before their game at Boston Garden against the Quebec Nordiques.

Bailey died on April 7, 1992, at the age of 88. He had outlived almost every player who took part in that vicious game in Boston when his life had hung by a thread. Red Horner, the Leaf who had impulsively imposed vigilante justice against Eddie Shore, was the last surviving player from that infamous 1933 contest. Horner lived long enough to participate in the 1999 closing ceremonies at the last NHL game ever played at Maple Leaf Gardens. He died on April 27, 2005, a month before what would have been his 96th birthday.

Scoring Summary

First Period
- 13:43 BOS Vic Ripley (assist: Harry Oliver)
- 16:30 TOR Hap Day (unassisted)

Second Period
- 18:34 TOR Hec Kilrea (assist: Hap Day)

Third Period
- 2:38 TOR Joe Primeau (unassisted) SH
- 16:35 TOR Hec Kilrea (unassisted)

4

March 26, 1936

*Eddie Shore Loses Cool;
Bruins Lose Playoff Series*

Star defenseman Eddie Shore was undeniably one of the greatest assets the Boston Bruins ever possessed. His volatility made him one of the most fiery and unpredictable players in the team's long and storied history. When under control, his fury drove him and his team to greatness. However, several times it got both Shore himself and his team into trouble. In effect, it was the price the Bruins paid for having Shore in their lineup. On March 26, 1936, it cost the Bruins a shot at the Stanley Cup.

By the 1935–36 NHL season, the Boston Bruins were a team in transition. Many of their star players from the late 1920s and early 1930s had departed the team or had retired from hockey. Bill Carson, Dutch Gainor and Lionel Hitchman were all out of the league. Others, such as Dit Clapper, Tiny Thompson, Cooney Weiland and Eddie Shore, remained in the Boston fold and were still productive. Thompson was the recipient of the Vezina Trophy as the NHL's stingiest goaltender. Shore, Boston's captain, won the Hart Trophy as the league's MVP at age 33. Nevertheless, the Bruins were a run-of-the-mill club in 1935–36, winning just two more games than they lost over their 48-game schedule.

Being in the middle of the pack was not such a bad thing, however. The NHL pack was large and nearly indistinguishable that season. It could be argued that every outfit in the league in 1935–36 was a mediocre one and that there really was no dominant NHL club that season. Detroit and the Montreal Maroons had the best results among the eight teams. Neither club's record was especially eye-catching. The Red Wings, regular-season champions of the American Division, were just 24–16–8 for 56 points. The Maroons likewise accrued 54 points with their 22–16–10 mark to top the Canadian Division. The Stanley Cup

4. March 26, 1936

chase was truly a wide-open one, perhaps as unpredictable as it ever was.

Boston managed to squeak into one of the six available playoff berths by finishing second behind Detroit. It was a mighty struggle, though. The Bruins, Chicago Blackhawks and New York Rangers all finished tied at 50 points. (Chicago lost their final four regular-season games to make the American Division race extremely tight.) Despite

Boston's Jim O'Neil was saddled with the feminine nickname "Peggy." Its likely origin was the title of an Irish song. During the first game of the 1936 playoffs, O'Neil, hardly known for offensive prowess, scored one of three Boston goals to seemingly give the Bruins an unapproachable 3–0 lead in their total-goals series versus Toronto (courtesy Boston Public Library, Leslie Jones Collection).

winning their final four games of 1935–36, the Rangers were assigned last place, however, thus missing the 1936 postseason, as they only won 19 games to Boston's 22 and Chicago's 21. NHL fans would not experience another playoff race so close until 1970.

Under the curious playoff format of the time, the two divisional champions (Detroit and the Montreal Maroons) met in a best-of-five series with the winner getting a trip to the Stanley Cup finals. The two second-place teams (Boston and Toronto) would play a two-game series in which total goals would determine the winner, as would the two third-place teams (Chicago and the New York Americans). All three NHL playoff series would begin on Tuesday, March 24.

The Toronto-Boston clash opened at Boston Garden. Boston entered the game with a positive distinction: In the seven previous times the club had qualified for the postseason since entering the NHL in 1924, Boston had never lost any game to begin the playoffs. The Bruins kept that mark intact, playing very well in front of an adoring home crowd greater than 14,000 at their sold-out building. Boston completely stifled the Maple Leafs' offense and scored thrice. After struggling in the first period to create offensive chances, those three goals all came from players largely unaccustomed to scoring in 1935–36: Eddie Shore, Jim O'Neil and Lorne Duguid. (O'Neil had acquired the oddly feminine nickname "Peggy" from the title of a popular Irish song from the 1920s.) The threesome had combined for exactly six tallies during the regular season. "They have been valuable in many ways, have kept faithful training and have been good to their mothers, wives and sweethearts," Victor O. Jones quipped in the March 25 *Boston Globe*, "but they've scored precious few goals."[1] Two of the goals, both scored in the second period to give the home team a 2–0 lead, came with Boston on the power play.

Boston goalie Cecil (Tiny) Thompson played excellently, as usual. He had recently been named the Bruins' MVP in a poll of newspapermen, receiving nine of a possible 11 votes. Jim O'Neil was also outstanding in the Bruin victory, as was Eddie Shore. Still Boston's biggest star and drawing card, Shore received plaudits from a great many writers and fans alike. Jones summarized Shore's tremendous presence in Game One this way:

> Next to O'Neil, the standout player was.... Eddie Shore. He played himself practically senseless. He rushed comparatively little except when the Leafs were shorthanded, when he led Boston with headlong, irresistible energy. He passed to O'Neil and made the second goal himself. Also, he was superb on defense.
>
> Shore bounced Art Jackson, later rocked [Joe] Primeau, and wound up the

4. March 26, 1936

first period by stepping into Charlie Conacher and throwing him over his shoulder some six feet.[2]

Boston's 3–0 advantage heading into Game Two, by precedent, should have been ample to guarantee a series victory. Victor O. Jones figured the Bruins advancing to meet the best of the third-place winners was a lock. He penned in the *Globe*, "Unless the B's drop tomorrow's game in Toronto by more than three goals, they'll remain in the cock-eyed series for the old mug."[3] The *Montreal Gazette*'s sports editor agreed. "Three goals will look like three dozen" declared D.A.L. MacDonald. "The Leafs have the pleasant problem of trying to solve the all-star Boston defense for three tallies before they can even hope for a fresh start."[4]

Billy Bell had done a passable job in refereeing the first game of the Boston-Toronto series as the match's head referee—at least as far as the winners and the Boston media were concerned. He was backed up by

Boston's Eddie Shore has been compared to Ty Cobb for the intensity with which he played his sport. Shore was the first NHL defenseman to regularly advance the puck into the offensive zone to create scoring opportunities. His unbridled fury often got him into hot water, however. His #2 jersey has been retired by the Bruins (courtesy of the Boston Public Library, Leslie Jones Collection).

Odie Cleghorn, an official with a very spotty reputation. However, in Game Two, the two men switched duties. Thus, Cleghorn would be the man in charge of calling penalties and making other key decisions in Toronto.

Even before the return match in Toronto on March 26, Cleghorn would not have won any popularity contests in Massachusetts. A former player and coach who played a combined 10 NHL seasons for Montreal and Pittsburgh from 1918 through 1928 before taking up officiating, Cleghorn had worked a crucial Toronto-Boston playoff game in 1933 contested at Maple Leaf Gardens. In it, Alex Smith apparently had scored a game-winning goal for the Bruins, but Cleghorn's quick whistle on the play nullified it. The Leafs ended up winning that contest. Less than a year later, Cleghorn was also the man in charge of the infamous game, held at Boston Garden on December 14, 1933, when Eddie Shore blindsided Toronto's unwary Ace Bailey. The Boston defenseman was angered by Cleghorn not calling a penalty on Toronto's Red Horner and violently ran at the first Leaf in his sites. Shore's dubious "check" ended Bailey's hockey career and very nearly his life. Cleghorn was widely criticized that night on both sides of the border for his excessively lenient approach to NHL officiating. He was widely blamed for that game getting out of hand. It was not only the Bruins who had a history of gripes with Cleghorn's refereeing. In a 1935 game, Cleghorn was nearly chased out of the Montreal Forum by the entire Canadiens roster after he made a controversial penalty call against the Habs. When a few Canadiens began to manhandle him, Cleghorn had to be rescued from harm by his partner—Billy Bell.

Despite his team being down by a daunting three goals after the first contest, Toronto coach Dick Irvin remained typically cheerful and hopeful heading into Game Two. He reflected on his personal hockey history for a harbinger of good things that might happen. He found it. With optimism in his voice, Irvin told Victor O. Jones, "I just remembered this is the 23rd anniversary of my biggest night. I scored nine goals for the Winnipeg Monarchs against Toronto in the final game of the Allan Cup championship [the Canadian amateur hockey crown] right here in Toronto. The final score was 9–2."[5] Irvin, of course, hoped his Maple Leafs would be equally blessed with goals against the favored Bruins.

Toronto's hockey fans had certainly not given up hope that their favorites could stage an unlikely comeback to take the series. The 12,000 seats at Maple Leaf Garden sold out quickly for the return match between two of the NHL's greatest rivals. Special tickets for 2,000 standees were also purchased in short order when no more seats were available. The buyers saw a very memorable contest.

4. March 26, 1936

What passed before their eyes was a stunning 8–3 Toronto win to give the Leafs the playoff series by an aggregate score of 8–6. The implausible result was nothing short of startling. During the 1935–36 regular season, the greatest number of goals the Bruins had allowed in a single game was five. That had happened twice—once with the Maple Leafs as Boston's opponents. The Bruins had not surrendered eight goals in a game in more than two years. The man generally considered Boston's hero of Game One, Eddie Shore, was certainly the goat of Game Two.

Things started out well for Boston. Bill Cowley, a promising 23-year-old center, scored for the visitors on a nifty backhand at the 1:36 mark of the first period. Boston's fast 1–0 lead gave them a 4–0 overall advantage. The score remained unchanged until the eighth minute of the second period. A gambler could have likely gotten very sizable odds if he was bold enough to risk a dollar or two on Toronto rallying from a four-goal deficit at that point in the series.

However, the proverbial roof was about to cave in on the Bruins. The catastrophe was due, in part, to Eddie Shore's short temper and hockey's rules regarding penalties in the 1930s. In 1936 teams could score more than one goal on a power play situation, even if the penalized player had committed only a minor infraction. Additionally, any player who received a misconduct was not only banished from the ice for 10 minutes, but his team also played shorthanded for two minutes. Toronto took advantage of the former by scoring twice within 30 seconds on the power play while Shore was serving a two-minute minor penalty. The goals came from King Clancy at 7:25 and Charlie Conacher at 7:55. Suddenly, the Maple Leafs were leading 2–1 in Game Two. More importantly they had narrowed Boston's lead in combined goals to 4–2.

The turning point of the game occurred when Red Horner scored a highly contentious even-strength third goal for Toronto at 11:35. The Bruins howled that Horner was improperly in the crease impeding goaltender Tiny Thompson. Furthermore, the visitors claimed Horner had illegally kicked the puck into the Boston net! Either transgression, if called, would have nullified Toronto's goal. Somehow it was permitted to stand. Shore passionately protested the goal, banging his stick on the ice to emphasize his disagreement with the referee. According to the account published by renowned hockey historian Brian McFarlane, this is what occurred:

> King Clancy said [to Shore], "Horner *was* in the crease. What's more, [Cleghorn] gave you the cheapest kind of penalty. I wouldn't take that kind of nonsense from anybody." While Shore was talking, Clancy placed the puck on his stick.

[Shore] fired it at Cleghorn, catching the startled referee in the backside. Cleghorn [handed] Shore a ten-minute misconduct. From that moment, the Bruins were lost. Charlie Conacher scored three goals and assisted on a fourth.[6]

Worse still for Boston, shortly after Shore was sent to the box, two other Bruins were also penalized, giving the Leafs an extended two-man advantage for a lengthy time. All the while, Shore sat glumly in the sin bin with his head bowed. The Maple Leafs scored twice during their power play and added a sixth goal once the penalty box had finally been cleared of Boston players. Bill Cowley got one goal back for Boston in the final seconds of the second period, but the Game Two score had Toronto ahead 6–2 and leading on aggregate 6–5. The outcome of the series was still up in the air, but the shifting dynamics of the game almost assured a Maple Leafs triumph. Toronto got two more goals in the third period to Boston's one to finish the night's scoring. The first of those Leaf markers was notched by Charlie Conacher, giving him a hat-trick on the night. Cooney Weiland scored for Boston with just under eight minutes remaining, cutting Toronto's lead to 7–6 on aggregate and giving the Bruins a decent shot at undoing the damage from Shore's time in the penalty box. However, about a minute later, Toronto's Buzz Boll responded. He added Toronto's eighth goal of the night to make the game 8–3 and restore the Leafs' two-goal overall advantage. No further goals came in the game's final seven minutes. The remarkable Maple Leaf comeback—also described as the horrible Boston collapse—was complete. Shore played virtually the entire third period for the Bruins but he could not make amends for his costly misconduct penalty.

The Bruins certainly thought they had repeatedly gotten the short end of the stick from referee Cleghorn. Victor O. Jones heartily agreed with those sentiments and was not afraid to share his opinions with his *Boston Globe* readers. Jones angrily wrote from Toronto, "Like a house of cards, Boston's high hockey hopes went crashing this evening when the Toronto Maple Leafs unleashed a terrific six-goal avalanche against a Bruin defense which had been weakened by some terrible refereeing on the part of Odie Cleghorn in the second period."

Jones continued, "The backbone of Boston's great defense, Eddie Shore, was canned for a total of 12 minutes in this period, and at one time sat for almost two minutes in the penalty box flanked by Jim (Peggy) O'Neil and Bill Cowley as six Leafs blinded the four Boston players left with a barrage of goals. Before Shore got back, the damage was irretrievably done."[7]

In a later edition of the *Boston Globe* published the same day, Jones was still more than mildly irked by what had transpired at Maple Leaf

Gardens and continued to vent. His commentary below ran under the attention-grabbing headline "Incompetent Officiating Ruins the Bruins" and the equally alluring sub-headline "Even Toronto Agrees Cleghorn Worst Ever."

> The fact of the matter, coldly stated, is that the Bruins are through for the year because Odie Cleghorn, who has proved himself incompetent before this, did another poor job of whistle-blowing last night. The Bruins might have won even with Odie having one of his characteristically poor nights if Eddie Shore, the world's greatest hockey player, hadn't lost his head as the result of Odie's work. But the combination of Odie calling them the way nobody else saw them, plus Eddie's fit of temperament, ruined the Bruins.[8]

The Bruins and their supporters were particularly upset with Cleghorn permitting Red Horner's goal in the second period to stand as legitimate. "Honest to God," said Boston goalie Tiny Thompson, who faced 47 Toronto shots because of the many Boston penalties, "that's the worst goal I've ever seen allowed. Not only was it [illegally] kicked in, my crease was so full of players that there was no room for me."[9] Lorne Duguid concurred. He claimed, "Horner was not only in the crease, I had his stick held over his head and he kicked [the puck] in."[10] Jones emphatically penned, "It was the worst piece of officiating I've ever seen. Nobody in Toronto thinks that Horner was outside the crease and nobody who was near that end of the rink thinks he did anything but kick it in."[11]

Toronto's general manager Conn Smythe, who had been displeased by the officiating in Game One, amusingly commented to Jones, "The refereeing was terrible in both games [of the series]. But our homer was better than your homer." Another member of the Leafs' management, Frank J. Selke, was moved to opine, "I don't think Odie Cleghorn will ever referee another NHL game."[12]

The Canadian Press report on the game that appeared in the following day's *Montreal Gazette* made no specific mention of Odie Cleghorn's atrocious officiating, only that the crowd at Maple Leaf Gardens was "hysterical"[13] as the home team's score steadily increased. It also pronounced that the Maple Leafs had pulled off "the greatest comeback in modern NHL history."[14] The news bulletins from Toronto were received positively at the Montreal Forum where the hometown Maroons were playing the Detroit Red Wings in Game Two of their series. As each Leaf goal was posted on the Forum's scoreboard, the cheers progressively got louder and louder as the Boston lead evaporated. The Maroon fans desperately needed something to cheer. They were witnessing their team endure their second consecutive shutout at home at the hands of the visiting Red Wings.

Jones concluded his angry tirade in the *Globe* with some thoughtful commentary on the state of the NHL. "This makes the third straight time that the Bruins have been jobbed out of Stanley Cup play by weird officiating in Canada," he wrote. "Hockey is strictly on the level as far as the players are concerned. It probably is, too, as far as the officials are concerned, but if the league continues to put whistles into the mouths of such incompetents as Odie Cleghorn, there are a lot of people who are going to lose faith in the great winter daffiness."[15]

With their controversial and wild comeback triumph over Boston in the books, Toronto advanced to the second round of the playoffs—in effect, a semifinal—where they confronted the New York Americans, a team that had never gotten very far in previous postseason play the few times they had qualified to compete for the Stanley Cup. The Americans had ousted the Chicago Blackhawks in their two-game, total-goals

Charlie Conacher (center) notched a hattrick in Toronto's controversial 8–3 win over Boston during the 1936 playoffs which was decided on a two-game, total-goals basis. The Maple Leafs overcame a daunting three-goal deficit after Game One. Largely because of how Game Two unfolded, the NHL scrapped that format the following spring (courtesy of the Boston Public Library, Leslie Jones Collection).

series. (Like the Bruins, the Americans had won the opening game at home, 3–0. Also like the Bruins, the Americans lost Game Two on the road. Fortunately for them it was by a close 5–4 score, so New York still prevailed by a 7–5 aggregate.) The Maple Leafs defeated the Americans two games to one in a best-of-three series, but Toronto fell in the best-of-five Cup finals to Detroit, three games to one.

It was probably no coincidence that the NHL scrapped its total-goal playoff series the very next season. It would come too late for Eddie Shore and his teammates, but never again in Stanley Cup play would one game's score carry over into another.

Scoring Summary

First Period
- 1:36 BOS Bill Cowley (assist: Roger Jenkins)

Second Period
- 7:25 TOR King Clancy (assists: Jack Shill, Joe Primeau) PP
- 7:55 TOR Charlie Conacher (assists: Jack Shill, Joe Primeau) PP
- 11:35 TOR Red Horner (assist: Art Jackson)
- 16:55 TOR Charlie Conacher (assist: Art Jackson) PP
- 17:58 TOR Busher Jackson (assists: Charlie Conacher, Pep Kelly) PP
- 19:13 TOR Buzz Boll (assists: Bill Thoms, Frank Finnigan)
- 19:48 BOS Bill Cowley (assist: Jim O'Neil)

Third Period
- 10:58 TOR Charlie Conacher (assist: Joe Primeau)
- 12:02 BOS Cooney Weiland (unassisted)
- 12:53 TOR Buzz Boll (unassisted)

5

April 2, 1939
Mel Hill Scores His Third Overtime Goal in One Series

Mel Hill, one of the stars of the Boston Bruins' 1939 Stanley Cup team, had the nickname "Sudden Death" foisted upon him that spring. It was a well-earned moniker. Three times in Boston's nail-biting seven-game triumph over the New York Rangers in a Stanley Cup semifinal, Hill recorded overtime goals. It is an accomplishment still unmatched today. Given the combination of circumstances, pure luck and opportunity that must be present for such a feat, it may never be duplicated.

John Melvin (Mel) Hill was born in Argyle, Manitoba, on February 15, 1914. (Some sources list 1915 as his birth year.) Hill's formative years were spent in another Manitoba community, Glenboro. A fine all-around athlete, Hill was also a soccer player of some repute. He was selected to join a group of all-star amateur players in Saskatchewan to compete against touring professional clubs from both England and Scotland once the 1938–39 NHL season had ended. Perhaps Hill was chosen because of his newfound fame, for just a few months earlier, the youthful hockey player had achieved one of the sport's most memorable feats.

Esteemed hockey historian Stan Fischler once asked rhetorically, "How would you like to have a nickname like 'Sudden Death'? If you happened to be John Melvin Hill from Glenboro, Manitoba, it was not a problem. There has never been another NHL player known to have that sobriquet. It fit Hill as accurately as it did his shot."[1]

Prior to the 1939 Stanley Cup playoffs, Hill—who had once been property of the New York Rangers—did not garner a tremendous amount of attention from hockey journalists. Officially listed at 5'10" and 175 pounds but appearing considerably smaller, Hill was a capable but not an especially spectacular member of a very good Boston Bruins outfit, noted for its fine collection of young talent. It comfortably finished first in the seven-team NHL in the 1938–39 season with a 36–10–2 record. They were the class of the league. Hill had notched 10 goals for Boston. Six of his teammates had scored more frequently.

With the Montreal Maroons ceasing operations after 1937–38, the NHL generously allowed six of its seven clubs to qualify for the playoffs. (Only the last-place Chicago Blackhawks, the defending Cup champions from 1937 to 1938, missed out on postseason play.) In a format that seems utterly bizarre by modern standards, merit was thrown out the window. The top two teams from the regular season—the Bruins and the Rangers—would meet in the opening round of the playoffs in a best-of-seven series with the winner advancing directly to the Stanley Cup finals. The remaining four teams would play each other in best-of-three affairs to determine the other Cup finalist for 1939. In another odd decision by the league, the third- and fourth-place teams faced off in one series while the fifth- and sixth-place clubs met in the other.

The Boston–New York series—essentially a Stanley Cup semifinal—was the first one in modern NHL history to be scheduled for seven games. Games One, Four and Six were slated for Madison Square Garden, the others for Boston Garden. After the first three contests, not many hockey fans or writers figured it would go the distance. Boston leaped out to a daunting three-game lead that seemed utterly insurmountable for New York to overcome. Things were going according to form as Boston had finished 16 points ahead of the runner-up Rangers in the league standings.

The Bruins had to work diligently for their victories, though. They won the first two contests in overtime periods. Mel Hill earned a place in Bruins lore by scoring the winning goal in both games. Game One, on March 21, took nearly three full overtimes before Hill ended things with 35 seconds left in the third extra period. Boston won it, 2–1. Two nights later, Hill took care of business in far less time. His winning tally came just 8:24 into the first overtime session. Boston won that game, 3–2. The most interesting development was that Bert Gardiner replaced Davey Kerr in net for the Rangers after Game One and stayed there for the rest of the series. Kerr had played every minute of all 48 games for New York during the regular season—and had only missed one game since 1934. He had apparently been injured sometime during Game One but steadfastly continued through nearly six periods of play.

Years later, Hill told an interviewer, "The first game was a real endurance test. It went on for three overtimes. Bill Cowley fed me a pass down the wing and I beat [New York goalie] Davey Kerr with a high shot to put us ahead in the series. I scored … again the following night [sic] in overtime, and we took a 2–0 lead [in the series] over New York."[2] A solid 4–1 Boston home win in Game Three on March 26, in which Milt Schmidt scored twice for the victors, seemed to put the Bruins in total control of the series.

Victor O. Jones of the *Globe* confidently wrote what most Boston fans were thinking after Game Three: The Boston-New York playoff series was as good as over. "Displaying the puissant team strength and their individual brilliance," he penned, "the Boston Bruins made it three straight [wins] versus the New York Rangers at a jam-packed Garden last night. The B's need only one more victory to advance to the final round. They expect to capture that in New York tomorrow. Hardly anyone ... who witnessed their triumph last night believes that the B's can be beaten."[3] The Bruins had a right to feel invincible: Including the end of the regular season, Boston had won 11 consecutive games.

To their credit, the Rangers did not fold despite the highly unfavorable situation facing them. New York won Game Four, 2–1, on March 28. They won by the same score two nights later at Boston Garden. This was

The New York Rangers provided formidable opposition to the Bruins for most of the 1930s. Famed coach Lester Patrick is center in this photograph. Two of the players shown here on Lester's right are his son, Muzz Patrick, and Alex Colville (courtesy Boston Public Library, Leslie Jones Collection).

an overtime triumph in which Clint Smith notched the winner. Suddenly there was doubt among the Bruins players and their fans about the series' outcome. After New York took Game Six at Madison Square Garden by a 3–1 margin on Saturday, April 1, Boston's lead had evaporated. The series was tied, but momentum was clearly on the side of the Rangers.

It was reported that the Bruins and Rangers, by chance, happened to ride the same train into Boston following Game Six on Saturday night. There was no fraternizing; the two teams' respective sleeper cars were situated well apart from one another. Decisive Game Seven would be played the very next night at Boston Garden.

The eyes of the hockey world, of course, turned toward Boston. According to the *Boston Globe*, the betting odds for Game Seven fluctuated wildly throughout Sunday, with the visiting Rangers being favored 10:7 at one point. By game time, bettors could pick either team and expect to get 6:5 odds from bookmakers.

In a thoroughly classy gesture, ex-Bruin goalie Cecil (Tiny) Thompson sent his former teammates an encouraging telegram before Game Seven. It read, "Tonight's the night." Thompson, 35, who had been Boston's excellent and unrivaled goaltender for a decade, was suddenly (and shockingly, to many fans) traded by Art Ross to Detroit early in the 1938–39 season for another veteran goaltender, Normie Smith. Smith never played a game for Boston. Ross was merely making room on the Bruins' roster for a promising American-born netminder named Frank Brimsek who was 12 years younger than Thompson. Thompson's Red Wings had been eliminated from the playoffs by Toronto the day before.

Despite their team being on the verge of an epic collapse, the Boston fans turned out in record numbers on Sunday, April 2 to witness the outcome of Game Seven. By the time the puck was dropped at 8:30 p.m., nearly 17,000 spectators had squeezed into cozy Boston Garden—a record attendance which likely tested the elasticity of the building's fire code. Remarkably, it was the third time in the four games played in the Hub that a new, single-game attendance record for a hockey match in Boston had been set. The 16,981 paying customers who passed through the arena's turnstiles that night witnessed a classic.

Plenty of hopeful Ranger fans made the trip to Boston too, some extravagantly traveling by passenger airplane to the game. They—and those plebeians who had mundanely traveled by railroad—were assured that their return flights and trains back to Broadway would be held up until the hockey game at Boston Garden had concluded, whenever that might be. Obviously, another long overtime battle between the Rangers and Bruins was not beyond the realm of possibility.

Somewhat surprisingly, the two teams did not play cautiously considering the game's enormous importance. There were plenty of scoring chances for both clubs, but goaltenders Frank Brimsek and Bert Gardiner showed no weaknesses. The game was deservedly deadlocked at 0–0 after the opening 20 minutes of action.

The tension in Boston Garden was palpable. Repeated shouts by hopeful Bruin fans of "It's in the bag" directed at the Rangers were proving to be far from true. One female fan was lauded by the *Boston Globe* for her pluckiness and dedication to the Bruins. She had been bloodied over her eye by a firecracker tossed randomly and dangerously into the huge crowd! She quickly returned to her choice seat with alacrity after being patched up in the Garden's infirmary. Two males, aged 24 and 16, were arrested in connection with the incident for "disturbing a public assembly."[4] Similarly, the *Globe* reported, "In the first period, a fight—or something—broke out on the crowd. It took four coppers to eject the single fan."[5]

Early in the second period, Boston's famed Kraut Line of Bobby Bauer, Woody Dumart and Milt Schmidt, backed up by the ageless Eddie Shore on defense, kept the puck in the Rangers' zone for three full minutes but could not manage a breakthrough score. Twice deflected pucks trickled past goaltender New York goalie Bert Gardiner but slid wide of the gaping net. The best Ranger chance of the period occurred when Neil Colville eluded a Dit Clapper check with some fancy stickhandling and moved in on Brimsek alone. The Boston netminder made a spectacular circus-type save to keep the game scoreless.

Nevertheless, the Bruins did open the scoring in the second period. At 15:52, Ray Getliffe got his first tally of the 1939 Stanley Cup playoffs, accurately converting a pass by Gordie Pettinger. Getliffe's 25th birthday was the next day. Unbeknownst to him, he would still be in his hockey uniform when the clock crept past midnight. Like teammate Mel Hill, Getliffe was also a former Ranger. So was Pettinger.

The partisan home crowd loudly celebrated Getliffe's go-ahead goal, but the Boston lead did not last very long. New York quickly rallied and leveled the score within two minutes of falling behind. Murray (Muzz) Patrick tied the game at 1–1 with a screen shot from the Boston blue line that Frank Brimsek clearly did not see. (It was also Patrick's first goal of the playoffs.) A biased scribe from the *Globe* unkindly derided Patrick's marker as "a cheap Ranger goal,"[6] but it counted as much as Getliffe's.

There was no further scoring in the second period—although a bit of comic relief was enjoyed by the tense crowd when a linesman could not get out of the way of the play fast enough and was accidentally

5. April 2, 1939

bowled over by Boston's Jack Crawford. Nor was there any scoring in the third period. The drama was becoming too much to bear for some spectators. During the third period, a very ripe grapefruit was hurled from the second balcony. It was apparently intended for the vicinity of the New York bench, but it did not possess enough steam to reach its target. Instead, it struck a hapless fan on top of his head where it disintegrated into smithereens. A few Rangers were spattered by bits and juice. Ranger coach Lester Patrick quickly erected a wall of blankets behind his team to prevent further long-range missile attacks. Another overtime finish beckoned as the sound of the claxon wafted through Boston Garden after 60 minutes of regulation play.

When the Bruins came onto the ice to begin the extra period, a band struck up "Marie," a march that had become popular in Boston. The familiar tune did not inspire any dramatics. Boston's best chance in the first overtime period was a sustained bit of pressure that began with Eddie Shore stealing the puck from Murray Patrick in the New York zone. A centering pass resulted in two shots on goal by Roy Conacher and one each by Bill Cowley and Mell Hill. Bert Gardiner stood firm in the Ranger net, however, and thwarted the home team's momentum.

After the first 20-minute extra session expired without a goal being scored by either team, NHL rules mandated a thorough resurfacing of the ice be completed—not just a mere scraping of excess snow. This requirement extended the break to a lengthy 30 minutes before the game's fifth period began.

During the second overtime, Victor O. Jones of the *Boston Globe* noted, "By this time, of course, the refs [sic] weren't calling anything in the way of fouls." However, he added, "Play was reasonably clean as neither side wanted to risk a penalty just in case the referee wanted to go home."[7] During that frame, a 39-year-old fan named Emmanuel Burman collapsed in his seat and was swiftly transported to Boston City Hospital. The diagnosis was "malnutrition combined with over-exertion and excitement."[8] He was discharged and sent home a few hours later. Like the first overtime period, the second overtime session failed to generate a goal.

The third overtime period did produce two penalties—but they were of the offsetting variety so neither team gained any advantage. Five minutes into the frame, Boston's Mel Hill and New York's Muzz Patrick were each handed minor penalties. The extra space on the ice did not produce any significant scoring chances. However, not long after the penalized players returned to the ice, the game's decisive incident finally occurred. Stan Fischler described how the key moment unfolded:

[Eddie] Shore started a Boston counterthrust. He skimmed the puck to [Roy] Conacher, who fired a heavy shot at Gardiner.

Gardiner was forced to extend himself, but made the save and kept play alive by tossing the puck deeper into the Rangers' zone. He assumed that a teammate would recover it and move it into the Bruins' end.

This time, however, the Rangers defensemen were slow and outhustled by Cowley, who snared the puck behind the net. Hill knew what he had to do—and he did it.

Camped out at his favorite spot, in front of the Rangers crease, Hill did not have to wait long for the puck to come to him. Before Gardiner could properly react, Hill scored the biggest goal of his young hockey life.

When the red light flashed at 8:00, not only had Boston won the series, but Hill had earned a nickname forever.[9]

Hill himself recalled being very patient in scoring his winning goal. "Cowley fed me a pass from behind the net and I was right on top of Rangers goalie Bert Gardiner," he remembered. "I held the puck for a second and then flipped it up into the net on the short side. The fans went wild. It was a tremendous thrill to win a series for my team."[10]

Victor O. Jones gleefully described the moment of victory for his *Boston Globe* readers. "Little Mel Hill, the Sudden Death Kid, early this morning ended one of the greatest hockey games and one of the most fiercely fought Stanley Cup series in history when his goal brought victory to the Bruins against the New York Rangers in the seventh and deciding game of their bitterly contested campaign."

Jones continued, "The end came after exactly 108 minutes of play, with Bill Cowley recovering a wild shot of Roy Conacher's and feeding Hill a perfect pass. Hill, whose overtime goals on passes from the same Cowley already won the first two games, took his time and blasted a fine forehander past Bert Gardiner from 20 feet out."[11] Boston Garden's clock read 12:30 a.m.

Wild scenes of celebration soon followed. Jones wrote,

> The scene following Hill's goal ... almost beggars description. Ten-inch salutes were exploding all over the ice. Hill was torn almost limb from limb by his mates. The crowd was frantic, littering the ice with hats, coats, umbrellas, and everything they could throw. Fans were dancing in the aisles, kissing each other, whooping like Indians at the release from their long pent-up emotions, with sheer relief from the agony of putting their hearts through a wringer for four solid hours.[12]

A group of confident and highly creative Bruin fans had certainly arrived at Boston Garden well prepared for a victory for the home team. According to an amusing blurb in the *Globe*, they had brought along a funeral wreath which they paraded through the lobby and hung on the

5. April 2, 1939

Rangers' dressing room door "with great ceremony"[13] immediately after Hill's game-winning goal.

One advantage the Bruins earned (and frankly deserved) by winning the grueling seven-game series between the league's top-two teams was the choice of playoff dates for the final. It was widely assumed that Boston coach Art Ross would take the maximum break allowed by the NHL before beginning their Stanley Cup finals versus Toronto. "The Bruins are weary and battered," wrote Jones, "but the tonic of last night's win ought to help them."[14] The Maple Leafs had played and won two best-of-three playoff series versus the New York Americans and the Detroit Red Wings before the Bruins had finished their seven-game epic clash versus the Rangers. Toronto earned their spot in the Cup finals with a 5–4 overtime win over Detroit on April 1—the same night New York had evened their series with Boston at three games apiece. Toronto had finished the 1938–39 regular season in third place, one game below .500, with 47 points.

The Boston-Toronto series for the Stanley Cup began on Thursday at Boston Garden, giving the Bruins four days' rest to recuperate from their marathon encounter with the Rangers. In another first for the modern NHL, the finals were also a best-of-seven affair. Boston won the opener, 2–1, but the Maple Leafs took Game Two with a 3–2 overtime triumph. Toronto was heading home in good shape, but Boston reasserted their superiority with solid 3–1 and 2–0 wins at Maple Leaf Gardens. On April 16, the Bruins returned home and won the second Stanley Cup in franchise history with a 3–1 win over Toronto to take the finals in five games. Hill scored the game's opening goal. The overmatched Leafs had scored just six goals in the series to the Bruins' 12. Despite the crazy playoff format, quality had persevered in the end.

"It was exactly 10 years since the Bruins won their other Stanley Cup," wrote Victor O. Jones in the next day's *Globe*. "Since then, they've had many a fine team, but never one so fine as this one." Jones claimed, "Boston's youngest team in history all played up to their best form in overwhelming a gallant but lesser team."[15]

Had there been a Conn Smythe Trophy for playoff MVP in 1939, the Bruins had several candidates. Rookie goaltender Frank Brimsek had undeniably been excellent in Boston's dozen playoff games. However, Mel Hill would have likely been named the winner. After all, Boston would have lost to the Rangers without Hill's heroics. Hill had scored six goals and added three assists during the 1939 playoffs.

The remainder of Hill's NHL career saw him win another Cup in Boston in 1941 and a third as a member of the Toronto Maple Leafs in 1945. His stats are rather ordinary. Over his career, Hill ended up playing slightly more regular-season games for Toronto than he did for Boston—plus one year with the Brooklyn Americans. Yet Hill is first and foremost a Bruin in the eyes of most hockey historians because of one dramatic seven-game series. In all the years since the 1939 Stanley Cup playoffs, only two other NHL players have ever scored three overtime goals in a single postseason (Maurice Richard in 1951 and Corey Perry in 2017). Hill alone did it within the confines of one playoff series.

Mel Hill is one of just four Bruins that have scored at least three playoff overtime goals. Like Hill, both Terry O'Reilly and Brad

Not generally a high-scoring player, Mel Hill was unquestionably the hero of the 1939 Stanley Cup playoffs for Boston, remarkably scoring three game-winning overtime goals in a single playoff series versus the New York Rangers. The unlikely feat forever affixed him with the nickname "Sudden Death" (courtesy Boston Public Library, Leslie Jones Collection).

Marchand have recorded three postseason game-winning tallies. Only Patrice Bergeron has four—and it took him a span of 16 years to do it.

Hill, who spent his post-hockey life as the owner of a company that bottled soft drinks, died in 1996. Nevertheless, his fame lives on. As Hill's biography page from the Manitoba Sports Hall of Fame accurately points out, whenever there's a long overtime game, it is not uncommon for an announcer, even today, to wonder aloud, "Where is Sudden Death Hill?"

Scoring Summary

First Period
- No scoring

Second Period
- 15:52 BOS Ray Getliffe (assist: Gord Pettinger)
- 1745: NYR Muzz Patrick (assist: Mac Colville)

Third Period
- No Scoring

First Overtime
- No Scoring

Second Overtime
- No scoring

Third Overtime
- 8:00 BOS Mil Hill (assists: Bill Cowley, Roy Conacher)

6

March 16, 1944

Bruins Score Nine Times—But Lose

It was almost one of the greatest comebacks in NHL history. Instead, their March 16, 1944, entered the books as a game where the Boston Bruins scored nine goals against the Red Wings at the Detroit Olympia ... and lost. Never before or since have the Bruins scored so often in a single game in a losing effort.

If one quickly glances at the score and date it was played, one could easily assume the clash that Thursday night was a meaningless late-season game in which one or both teams did not have much to play for. That would only be half right. With the 1943–44 NHL season winding down, the Red Wings were locked into second place in the six-team NHL. The game was certainly meaningful for the fifth-place Boston Bruins, however. Though it was a slim one, the Bruins had a mathematical chance of catching the fourth-place Chicago Blackhawks for the league's fourth and final playoff spot. Everything had to fall into place for Boston, however, with no margin for error. Thus, a Bruin victory in Detroit was absolutely essential if the unlikely scenario had any possibility of occurring.

One thing was beyond certain in the NHL standings at that point in the season: The Montreal Canadiens were miles ahead of everyone else and it would take a handful of miracles for the Habs not to hoist Lord Stanley's coveted silverware that spring. If ever a year's Stanley Cup winner was a foregone conclusion, it was that particular campaign. The Montreal Canadiens romped through their 50-game schedule because of the "zombies" in their lineup. That curious term requires some explaining to anyone who is not a Canadian history buff.

During the Second World War, the debate over conscription— forced military service for able-bodied young men—was easily the most divisive issue in Canada. Most of English-speaking Canada was strongly in favor of it; French-speaking Quebec was almost entirely opposed to it. A typically Canadian compromise was eventually reached by the federal politicians: Conscription would be instituted by the national government, but draftees could choose to serve in "home defense units" stationed in Canada, far away from the dangerous combat zones. It also allowed such draftees to generally go about their regular lives, only being called upon to serve if Canada was in danger of attack by Japanese or German forces. This option, not surprisingly, was an enormously popular one among francophones. Because home defense units were in limbo between being active and inactive, critics compared them to the zombies seen in Hollywood horror flicks who existed in a state somewhere between the living and the dead. Thus, the term "zombie" became a pejorative one. Of course, Canadian soldiers who did volunteer to put their lives on the line overseas generally held zombies in very low esteem, as is shown in this stanza from a bit of doggerel discovered in 2019 in the diary of Lance Corporal Gerald DeMerchant of New Brunswick who was enduring enemy fire in Europe:

> *If by chance we are so lucky,*
> *As to safely reach the Rhine,*
> *We would rather fight the zombies,*
> *Than the Jerries any time.*[1]

The strong prewar NHL clubs—Boston and New York especially—lost most of their rosters and just about all their star players to the manpower demands of Canada's military. (Frank Brimsek, Boston's excellent netminder, was a Minnesotan who enlisted in the U.S. Coast Guard.) The Montreal Canadiens, heavily laden with French-Canadians, had been barely affected by the war. Their most prominent zombie was 22-year-old Maurice Richard, who scored 32 goals for the Habs in the 1943–44 season. As non–Canadian pro hockey players were scarce, the other five NHL teams scrambled mightily to find decent personnel who were exempt from military service due to age or some other disqualifying feature. Thus, it was hardly surprising that the Habs held an enormous lead in the standings as the final weekend of the 1943–44 season approached. Montreal lost just five games all season. Their closest pursuers, Detroit, tasted defeat 18 times. Meanwhile, the Boston Bruins muddled through most of the war years without the superb players that had been the heart of their Stanley Cup teams of 1938–39 and 1940–41. In 1942–43 they still had enough talent to reach the Cup finals. In 1943–44, however, the Bruins—now without Brimsek guarding their cage—did not look like a championship outfit to even their most optimistic supporters.

It was a little bit surprising that the Bruins were still in the running for a spot in the Stanley Cup playoffs on March 16. Boston had endured a six-game losing skein from February 13 to March 2 that nearly ruined their chances. Yet they managed to stay hopeful about the postseason by losing just one of their next five games. Boston was on a modest two-game winning streak when they stepped onto the ice at the Detroit Olympia for their 49th game of their 50-game schedule. The on-the-ropes Bruins had already survived one elimination game two days earlier, on March 14 by upending the Chicago Blackhawks, 6–4, in front of friendly home supporters at Boston Garden. The Bruins were still clinging to life, but it was a tenuous connection. Boston would have to win both their final games while the Hawks would have to lose all three matches left on their schedule. If that happened, both teams would finish 1943–44 with 47 points and identical won-lost-tied records. Goals-scored would be the criterion used break the deadlock—and

Scribes and fans alike questioned Art Ross' decision to abruptly trade longtime Boston goaltender Tiny Thompson in 1938 to open the job for minor-league netminder Frank Brimsek. Ross' wisdom was soon apparent. Brimsek quickly earned the apt nickname "Mr. Zero" for his habit of recording shutouts. He had 10 in his rookie NHL season. Brimsek's steadiness led the Bruins to the 1938–39 Stanley Cup and another championship two years later (courtesy Boston Public Library, Leslie Jones Collection).

Boston held a sizable edge over Chicago in that department. "Fantastic as it sounds," wrote Jerry Nason in the March 15 edition of the *Boston Globe*, "the Bruins are still nursing a tiny flame of hope for an NHL playoff berth."[2]

The Boston-Detroit game started out typically; there was no sign that a whopping 19 goals would eventually be scored by the two clubs. The first tally did not come until the 7:05 mark of the first period. Detroit's Carl Liscombe beat Boston goalie Maurice Courteau, a 30-year-old from Quebec City, to give the home team a 1–0 lead. More than ten minutes elapsed without another score. Boston leveled the game at 18:09 on Jack Crawford's unassisted goal. It was the first of many Bruin shots that would elude Detroit goaltender Connie Dion. (Dion had served in the Canadian Army at the start of the war, but he was discharged in 1943.) As was commonplace of the era, teams did not carry spare goalies, so both Courteau and Dion would have to play the entire 60 minutes regardless of the score. Just 20 seconds after Crawford's marker, Detroit retook the lead on a goal by 32-year-old future Hall-of-Famer Syd Howe. (Howe's seasonal goal total would match his age in 1943–44.) Despite the flood of goals that followed in the topsy-turvy game, the Red Wings would not relinquish their advantage at any time before the final buzzer sounded.

Detroit began the second period in a frenzy, scoring three times in the opening three and a half minutes to assume a 5–1 lead, with Don Grosso (who would conclude his NHL career in 1947 as a Bruin), Bill Jennings and Mud Bruneteau doing the damage for the Red Wings. Bill Cowley got a goal back for Boston at 5:01. Four minutes after Cowley's tally the teams scored four times—twice apiece—to give Detroit a 7–4 lead after 40 minutes of play. Former Toronto Maple Leafs star, 33-year-old Ralph (Busher) Jackson, got the two Bruins goals. An ex-Bruin from the club's recent glory days, Frank William (Flash) Hollett, who was almost 33 himself, scored one of the Detroit markers.

The third period was a thoroughly wild 20 minutes of hockey. Detroit scored first. At 4:09, Carl Liscombe got his second goal of the game as Detroit's lead rose to a seemingly secure 8–4. Midway through the period, in a span of about five minutes, each team again scored a pair of goals. Herb Cain and Jack Crawford got the two for Boston. (Cain would lead the NHL in scoring in 1943–44, notching a record 82 points; teammate Bill Cowley would finish second with 71.) Detroit's scores came from the reliable sticks of Carl Liscombe (his third goal of the game) and Bill Thomson. Thomson's goal, at 15:08, put the Red Wings in front 10–6. Under normal circumstances, that tally should have decided matters.

But this was not a normal NHL game. With their playoff chances rapidly dwindling, Boston committed totally to the offense and got some positive results, albeit a smidgen too late. Bill Cowley made it 10–7 at 17:31. At 18:57 Busher Jackson got his third of the game to make it a 10–8 contest. Moments later—17 seconds later, to be exact—Cowley became the second Bruin to record a hattrick. Suddenly the score was 10–9 for Detroit. That was as close as Boston got to catching the home team, but they gave the Red Wings and their 7,932 fans scattered around the Olympia a mighty scare. The unnamed Associated Press correspondent wrote that the Bruins' valiant rally was not quashed by the badly reeling Detroit club, but instead it "was smothered by the final horn."[3]

The loss in Detroit turned out to be the final NHL appearance for Boston goaltender Maurice Courteau. He had played six games for the Bruins, won two and lost four, and had allowed 33 goals. His goals-against average was an unflattering 5.50.

The combined offensive output of the Red Wings and Bruins set a modern (post–1926) NHL record and tied the all-time mark set in a 1920 game when Montreal trounced the Quebec Bulldogs, 16–3. (That rout occurred in Quebec City!) All these years later, one stat from the March 16, 1944, game catches the eye: All 19 goals were scored at even strength! There was only one penalty called during the entire game. It was a minor infraction whistled on Boston's Pat Egan in the first period. Detroit did not capitalize with the subsequent man advantage.

Had the Bruins managed to defeat the Red Wings that night, their hopes for a fourth-place finish would have remained alive, as Montreal edged Chicago, 3–2, at the Forum in the only other NHL game contested that Thursday evening. Thus, a potentially dramatic weekend for the Bruins and Blackhawks went out the window with Boston's 10–9 defeat. For Boston, the loss at the Olympia was becoming the norm. The Bruins failed to win any of their five games played in Detroit's home building in 1943–44. They fared only marginally better at home versus the Red Wings, recording a single win and a tie in five games.

Undoubtedly dispirited and with absolutely nothing to play for, Boston lost badly in Toronto two nights later to conclude their 1943–44 campaign on a sour note. The score that Saturday at Maple Leaf Gardens was 10–2 for the home team. Toronto was up 5–0 after about 23 minutes of play and never faltered. It was the sixth time in that 50-game season that the porous Boston defense had surrendered at least 10 goals in a game. It also marked the first instance in club history in which the Bruins had allowed double-digit goals in consecutive games—a dubious feat that would not be repeated by any Bruin squad until December 1965.

6. March 16, 1944

Boston's goalie on March 18 was a 35-year-old from Owen Sound, Ontario, named Benny Grant who had begun his NHL career with Toronto back in the 1928–29 season. The next day's *Boston Globe* called him "hapless."[4] He bravely faced a barrage of 54 shots from the Leafs. It was his one and only NHL game as a Boston Bruin.

Chicago did better than expected with their fourth-place playoff spot. In an upset, the Blackhawks, who had finished the regular season a game under .500 with a 22–23–5 record, ousted the second-place Red Wings in five games to reach the Stanley Cup finals. As expected, Montreal promptly dispatched Chicago in four straight games. It did, however, require a sparkling comeback from a 4–1 third-period deficit and

Despite often being injured, Bill Cowley managed to play 508 regular season games with the Bruins from 1935–36 to 1946–47, scoring 190 goals. From 1944 to 1952 he held the NHL record for career assists. For a time, Cowley was the NHL's all-time leader in points. He was one of the few pre-war Boston regulars who did not join the military (courtesy Boston Public Library, Leslie Jones Collection).

an overtime goal by Toe Blake for the Habs to win the final game, 5–4.

In the first line of his coverage of the Habs' Cup triumph, Dink Carroll of the *Montreal Gazette* joyfully wrote what would become the regular celebratory cry among Montreal hockey fans: "Les Canadiens sont là!"[5] ("The Canadiens are here!") Critics who disapproved of zombies playing NHL hockey in 1944 could cynically retort, "Well, they're certainly not over there!"

Scoring Summary

First Period
- 7:05 DET Carl Liscombe (assists: Mud Bruneteau, Bill Thomson)
- 18:09 BOS Jack Crawford (unassisted)
- 18:29 DET Syd Howe (assist: Mud Bruneteau)

Second Period
- 1:09 DET Don Grosso (assists: Adam Brown, Bill Jennings)
- 2:21 DET Bill Jennings (assist: Flash Hollett)
- 3:23 DET Mud Bruneteau (assist: Hy Buller)
- 5:01 BOS Bill Cowley (assist: Norm Calladine)
- 9:51 DET Flash Hollett (unassisted)
- 11:06 BOS Busher Jackson (assist: Herb Cain)
- 11:51 BOS Busher Jackson (assists: Herb Cain, Art Jackson)
- 15:34 DET Adam Brown (assists: Don Grosso, Cully Simon)

Third Period
- 4:09 DET Carl Liscombe (assist: Syd Howe)
- 10:06 BOS Herb Cain (assist: Jack Crawford)
- 10:12 DET Bill Thomson (unassisted)
- 14:43 BOS Jack Crawford (unassisted)
- 15:08 DET Carl Liscombe (assist: Syd Howe)
- 17:31 BOS Bill Cowley (assists: Bep Guidolin, Jack Crawford)
- 18:57 BOS Busher Jackson (assists: Herb Cain, Bill Cowley)
- 19:13 BOS Bill Cowley (assists: Herb Cain, Busher Jackson)

7

January 21, 1945

Bruins Rout Rangers, 14–3

Roger Birtwell of the *Boston Globe* accurately but cruelly described the January 21, 1945 New York Rangers-Boston Bruins game succinctly in the opening paragraph of his coverage the next day: "Eleven thousand fans thronged the Garden last night to see a hockey game, but they wound up seeing the Bruins hold target practice instead."[1] Birtwell was referring to the home team's merciless 14–3 demolition of the lowly New York Rangers. The eye-catching Boston scoring barrage remains the greatest single-game output in the team's long history.

By the 1944–45 season, the NHL was top-flight hockey in name only. Most of the league's best players were serving in the military; as most NHLers were Canadians, it was that country's armed forces that possessed all the elite hockey stars. The two teams that were affected most were the Boston Bruins and New York Rangers. Before the war began siphoning the world's top players into more important duties, those two clubs were undoubtedly the NHL's best. By the last year of the war, the Bruins and Rangers were largely laughingstocks, barely able to stock their teams with adequate players who, for some reason or another, had managed to elude military service.

Near the end of 1944, Art Ross had publicly labeled his Bruins as "the worst team I ever saw."[2] At the time, Boston possessed a mediocre—but hardly horrible—record of 8–11–1 after 20 games, so Ross was clearly engaging in negative hyperbole. The criticism must have worked on some level, however, as Boston managed to squeak into the playoffs in the six-team NHL with an unspectacular fourth-place mark of 16–30–4. Five members of the 1944–45 Bruins would play their only NHL hockey during that final wartime season.

Despite Ross' disparaging superlative about his club, the New York Rangers were an even more pitiful bunch than the Bruins ever were during that period. By the mid-1940s, they were frequently losing games with double-digit scores run up by their opponents. Four times during the war years, the Bruins scored at least 10 goals in a game against the Broadway Blueshirts. It did not involve Boston, but one such horrendous New York loss was a notable 15–0 setback to Detroit on January 23, 1944. It remains the most lopsided shutout in NHL history. (In a 2016 article about that game written by Richard Bak for a Detroit hockey fans' website, the Red Wings historian noted that the score could have been worse. A sixteenth Detroit goal was waved off by the referee because the puck crossed the goal line a fraction of a second after the third period had ended.) That season New York goaltender Ken McAuley played in all 50 of his team's games (less one period in which future Hall-of-Famer Harry Lumley made his NHL debut). McAuley lost 39 games and he allowed 310 goals while doing so. His awful goal-against average of 6.24 still stands as the worst seasonal mark ever by an NHL goalie who played at least 25 games. The Rangers won just six games in 1943–44 and are usually high on most hockey historians' lists of the worst NHL teams of all time.

As the 1944–45 NHL season approached, Ranger coach Frank Boucher was hoping to have one of their best pre-war players, Bryan Hextall, available. However, he was not permitted to travel outside of Canada as he had registered as a farmer with the Saskatchewan War Mobilization Committee to avoid military duty. The board took Hextall at his word—but ruled that a farmer was a farmer, not a professional hockey player. He could not be both. With many NHL teams struggling to fill roster spots, the Rangers were hopeful of at least making the playoffs.

Entering the January 21, 1945, game at Boston Garden, the Rangers were a weary, discouraged and luckless bunch that Sunday evening. Wartime travel and fuel-consumption restrictions had reduced the number of passenger trains in operation throughout North America. The Rangers' game on Thursday, January 18 in Detroit started three hours late because of missed railroad connections. The contest at the Olympia did not end until 12:56 a.m. Detroit won the game, 7–3. The lateness of the finish caused the Rangers to miss their overnight train heading towards Montreal via Toronto. The Rangers arrived in Montreal several hours behind schedule on Friday. They played in Montreal on Saturday night, January 20, and promptly lost three players to injuries, including rugged Grant Warwick, who suffered a severe attack of stomach ulcers that required him to be hospitalized. The Rangers dropped that game to the Habs by a respectable 5–2 score. The next stop scheduled on New York's road trip was Boston. Despite their recent poor showings, the Rangers could be somewhat confident, having beaten the

Bruins in their most recent meeting, 5–1, at Madison Square Garden on January 11. A New York win would lift the Rangers into a fourth-place tie in the NHL standings.

In its Sunday edition, the *Boston Globe* foresaw an easy win for the Bruins that night. An unnamed scribe opined,

> There's a hockey game at the Garden tonight that the home team—unless it takes a fearful outwitting—is in a spot where it almost can't lose.
>
> For the Bruins tonight play the Rangers. While the Bruins have been having a nice fat rest since their victory over Toronto last Tuesday, the Rangers have been getting knocked around the country in pretty vigorous style.[3]

Alas, more travel complications befell Frank Boucher's club. The Rangers arrived in Boston for their Sunday night game just 100 minutes before the scheduled time for the opening faceoff. Unfortunately, their equipment was delayed. The railway baggage car carrying New York's sticks, skates and uniforms was wrongly removed at Concord, New Hampshire. By the time the error was rectified, the Rangers' hockey gear finally showed up at Boston Garden nine minutes after the game

Art Ross sits between the two Jackson brothers circa 1944. Harvey (Busher) Jackson (left) had been a star player for years with Toronto. Art Jackson was a steady performer, scoring 94 goals in seven seasons for the Bruins (courtesy Boston Public Library, Leslie Jones Collection).

was supposed to have begun. Journalist Roger Birtwell amusingly noted in his report for the *Boston Globe*, "When 'The Star-Spangled Banner' was played, the Rangers were still in the dressing room yanking on their skates."[4]

Boston team president Weston Adams, a Lieutenant-Commander in the U.S. Navy, was home from the Pacific Theatre to see his beloved Bruins orchestrate the historic blowout. Remarkably, the Boston goals did not initially come at a furious pace from the opening faceoff. Half the first period had elapsed before the red goal light flashed. The first one was scored by Jack Crawford at the 11:31 mark. That initial tally seemed to open the floodgates. Bill Cowley scored two goals spaced just 24 seconds apart at 18:23 and 18:47. According to Roger Birtwell, Cowley "rammed the first between [Ranger goalie Ken] McAuley's skates like a guy digging a hole with a crowbar."[5] By the time the first period concluded, the home team held a very secure 5–1 lead.

At one point in the second period, Boston scored three times within 46 seconds (including a pair of goals 19 seconds apart and an assist by Frank Mario), and four times within 80 seconds, the last mark setting a new NHL speed record for accruing a quartet of goals. Boston Garden's scoreboard showed the Bruins ahead 10–1 when the second intermission mercifully came for the Rangers.

To their credit, New York still put forth a reasonable effort during the final stanza even though they had no legitimate hope of staging a comeback. The Rangers had their best results in the third period, scoring twice. But Boston gave no thought to reining in their lethal attack, however. The Bruins added four more goals in the final 20 minutes, including another two from Bill Cowley, to give him four on the night. That individual sum tied a club record. Ken Smith, a rookie, also had a hattrick for the victors. Frank Mario scored twice for Boston, his pair of goals coming just 19 seconds apart in the second period. Rookie Bill Cupolo's significant contribution to the Boston win was hardly noticed: he got four assists. (Cupolo was one of the five transient Bruins who would never again play in the NHL after debuting in the 1944–45 season.) The humiliating loss was the Rangers' fourth in a row. Overall, the Bruins notched more goals than assists by a 14:12 ratio. (This was largely due to a recent directive from the NHL designed to reduce the number of debatable assists awarded on goals—a decision unpopular with the players on all six clubs.) Those 14 Boston goals bettered the old club record by one. The Bruins' 13-goal game also came against the downtrodden wartime Rangers. It occurred the previous season, on January 2, 1944. At the time, many Boston hockey writers thought such an orgy of goals might never be duplicated by the Bruins. Boston managed to outscore the other four NHL teams that also took to the ice on January 21, 1945. Montreal, Detroit, Chicago and Toronto combined to score only 13 goals at the Montreal Forum and Chicago Stadium.

A bit of levity occurred shortly following the Bruins' twelfth goal. Boston Garden public-address announcer Fred Russo dutifully passed along a personal message to a specific ticketholder: "Tom Mallory, Jr: Go to the poultry show at once." Another patron, apparently bored by the historic rout he was witnessing, shouted loudly, "Why don't we all go?" The off-the-cuff remark drew a huge laugh.

Of course, the football-type score from Boston Garden caught the attention of newspaper readers the following day. "Against the glassy-eyed goalie of a leg-weary, injury-riddled, travel-worn New York Ranger team," wrote Roger Birtwell in his summary for the *Boston Globe* the next day, "the Bruins rang up 14 goals—the largest number ever made by a Bruin team—and buried their rivals." Birtwell further commented, "At the end of the game, Ranger goalie Ken McAuley went wobbling off the ice after making 46 saves, more than three times the 15 made by Paul Bibeault of the Bruins."[6]

The Canadian Press report on the weekend's NHL games stated the obvious about what had occurred in the Hub on Sunday "[The Bruins]" it stated, "showed the Rangers there would be a struggle if the latter team tried to move into fourth place."[7] The Associated Press was content to report that Boston's "terrific scoring ... enabled the Bruins to strengthen their grip on the fourth-place playoff berth."[8]

Harold Kaese, another member of the *Boston Globe*'s sports department, echoed those same sentiments with an odd analogy. He wrote on January 22, "The 14–3 beating the Rangers took at the hands of the Bruins at the Garden last night may turn out to be a hockey equivalent of Stalingrad. The Rangers' playoff bid now seems hopeless. The Bruins seem sure to qualify. They have routed the enemy at the critical moment."[9]

Kaese also sympathized with the vanquished, pointing out the Rangers had no ally in the league's schedule-maker, having been saddled with a difficult road trip compounded by an impossible train schedule. "The Rangers were dead, dead on their skates," the scribe noted. "The Bruins flew around them, scoring five goals in the first period, five in the second and four in the third. It would have been merciful if they had shortened the periods. The Bruins were glad to win, but even they did not enjoy the score."[10]

An Associated Press report on the weekend's hockey action

presciently noted, "With the National Hockey League teams about three-fifths of the way through their schedules, the loop standings began to take on an appearance that might not change from now to the end of the season."[11] That indeed proved to be the case. The standings after the circuit's January 21 battles—with Montreal, Detroit, Toronto and Boston holding the NHL's four playoff spots in that order—would remain unchanged through each team's 50 games.

Remarkably, the Rangers put the horrible shellacking at Boston Garden behind them and won their next game—a 4–3 triumph in Chicago on Wednesday, January 24. The Blackhawks were residing in the league cellar at the time and appeared to be destined to finish the 1944–45 season there. Still, more than 10,000 fans turned up. In a see-saw game, the Rangers thrice took one-goal leads only to see the hometown Blackhawks rally to tie the score three separate times. Kilby MacDonald scored his second goal of the game at 13:03 of the third period to give New York a fourth advantage they would not relinquish. The breaks went the Rangers' way, for a change. A New York goal scored by Ab DeMarco in the second period was, according to the Associated Press, hotly disputed by the home team.

On the other hand, the hockey gods may have punished the Bruins for coldly running up the score against the badly depleted Rangers. Boston proceeded to lose four straight games after their one-sided win. The team lost the services of player-coach Dit Clapper who had been injured in Boston's 5–4 home loss to Detroit on January 23 when his attempted bodycheck on former Bruin Marty Barry went badly awry. Moreover, the Bruins found themselves on the wrong side of a double-digit score six days after routing the Rangers when they fell to the Canadiens in Montreal, 11–3, on Saturday, January 27. The sudden Boston losing streak gave the Rangers a glimmer of hope.

The next time the Rangers and Bruins faced off was exactly two weeks after the 14–3 game, on Sunday, February 4. It was again played at Boston Garden with perhaps 8,000 fans passing through the turnstiles in hopes of witnessing another Boston rout. (It was a seemingly inflated attendance figure that was challenged by a skeptical Harold Kaese of the *Boston Globe*.) Instead, they were treated to a very competitive hockey match. Proving that wartime hockey was a wildly unpredictable enterprise, New York battled the Bruins to a 3–3 deadlock in a game described by the Associated Press as "unexciting." Rangers coach Frank Boucher had a more complete roster at his disposal this time—and they arrived at Boston Garden in plenty of time. The visitors rallied from a 3–1 deficit to earn the point. The tying goal came with about four minutes left on the clock when Bucko

McDonald launched a long shot at the Bruin net. His teammate, Fred Thurrier, was positioned well to knock home a juicy rebound generously provided by Boston goaltender Paul Bibeault. The 14–3 debacle was apparently ancient history; no mention of the club's most recent clash was made by the *Globe*.

The tie was obviously better for the Rangers than the 11-goal loss had been to them 14 days before, but prior to the contest Frank Boucher had called the February 4 game a must-win for his club. The Rangers were running out of opportunities to catch the Bruins for fourth place—the final playoff position—in the NHL. Despite picking up a point with the draw, according to Boucher's perspective, the result was a wasted opportunity for the Rangers to whittle away at Boston's small lead over them in the league standings. Boston faced New York three more times before the 1944–45 campaign concluded. Each team won one time while one game finished in a 4–4 tie.

When the official NHL statistics for 1944–45 were finalized after the 150th and final regular-season game was entered into the books, the record showed the Bruins and Rangers had faced each other ten times. Boston ended up with a slight edge, having won four games. New York won three. The other three ended in ties. In those ten contests, Boston scored 51 goals to New York's 35. About 27.45 percent of those Bruin scores had occurred in a large bunch on the third Sunday in January. Thus, it can be reasonably concluded that Boston's 14–3 thumping of the New York Rangers on January 21, 1945, was truly a statistical aberration.

More than two years would go by before the Boston Bruins put together another 10-goal outburst in a regular-season game. It was on Wednesday, February 12, 1947. That night the Bruins romped to a decisive 10–1 victory at Boston Garden. The home team unabashedly tried for double-digits as the final Bruin goal, scored by future Boston coach Bep Guidolin, came with just 15 seconds remaining on the clock. The victims of the onslaught that night were once again the New York Rangers.

Scoring Summary

First Period
- 11:31 BOS Jack Crawford (assist: Gino Rozzini)
- 14:27 BOS Ken Smith (assist: Bill Cupolo)
- 16:48 NYR Ken Hunt (assist: Kilby MacDonald)
- 18:23 BOS Bill Cowley (unassisted)
- 18:47 BOS Bill Cowley (unassisted)

Second Period
- 6:34 BOS Bill Thoms (assist: Dit Clapper)
- 7:08 BOS Frank Mario (assists: Ken Smith, Dit Clapper)
- 7:27 BOS Frank Mario (assist: Bill Cupolo)
- 7:54 BOS Ken Smith (assists: Bill Cupolo, Frank Mario)
- 13:31 BOS Herb Cain (unassisted)

Third Period
- 2:42 NYR Fred Hunt (assists: Joe Shack, Kilby MacDonald)
- 3:21 BOS Dit Clapper (unassisted)
- 4:45 BOS Bill Cowley (assist: Bill Thoms)
- 9:50 NYR Ab DeMarco (assist: Bucko MacDonald)
- 15:47 BOS Bill Cowley (assist: Herb Cain)
- 16:40 BOS Ken Smith (assist: Frank Mario)

8

March 18, 1952

Bobby Bauer Scores in One-Game Comeback

There was magic in the air on Tuesday, March 18, 1952. It was a truly special night at Boston Garden as nostalgia came alive. For just one evening, all three parts of the Boston Bruins' famed Kraut Line were reunited in a regular-season game versus the Chicago Blackhawks.

The game was originally supposed to honor two active but aging Bruins, Milt Schmidt and Woody Dumart. It did and then some. But those in attendance were also treated to a one-off return to the Boston lineup for 37-year-old Bobby Bauer, who had last played an NHL game in 1947. To the delight of the 12,658 fans who bought tickets, the Bruins shut out the visiting Chicago Blackhawks, 4–0. Schmidt scored once (his 200th NHL goal) and assisted on the other three Boston tallies. Bauer shook off the accumulated rust to notch a goal and an assist. It was about as perfect a night as a follower of the Bruins could have imagined.

The Bruins and their fans showed their admiration for Bauer, Schmidt and Dumart to the tune of about $20,000 in gifts and cash—certainly an eye-catching total in the early 1950s. During a 30-minute pregame ceremony attended by NHL president Clarence Campbell, the tokens of esteem kept piling up in front of the three beloved gentlemen. They included gold watches from the league, silver trays and pitchers from the Boston media, movie cameras from a Bruins fan club in Plymouth, Massachusetts. Bicycles for the players' children were purchased by the arena ushers and other staff members at Boston Garden. The three men's wives—whom the event's organizing committee collectively referred to as "Mrs. Krauts," also received a bevy of expensive gifts as mementoes. (By coincidence, it was also Marie Schmidt's birthday.) The *Boston Globe* called it "the greatest testimonial in hockey history."[1] Following the speeches and presentations, a hockey game had to be played that night on Garden ice. It was an important one at that. A

Boston victory would mathematically secure the home team the fourth and final berth for the 1952 Stanley Cup playoffs ahead of the New York Rangers.

"It was a night that comes only once in a lifetime," Schmidt told Herb Ralby of the *Boston Globe* while peeling off his perspiration-soaked uniform in the Bruins' dressing room. Ralby described the Boston captain as "beaming and deeply thrilled."[2] It was also a deserved honor. At their peak, the Kraut Line was the NHL's most productive goal-scoring outfit. It carried the Bruins to two Stanley Cups, in 1938–39 and 1940–41. Had it not been for the onset of the Second World War, there likely would be a few more Cup banners fluttering in Boston today.

Milt Schmidt, Bobby Bauer and Woodrow (Woody) Dumart were all born in the same Canadian city—Kitchener, Ontario—within a span of about two and a half years between 1915 and 1918. German immigrants and their descendants were the predominant ethnic group, so much so that the municipality was called Berlin from its founding

The most prominent offensive unit during the NHL in the late 1930s and early 1940s was Boston's famous Kraut Line, comprised of three superb players of German ancestry: Bobby Bauer (left), Milt Schmidt (center) and Woody Dumart. They were boyhood friends from Kitchener, Ontario. The Bruins fell on hard times when their wartime duties called (courtesy Boston Public Library, Leslie Jones Collection).

until 1916. Although all three boys were excellent overall athletes, they especially excelled at hockey. They frequently competed on the same teams—including an elite amateur club called the Kitchener Greenshirts—creating a chemistry that was undeniable. They advanced to the minor pro ranks together. At some point in 1936, Albert Leduc of the Montreal Canadiens comically dubbed them "the Sauerkraut Line." It was eventually abbreviated to the Kraut Line. Such a moniker would not likely pass the politically-correct test today, but no one seemed to care very much at the time—especially the three players. They found the collective nickname amusing.

Dumart—the middle man by age—was the first of the trio to crack the Bruins' lineup. (He played one game for Boston in 1935–36.) By the end of the next season, all three were playing in the Hub and making an impression on fans, writers and opponents throughout the NHL. Clearly, they were the Bruins' strongest hope for the future.

The men got along splendidly on and off the ice. They made a point of negotiating their contracts as a threesome instead of as individuals, figuring it would be an effective ploy to get the best deal. For a while, the trio shared a one-room apartment in Brookline, Massachusetts. In 1939–40, they finished one-two-three in NHL scoring. To date, it is a feat matched by only two other lines in NHL history. Together they combined to play 1,887 NHL games—every single one of them for the Bruins.

As two-time Stanley Cup champions the entire Bruin trio enjoyed popularity well beyond Boston. Following the 1941 triumph, Bruin veteran Aubrey (Dit) Clapper coaxed many of his teammates to form a charity softball team to face a team comprised of other NHL players. Their first stop was Clapper's hometown of Peterborough, Ontario, where an estimated 5,000 people turned out to see Boston's famous Kraut Line and its supporting cast of hockey heroes. An amusing incident occurred during the contest: At some point in the game, Bobby Bauer smashed a long drive that landed just inside the left-field foul line. There was no outfield fence at the ballpark, so the ball kept rolling and rolling while outfielder Murph Chamberlain of the Montreal Canadiens fruitlessly tried to chase it down. The ball eventually rolled through the open doorway of a distant building. Chamberlain had no idea it was a women's public restroom, so he unhesitatingly stormed in after it. Seconds later, two terrified gals came running out of the restroom screaming—followed closely by Chamberlain who had the ball in his hand. Bauer could have easily circled the bases three times before it was relayed back into the infield. Apparently, most of the overflow crowd was doubled over in laughter at the sight of the pair of frightened females fleeing out the door. When the side was retired, Chamberlain received a deserved standing ovation for his spirited display of determination—pointless as it was—as he trotted from his outfield position to his team's bench.

All three members of the Kraut Line joined the Royal Canadian Air Force during the Second World War. On Tuesday, February 10, 1942, at the conclusion of their last home game before they departed for military duty, the men were carried off the Boston Garden ice by both their Bruin teammates *and their opponents from Montreal*! "The attitude, the feelings the Montreal Canadiens had for the Krauts that night was fantastic," Schmidt recalled more than 60 years later. "What more could you ask for?"[3] Fittingly, the threesome had accounted for 11 points in Boston's easy 8–1 victory. During an emotionally charged postgame ceremony, each man received gifts from the club, including his full salary for the 1941–42 season. The Boston hockey writers organized a farewell party for them at a local hotel.

Since things German were not especially popular in America and Canada during the war era, the press tried to come up with an alternative nickname for the Kraut Line. "The Kitchener Kids" seemed to get the best response, but fans in Boston and elsewhere generally preferred the original. After the war, the Bruins figured their fans would still resent the Germanic nickname, so the club held a contest to rename the Kraut Line. The winner was The Buddy Line—which lasted perhaps a month before the Kraut Line was reinstated under its famous name. Schmidt, Bauer and Dumart did not give up hockey entirely during the war. Not too surprisingly, they joined the Canadian air force's hockey team almost immediately. They led the RCAF Flyers to the 1942 Allan Cup—emblematic of national amateur hockey supremacy in Canada. (Yes, somehow all three members of the Kraut Line were reinstated as amateurs in 1942.) Meanwhile, with their best line otherwise occupied, the Bruins began slowly descending from a top-flight NHL team to a bottom-feeder. Although Milt Schmidt won the NHL's MVP in 1950–51, Boston would not be a first-place club again until 1970–71.

The March 18, 1952, *Boston Globe* hyped the return of the Kraut Line to Boston Garden ice after an absence of five years. Journalist Herb Ralby noted, "The nostalgic touch of the great line reunited is expected to lure old-time puck pecans [sic] out of hibernation tonight when the Bruins tangle with the tail-end Chicago Blackhawks at the Garden."[4] The Bruins, who had been faring poorly at the gate for most of the 1951–52 season, looked forward to the anticipated strong turnout, something that was not always the case at the Garden's turnstiles in the early 1950s. "Although there are still plenty of tickets available," wrote Ralby,

8. March 18, 1952

"the season's largest crowd is expected to watch Bobby Bauer in his first NHL game since the spring of 1947."[5]

Bauer was not exactly coming into the game unprepared. During the 1951–52 hockey season, he was coaching the Kitchener-Waterloo Dutchmen in the Canadian senior amateur ranks, and taking more than just an occasional shift or two: he scored eight goals and had 10 assists for that club. Bauer was also the owner of the Dutchmen, so he had the luxury of an autocrat in calling the shots regarding the team's personnel matters.

"This is the biggest game of the season, as far as I'm concerned," declared Boston coach Lynn Patrick, who planned on giving the Kraut Line a regular shift versus Chicago. "I don't think we are weakening ourselves by using Bobby Bauer. He still can play well enough to check many of the fellows playing today with brains alone."[6] For old times' sake, Bauer would be given his old #17 jersey to wear one last time. This required some juggling as Dave Creighton was presently assigned #17 in the Boston lineup. Creighton instead wore #4 for this special night without any hesitation.

Gritty Ed Kryzanowski had given Boston a 1–0 lead, beating Harry Lumley with a first-period power-play goal at 17:14.

The highlight of the night was probably Boston's second goal. It was scored by Milt Schmidt—his 200th in NHL competition. Assists went to both Bauer and Dumart. Bauer had the foresight to retrieve the puck out of the Chicago net and hand it to Schmidt as a souvenir. The crowd erupted in cheers when the announcement was made over Boston Garden's P.A. system: "Boston goal scored by Schmidt. Assists from Dumart and Bauer." No one had heard that familiar refrain in five years.

"Milt's tally was a typical Kraut production,"[7] wrote Tom Fitzgerald in the next day's *Globe*. A nifty three-way passing play concluded with Schmidt driving home a shot from about six feet in front of Lumley. The time of the goal was 12:58 of the second period. Up until that point, the three men operated as a single line, but the pace of the game was starting to show on the 37-year-old Bauer who readily admitted afterward that he was tiring badly at the end of each shift. Bauer only saw occasional shifts for the rest of the game—but he did score a goal.

About seven minutes into the third period, "Schmidt sent in a good leading pass to Bauer," wrote Fitzgerald. "Brainy Bobby demonstrated his old mastery."[8] It was an aesthetically pleasing tally. Bauer swung around Chicago defenseman Lee Fogolin and then deked Lumley out of position. He backhanded a shot high into the gaping net.

"While Bauer played as if he could still perform in the NHL with conditioning," wrote Herb Ralby, "it was definitely his last game." Bauer himself confirmed this fact in a postgame interview. "I came down just for Milt and Pork [Bauer's nickname for Dumart]," he said. "I don't think I could play as well again. It was just an emotional lift tonight. I think I'd go downhill after this game."[9]

Seven minutes later, Boston put the game totally out of Chicago's reach. Réal Chevrefils got the Bruins' fourth goal, knocking home a rebound from an Ed Kryzanowski shot. Schmidt got an assist on that goal too.

Overshadowed by the hoopla about the Kraut Line was the excellent netminding displayed by Boston's Jim Henry. He notched his seventh shutout of 1951–52.

Years later Schmidt joyfully recalled to hockey historian Stan Fischler. "How could I ever forget that game?" Schmidt said. "Bobby comes back, I get my 200th [goal]; Bobby scores, and we clinch a playoff berth."[10]

The *Globe*'s indefatigable Tom Fitzgerald did some thorough digging into the Bruins' club record book and found some quirks regarding Schmidt's milestone score. "Milt's goal was freighted with coincidences," he wrote. "It was in Chicago on March 11, 1937 that he got his first major league tally. It was against Chicago here on February 5 [of this season] that Dumart got his 200th."[11]

Schmidt and Dumart continued to play for the Bruins a while longer. Dumart retired at the end of the 1953–54 season. Schmidt lingered until partway through the 1954–55 campaign, giving up playing to become the new Boston coach 30 games into the season. Bauer promptly returned to senior amateur hockey, coaching Canada's Olympic team in both 1956 and 1960, winning medals on both occasions, but not the gold—which was looked upon as a failure by most Canadian hockey fans.

Bauer did not live long, though. On September 17, 1964, Bauer died of a heart attack while engaging in a round of golf. He was just 49. Schmidt was given the sad news while running a Boston practice. He was visibly shaken by it. In contrast to their linemate, both Dumart and Schmidt enjoyed long lives. Dumart lived to be 84, passing away in 2001. Schmidt lived to be 98. Before his death from a stroke in 2017, Schmidt was the oldest living NHL player, the last man to have played in a league game during the 1930s, and the last opponent to have played against the Montreal Maroons who folded after the 1937–38 season.

Longtime Schmidt admirer Bobby Orr recalled, "He wasn't very big, but his heart was this big on the ice," spreading his hands wide to illustrate his point. "And that's how he played. He was a great player and a wonderful individual. He's a great man and a great friend to all of us."[12]

Scoring Summary

First Period
- 17:14 BOS Ed Kryzanowski (assists: Réal Chevrefils, Milt Schmidt) PP

Second Period
- 12:58 BOS Milt Schmidt (assists: Woody Dumart, Bobby Bauer)

Third Period
- 6:40 BOS Bobby Bauer (assists: Milt Schmidt, Réal Chevrefils)
- 13:41 BOS Réal Chevrefils (assists: Milt Schmidt, Ed Kryzanowski)

9

April 8, 1952
The Rocket's Greatest Goal Sinks the Bruins

"The 14,508 rabid Montreal partisans staged a hysterical demonstration of several minutes, littering the ice with programs and millinery following the great individual feat of their old hero, [Maurice] Richard."[1] That was how Tom Fitzgerald of the *Boston Globe* described the aftermath of the surreal, Hollywood-type climax to a Stanley Cup playoff game and series. A seriously injured and clearly groggy Maurice (Rocket) Richard of the Montreal Canadiens had inflicted the tough loss on a plucky Boston Bruins crew who nearly staged a major upset.

Fitzgerald did not quite believe what he had seen. The scribe was not alone. Many other ticketholders at the Forum had trouble comprehending what they had seen, too. In retrospect, one thing is certain: Had the game occurred half a century later, in the best-case scenario, Richard would have been quietly sitting alone in darkness in the Habs' dressing room. More probably he would have been unhappily detained at a Montreal hospital waiting to be assessed for head trauma and likely kept overnight as a precaution. As no one in 1952 considered being knocked senseless as anything more than a minor inconvenience for a professional hockey player, Richard was allowed to leisurely return to the game at the Montreal Forum as if nothing at all had happened to him. That was fortunate for the victors.

There has never been a more dynamic player to don the jersey of the Montreal Canadiens jersey than Maurice Richard—nor is there ever likely to be another. If one merely reviews the long list of his awards, plaudits, and accolades one would be treated to a résumé that included Richard being named an NHL All-Star 14 times and having his name engraved on the Stanley Cup eight times. (Only four players had more.) At the time of his retirement, the Rocket held nearly 20 separate NHL records. More than six decades later he still holds or shares a handful of records, including most goals scored in the Stanley Cup finals (34), most goals scored in one playoff game (five—shared) and most overtime goals for one playoff season (three—shared). But the Rocket was much more than merely his statistics.

It is difficult for modern hockey fans to comprehend how important Maurice Richard was to the Montreal Canadiens and to the people who resided in the province of Quebec. He truly was an iconic figure in the most literal sense of the word—and he remained that way until the day he died. Hockey historian Dave Stubbs described the intense hockey superstar in a 2017 video interview for NHL.com,

> Rocket Richard was unlike anyone who ever came along in the NHL. He was always tested. He was booed. He was heckled. He ultimately became a symbol for French-Canadians. Books have been written, university theses have been done on the Rocket, on the importance of him [to Quebeckers]. All through it, Rocket maintained, "I'm just a hockey player," which is ridiculous because he was never just that.

NHL.com has its own similar assessment of Montreal's famous number nine:

> [Richard] was the most intense athlete the game has seen. He was everything that personified greatness. Winning at any cost was what he was all about. He was prepared to pay the price for every goal he scored, and no price was too high.

The most noticeable feature that teammates and opponents noticed about Richard was his eyes. During a game, his lamps transformed; they had a wild, almost maniacal look about them. (A few photographs have captured this odd and frightening aspect of Rocket's face.) In 2022, a list of the 60 toughest players in NHL history compiled by the website StadiumTalk.com slotted Rocket Richard at number-two, trailing only Tie Domi.

At the time of his retirement, Richard's 544 career regular-season goals were the most ever scored by an individual player. His 50 goals in 50 games in the wartime 1944–45 season established a record that became a benchmark for the league's elite to attempt to equal. (As of 2022, four players have joined Richard in this elusive club, matching or bettering his feat seven total times.) So important was the Rocket's impact on the league, that it awards a trophy in his name to the player who nets the most goals each season. The NHL waived its three-year requirement for entry into the Hall of Fame, allowing Richard to join its ranks in 1961 not long after his 1960 retirement. In that same year, the Montreal Canadiens retired his #9. Richard was made an Officer of the Order of Canada in 1967. Upon his death in 2000, at age 78, Richard was given a state funeral. It was the first ever accorded to a Canadian athlete.

On the night of April 8, 1952, before an adoring throng at the Montreal Forum, 30-year-old Maurice Richard elevated his stature as a hockey superstar to phenomenal heights by performing a dramatic piece of wizardry and securing his place in Stanley Cup history. The Boston Bruins were his victims.

The 1951–52 NHL season featured the Detroit Red Wings romping through the 70-game regular season with a 44–14–12 record, accruing exactly 100 points to secure an easy first-place finish in the six-team circuit. Their closest pursuers were the Montreal Canadiens. The Habs were well in arrears of Detroit, finishing with just 78 points. The Red Wings subsequently crushed the Toronto Maple Leafs in four straight games in one Stanley Cup semifinal. Wings goalie Terry Sawchuk, sporting a crewcut and just 22 years old, recorded shutouts in the two games played at the Detroit Olympia. The Red Wings outscored the outclassed Maple Leafs by a 13–3 aggregate in the series.

Thankful for not having to face the seemingly unbeatable Wings right away, the fourth-place Boston Bruins instead were paired against a capable Montreal Canadiens outfit. Boston finished their regular season unimpressively, four games under .500. Common sense and the predictions of pundits went out the window, though. The Bruins would be embroiled in a magnificent fight with the far more skillful and star-studded bunch from Quebec. It was a tough, physical affair that went the seven-game limit to be decided. Boston had lost the first two games to the Habs badly, by embarrassingly one-sided scores of 5–1 and 4–0 at the Montreal Forum, before winning Game Three in convincing fashion at home, 4–1. The Bruins then tied the series with a 3–2 squeaker in Game Four at Boston Garden that featured referee George Gravel whistling only the most egregious fouls in what was becoming a playoff tradition throughout the NHL's corps of referees.

Boston had led Game Four 2–0 on goals by Milt Schmidt and Réal Chevrefils, only to see Montreal rally to tie the contest on a pair of goals scored by Floyd Curry. With the score level, overtime seemed imminent. However, promising youngster Fleming Mackell got the winner for Boston with about five and a half minutes left to play in the third period. Mackell, who had been born in Montreal not quite 23 years earlier, had missed the previous two games of the semifinal while battling a flu bug. "By their refusal to succumb to panic," wrote an impressed and hopeful Tom Fitzgerald in the *Boston Globe*, "the Bruins established themselves as reasonably good choices in this best-of-seven encounter which resumes in Montreal."[2]

Wagering a few dollars on Boston seemed even more reasonable after the visitors scored an upset 1–0 win at the Forum in Game Five to

9. April 8, 1952

(From left) Johnny Peirson, Fleming Mackell, Jim Henry and Leo Labine were mainstays in the Boston lineup in the early 1950s. Goaltender Henry, nicknamed "Sugar Jim," played in all 210 regular-season games the Bruins played from 1951–52 to 1953–54 (courtesy Boston Public Library, Leslie Jones Collection).

assume a surprising 3–2 series lead. Jack McIntyre got the only goal 3:30 into the third period. With the playoff shifting back to Boston for Game Six, suddenly the favored Habs were on the verge of elimination by the upstart club in black and gold. Momentum seemed to be on Boston's side: Counting the tail end of the regular season, the Bruins had won their previous nine home games.

Played before the first sellout crowd at Boston Garden in three years, Game Six was an intense double-overtime affair, a supremely physical contest that took its toll on everyone. Many players were battered and bruised. This trend even included coaching personnel. Canadiens coach Dick Irvin was struck by a puck from the stick of Boston's Milt Schmidt. The bloody wound required several stitches to his cranium. A more likely candidate to be injured by a flying disc was Boston goalie Sugar Jim Henry. He took a puck to the face that luckily just missed his eye. The impact was strong enough, however, to fracture his nose and blacken both his eyes. He was a sight. The game was delayed 17 minutes while Henry was bandaged in Boston Garden's infirmary and eventually sent back out on the ice. (This was par for the course and such resolve form goaltenders was expected. Even NHL teams did not carry backup netminders in 1952.)

Boston held a 2–0 first-period advantage on goals by Milt Schmidt and Dave Creighton, but Montreal clawed their way back to tie the game on a second-period goal by the unheralded Eddie Mazur—who had never played a regular-season NHL game—and another by Maurice Richard in the third frame. In the end it would be another little-known Hab, Paul Masnick, a recent call-up from Cincinnati who decided matters. After a long shot from Montreal's Doug Harvey produced a high carom, Masnick was the first player to see where the puck had descended. He deftly slapped home the tantalizing rebound sitting nicely for him at the side of Henry's crease to force a seventh game. The time of his goal was 7:49 of the second overtime. It was 11 minutes past midnight when the game was won by Montreal. "It provided a somewhat freakish end to the long contest that had left the athletes limp and weary and had drained the emotions of the crowd,"[3] wrote Tom Fitzgerald. Compared to Mazur, Masnick was a grizzled NHL veteran. The 20-year-old had scored the grand total of one regular-season goal in 15 games with Montreal in 1951–52. Masnick had played in an American Hockey League playoff game in Providence the night before. Game Seven would be played at the Forum two nights later.

Maskless NHL goaltenders were a gritty lot in the early 1950s. Sugar Jim Henry was a typical sample. Remarkably, the visibly wounded Henry would suit up in Game Seven for the Bruins despite spending much of the day alternating between hot and cold compresses on his eyes to keep the swelling down in his face so he could see. As difficult as that may be for fans of today's game to fathom, what would happen later in the game would considerably trump Henry's willingness to play in Game Seven.

The Forum's faithful fans did not have to wait long to show their appreciation for the Habs as Eddie Mazur scored just four minutes and 25 seconds into the first period of Game Seven. Undaunted, the Bruins leveled the score exactly eight minutes later off the stick of left winger Ed Sandford. It would be the final tally for the Bruins of the 1951–52 season. There was no scoring by either team in the second period as both netminders, Henry and Montreal's Gerry McNeil, turned away each shot they faced: a paltry seven for Henry and even fewer for McNeil—just five. The game was still tied 1–1 heading into the third period. As

9. April 8, 1952

excellent as the netminding and defensive play were, it would not be the major story of this game.

Despite a scoreless second period, high drama still came to the forefront in that stanza. What exactly happened varies depending on which source is consulted, but the outcome remains the same. There is no known video record of what occurred. (*Hockey Night in Canada*'s television broadcasts would debut the following season.) Most accounts agree that Maurice Richard rushed up the ice, carrying the puck for the Canadiens. Richard attempted to move around Boston defenseman Hal Laycoe. However, he didn't see the solidly built, 5'10" Leo Labine lingering behind his Bruin teammate until the very last second. It is worth noting that Richard and Labine had a longtime and heated rivalry with one another. They feuded constantly. With both their respective teams facing elimination, tension was running high, and fuses were unsurprisingly short. Labine, seeing an ideal opportunity to legally flatten his rival, planted his shoulder heavily into Richard's chest as he attempted to worm his way between the two Boston defenders. Richard accidentally took Labine's stick to the face before his head ricocheted off the knee of one defender—whose knee it was is subject to debate—ultimately striking the ice. Play was halted as Richard lay motionless. Blood poured out from a deep cut over Richard's left eye and covered his face. The Forum's fans were stunned into a shocked silence, many truly believing that Richard was dead. Roch Carrier, the French-Canadian author of *Our Life with the Rocket*, described the tense scene at the Montreal Forum this way:

> The Rocket collapses onto his back, spread-eagled, arms outstretched. Fans think of the crucified Christ. At this time of year, in the Catholic province of Quebec, thoughts are on Good Friday, the day when Christ died on the cross. The silence in the Forum is distressing. The people would like to get down on their knees. Easter, the day of His resurrection isn't far away, either.... Suddenly the Rocket moves. The crowd explodes. "Christ is resurrected!"[4]

Forum ushers hustled onto the arena's ice surface carrying a stretcher, but they were shooed away by team doctor Gordon Young. "You don't know this guy," Young told them. "He'd have to be dead to allow himself to be carried off like that."[5] Trainer Hector Dubois, physiotherapist Bill Head and teammate Bert Olmstead were also quick to arrive on the scene. They surrounded Richard, who eventually responded to smelling salts waved under his nose. Richard regained consciousness and, with the aid of his teammates and no stretcher, he gingerly made his way off the ice to the Canadiens' dressing room. Richard would temporarily fall unconscious again while Young stitched up the gash above his eye. Montreal club officials sensibly urged Richard to take the rest of the game off. Young's advice, too, was that he should not play.

The Rocket was clearly suffering the effects of a concussion in an era where such things were of considerably less concern than they are today. Blood still oozed out from under his formerly white bandages as Richard made his way from the Forum's infirmary to the Habs' bench, much to the pleasure of the startled hometown fans. By this time, the third period was well under way. Canadiens coach Dick Irvin stopped Richard to assess his condition. "He told me he was all right," Irvin recalled, "but he wasn't just then; he didn't even know the score of the game."[6] Richard's linemate Elmer Lach quickly apprised him of the situation. The score had remained unchanged for more than 43 minutes, still level at 1–1, with just over four minutes to play in the third period of Game Seven. Moments later with blurred vision, still dizzy, and possessing a mind that was less than clear, Richard could not recall the score. He asked about it again. Again, Richard was informed that his Habs were deadlocked with the Bruins. It was all the information Richard needed, despite his peering at the scoreboard with unfocused eyes. Lach later recalled the situation. "I caught Rocket squinting up at the clock and I asked him what was the matter. He told me his eyes weren't in focus, but just then it was time for a line change—and over we went."[7]

Seeing Richard on the bench from his vantage point up in the press box, Toe Blake, Richard's former linemate, turned to journalist Baz O'Meara of the *Montreal Star* and prophetically prophesized, "The Rocket will get one in the last five minutes."[8] What neither man could possibly know at the time was how stellar a goal it would be.

The fresh group of Montreal forwards (the Rocket, alongside Lach and Bert Olmstead) took to the Forum ice. The teams were playing four-on-four hockey due to offsetting five-minute high sticking penalties assigned to Hal Laycoe and Billy Reay. This gave Richard more room to operate. Emile (Butch) Bouchard, who had possession of the puck for the Habs, was surprised to see Richard on the ice and promptly fired him an accurate pass.

Richard, now in possession of the puck, raced past a pair of Bruins forwards, skillfully avoiding a Milt Schmidt poke check. With only the two defensemen (Bill Quackenbush and Bob Armstrong), remaining between Richard and the Bruin goal, Richard skated into the right corner of the Boston zone, slipping past Quackenbush, using one arm to hold the Bruins defender at bay, before making his way to the net. Richard then faked a shot to draw goaltender Jim Henry to his left post before skating past the unwary netminder and shooting the puck into

9. April 8, 1952

the unguarded far corner of the net, all the while surrounded by Bruins trying to dispossess him of the puck. There were three minutes and 21 seconds left to play in the third period when the red goal light flashed behind Henry. Predictably, the hometown fans were ecstatic, having just witnessed, all things considered, one of the most amazing goals ever to be scored in an NHL game. Sadly, there is no film of the spectacular goal, just a handful of still photos taken by various news photographers from assorted angles. The still-groggy Rocket received a four-minute standing ovation for his successful and superhuman effort.

Richard himself later described the moment. "My legs were all right, but I was dizzy," he said. "I heard the crowd yell, and by that time I was too dizzy to see."[9]

Bill Quackenbush commented afterwards on his unsuccessful strategy to deal with the racing Rocket. He stated, "I stayed with him all the way. [I] actually got him into the right corner and figured that that was that. But it wasn't--not with Richard."[10]

In a retrospective article penned nearly 70 years after it occurred, Stan Fischler of *The Hockey News* described Richard's famous score as "one moment in one game that has been embedded in hockey history as one of *the best goals*, in one of the most exciting playoff clinchers since the invention of the round puck."[11]

As time wound down, Henry was predictably pulled for an extra attacker by Boston coach Lynn Patrick in a desperate attempt by the visitors to score a game-tying goal. The ploy failed. All it did was give Billy Reay of the Canadiens the chance to pad his club's lead with an empty-net goal with 34 seconds left to play. The final score was 3–1 for the Canadiens. Boston had lost a heartbreaking playoff round to Montreal—a series they probably should have won. It was neither the first nor the last time that would occur in the teams' collective histories.

A headline in the next morning's *Montreal Star* excitedly proclaimed, "Richard's Glitter Goal Hurtles Habitants into Cup Final." A sub-headline in the accompanying story by Baz O'Meara alliteratively referred to the Rocket as the "maestro of momentum."[12]

One of the most dramatic hockey photos ever taken was snapped during the customary post-series handshake queue. It graphically shows a beaten, bruised and black-eyed Jim Henry gentlemanly locking hands with a bloodied and bandaged Maurice Richard in a mutual gesture of sportsmanship.

Other Bruins did not accept defeat quite so gracefully. Thirty-six years later, in a 1988 interview for *Sports Illustrated*, Boston's Ed Sandford recalled the scene in the visitors' dressing room. "After we lost the final game, everyone seemed to disappear. Hal Laycoe and I were left."

He continued, "We went to some restaurant in Montreal and ordered some food. Neither one of us was saying much. Finally, Laycoe says, 'To hell with this!' He stands up, turns the table upside down, and walks out the door. Stuff was everywhere on the floor. It's a mess. Waiters come running. I'm sitting there and I have to pay for it all!"[13]

After the postgame niceties had concluded, with his face still stained with blood, Richard eventually made his way to the Habs' dressing room where his father, Onesime, was patiently waiting for him. Suddenly overcome with emotion, the Rocket collapsed upon a bench as his father placed a comforting hand upon his famous son's shoulder. Just for a moment, the toughest man in professional hockey was sobbing uncontrollably.

With their remarkable semifinal victory over the Bruins secured, the Montreal Canadiens advanced to the 1952 Stanley Cup finals to confront the vaunted and well-rested Detroit Red Wings. It was unlikely the level of drama from the Boston-Montreal series would be repeated in the best-of-seven tilt for the Cup. It was not. With a healthy squad that featured the likes of Gordie Howe, Alex Delvecchio, Sid Abel and Terry Sawchuk against a tired Canadiens lineup that was mostly held together by bandages and willpower, it was little surprise that Detroit cruised to an easy series sweep. Montreal managed to get pucks across the goal line just twice in the entire series. Richard did not score either of them. Terry Sawchuk did not surrender a goal in any of the Red Wings' four home playoff games in 1952—a feat unmatched to this day.

One thing is certain: Had the April 8, 1952, game been played under modern NHL safety conditions, there is no chance the Rocket would have even seen the Montreal bench after such a devastating hit by Leo Labine, let alone step back onto the ice to continue in the game. Since 1979–80, all rookies entering the NHL have been required to wear protective helmets for the whole of their careers, so the days of players smacking their unprotected heads on the ice is long gone. Furthermore, since 1997, the NHL (in conjunction with its players' association), has implemented concussion protocols that are continuing to evolve as more about head injuries is learned. Under modern guidelines, Richard would have likely been kept off the ice for a lengthy time. However, not only did the Rocket suit up for Game One versus Detroit two nights later, but the feisty Richard also had his name recorded in the game's box score for having been penalized in the third period for roughing.

Years later Henry would reflect on the famous Richard goal that knocked his team from 1952 postseason competition: "I felt bad, of course, because he had just eliminated us from the playoffs," he said, "but I had to congratulate the Rocket because it was one of the greatest goals I had ever seen. It was no shame being beat [sic] by such a player."[14]

Boston coach Lynn Patrick was more succinct in his analysis of the goal that sent his team home for the summer. He glumly told one hockey scribe, "A truck would not have stopped Richard."[15]

Scoring Summary

First Period
- 4:25 MON Eddie Mazur (unassisted)
- 12:25 BOS Ed Sandford (assists: Fleming Mackell, Bill Quackenbush)

Second Period
- No scoring

Third Period
- 16:19 MON Maurice Richard (assist: Butch Bouchard)
- 19:26 MON Billy Reay (assists: Floyd Curry, Donald St. Laurent) EN

10

January 18, 1964
The Ultimate Outlier—Boston 11, Toronto 0

There is a truism in sports that unexpected outcomes are precisely why the games are played instead of having a computer generate the probable results and saving everyone a lot of time. Mild upsets happen every day in all levels of every sport. Those occurrences are what keep people tuned in. They just might see something wholly against what the experts are telling them will unfold.

The greatest example of "Who would have expected that?" in NHL history likely occurred on the evening of January 18, 1964. That chilly Saturday night in Toronto, the two-time defending Stanley Cup champion Toronto Maple Leafs suffered a humiliating trouncing at the hands of the lightly regarded, last-place Boston Bruins before a stunned home crowd and a national television audience in Canada. The score was, remarkably, 11–0 for the underdogs.

To say this was an unexpected outcome would be putting it mildly. "The Bruins rolled to an unbelievable 11–0 victory over the bewildered Toronto Maple Leafs," the *Boston Globe* giddily reported in its Sunday edition. While it was true that Boston entered the game riding a modest two-game winning streak, having recently beaten Toronto and Detroit, it was also a fact that by the middle of January the Bruins were firmly embedded in sixth place in the six-team NHL, 20 points out of a playoff spot, and in deep trouble. The Bruins had won just nine of their 41 games in the 1963–64 season prior to this jaw-dropping victory. Toronto, on the other hand, was in third place, but only four points out of the top spot in the standings. What occurred in Toronto's fabled home building on January 18 so stunned the ticketholders at Maple Leaf Gardens that a good percentage of them appeared to cheerfully switch allegiances—at least for one crazy night. They began enthusiastically chanting, "Go, Team, Go" for the bemused Bruins as Boston rolled up the score to double digits. This was quite a different experience for the Bruins, who had been routinely subjected to derisive chants at Boston Garden from disenchanted fans during the first three months of the season.

An unnamed Canadian Press correspondent summarized the fiasco succinctly. He wrote, "[The] Bruins were cheered lustily and the Leafs booed by a Toronto crowd of 14,011 that watched its heroes run into each other, fail to clear the puck, leave [Boston] attackers

Dean Prentice is best known as a member of the New York Rangers where he spent 11 seasons from 1952–53 through 1962–63. Prentice then spent three and a half years as a Boston Bruin where he was one of the key contributors in Boston's stunning 11–0 victory over the Toronto Maple Leafs on January 18, 1964 (Weekend Magazine/ Louis Jaques/ Library and Archives Canada/ e002505666).

uncovered, and even pass the puck to the Bruins. The Bruins were not only faster and slicker, but also stronger. Boston body checks sent Leafs flying in all directions"[1]

The end result was the most one-sided shutout in the NHL since the dark days of the Second World War when NHL teams were forced to operate with severely depleted and obviously substandard rosters. The league record was held (and still is held) by the Detroit Red Wings who mercilessly pummeled the pitiful New York Rangers 15–0 on January 23, 1944—almost 20 years to the day prior to the Bruins' 11–0 shellacking of the vaunted Maple Leafs. Apart from there being no global war raging in 1964, there was one other important difference: The Red Wings were playing a home game that night in 1944 at the Detroit Olympia; Boston was the *visiting* team when they soundly thumped Toronto.

"I recall seeing that score in the paper and thinking it was a misprint," wrote fan Dennis Bonvie on a hockey-discussion website in 2011. "There were no hockey box scores at the time in the local Connecticut newspapers. At first, I thought it must have been 1–0, then I thought it may have been 11–0 for Toronto. Anyway, [an NHL team] scoring 11 goals at the time was really unheard of."

The game was filled with anomalies. None of the 11 Boston goals came via the power play. No Bruin had scored three goals in a game since Murray Oliver managed the feat (versus the Maple Leafs at Toronto!) on December 23, 1961. On this night *two* Boston players notched hattricks: Andy Hebenton and Dean Prentice, the first time that twin accomplishment had happened since Boston's record-setting 14–3 demolition of the New York Rangers on January 21, 1945. (Prentice, in fact, got his three goals on just three shots on net!) It would be a year less four days before another Bruin scored three goals in a single game again. Boston's win gave them three consecutive victories—a feat the lowly Bruins had not achieved since March 1960. The last time the Bruins had scored as many goals in a game was on March 5, 1950, when they demolished the Chicago Blackhawks, 11–4, at Boston Garden.

After the opening faceoff, Boston wasted little time jumping into the lead. Gary Dornhoefer, a promising 20-year-old rookie, gave Boston a 1–0 edge after just 53 seconds of the first period, with assists coming from Johnny Bucyk and the aforementioned Murray Oliver. It was Dornhoefer's third goal in five games since joining the Bruins. His shot cleanly beat 32-year-old Don (Dippy) Simmons, a former Boston goalie who had played well for the Bruins versus New York and Montreal during the 1958 Stanley Cup playoffs. Simmons would make 27 saves this night—but he would be in the Toronto net for all 11 Boston goals. Toronto coach Punch Imlach could not pull Simmons from the game even if he wanted to do so—which he certainly did. The Maple Leafs had no backup goalie to relieve Simmons from the mounting misery. It was the fourth consecutive game in which Simmons had played goal for Toronto as Johnny Bower, the Leafs' other netminder, was sidelined with an injured hand.

The Boston rout was on. The goal judge seated behind Simmons for the first and third periods became the busiest man at Maple Leaf Gardens. In a penalty-free first period, Boston raced out to a virtually insurmountable 6–0 advantage over Toronto as Andy Hebenton and Dean Prentice each produced two-thirds of their eventual hattricks. Murray Oliver scored the other Boston goal. Rugged center Orland Kurtenbach uncharacteristically notched three assists in the first 20 minutes for the Bruins; he would record just 25 all season. To further demoralize the Leafs, Boston's sixth goal of the first period came with just six seconds left on the clock.

Things calmed down considerably in the middle frame as Boston added just a single goal to their lead in the second period. It came at the 12:27 mark as Andy Hebenton completed his hattrick to make the score 7–0 for the unstoppable Bruins. (Hebenton, playing his final NHL season—and his only one as a Bruin—scored 12 goals in the 1963–64 season, thus attaining a quarter of his total in this one game.) Frustration understandably began to mount among the Toronto players. When Boston's Bobby Leiter enthusiastically rode Toronto's Eddie Shack along the boards in a battle for the puck, Shack became momentarily airborne and his elevated skate exploded a pane of so-called shatter-proof glass near the Toronto blue line. Surprised spectators sitting near the impacted area began pulling smithereens out of their hair and clothing as Shack became enraged at the generally pacifistic Leiter. Fisticuffs ensued. The short battle can be seen on YouTube. (Sadly for Boston fans who had little to cheer about in the first half of the 1960s, the brief Shack-Leiter tussle is the only part of this historic rout that exists on that video-sharing website as of 2022.)

Apparently unsatisfied with the unfamiliar size of their lead, Boston methodically and mercilessly added four more tallies to the Maple Leaf Gardens scoreboard in the third period. Murray Oliver got the team's eighth Bruin goal and an assist on the team's tenth score, giving him two goals and a pair of assists for a productive four-point game. As impressive as that figure was, teammate Dean Prentice outdid him by 50 percent. He finished the lopsided contest with three goals and three assists on the night. The six points he accrued on January 18 accounted for a large chunk of Prentice's 39 points for the whole 1963–64 season. Johnny Bucyk scored Boston's tenth goal 7:04 into the final period. (Bucyk also had a four-point night, with a goal and three assists.) Jean-Guy Gendron concluded the Boston scoring orgy at 15:47. It came on Gendron's only shot on goal in the game. Overall, a dozen Bruins ended up recording at least one point. Prior to this game, Boston's highest goal output in 1963–64 had been eight versus the New York Rangers on December 7.

Fans generally paid little attention to the NHL's obscure plus/minus stats in 1963–64, but those numbers clearly showed who quietly had a great night for the triumphant visitors. Boston captain Leo Boivin and Ted Green, who both had just one assist, each finished the game at plus-six as did Dean Prentice and Andy Hebenton. On the reverse side of the ledger, two Maple Leafs endured a rough night in that same statistical category: Tim Horton was minus-six while Allan Stanley, who had played 129 games as a Bruin in the late 1950s, was an embarrassing minus-seven. Two other notable Toronto skaters (Dave Keon and George Armstrong) were each saddled with a godawful minus-five.

According to the *Boston Globe*, at the conclusion of the rout, the Maple Leaf Gardens crowd "rose in unison to give Boston a standing ovation as the team left the ice. Toronto slunk quietly into its chamber."[2] The *Globe* also noted that the game's three stars, as selected by *Hockey Night in Canada*, were justifiably all Bruins: Dean Prentice, Andy Hebenton, and Gary Dornhoefer. At least two of the applauding spectators were rooting for Boston without any hint of sarcasm. They were Dornhoefer's parents, residents of Kitchener, Ontario, who made the trip to Maple Leaf Gardens to witness their son play in the NHL for the first time in their lives.

Despite the passage of nearly 60 years, the 11–0 whitewash inflicted on the Maple Leafs that night in 1964 remains the most one-sided shutout victory in the Boston Bruins' century-long history. On the other side of the coin, the shellacking equaled the worst defeat in Toronto's history. The Leafs had fallen by exactly the same score to Montreal in a Stanley Cup playoff game on March 30, 1944.

Toronto's 20-year-old Pete Stemkowski, who went on to have a substantial NHL career that lasted until 1978, had the misfortune of playing his first big league game that night. Of course, he did not get any points for the Leafs in the shutout loss, but he did get his name in the contest's official record by serving a Maple Leaf bench penalty in the second period when the home team was caught with too many men on the ice.

Don Simmons did not receive many kind words about his performance in the Toronto net. "Simmons managed to stop 27 shots," declared the Canadian Press scribe, "but the rest of them were mainly short, low blasts fired into corners [of the net] while the goalie was on the other side or on his back."[3] The *Boston Globe* correspondent (who was not accorded a byline by his newspaper) did not mince his words, labeling Simmons as "hapless and helpless."[4] Boston coach Milt Schmidt was a little more sympathetic. "Don't blame Simmons," he told the Toronto *Globe & Mail*. "His defense was standing around like statues."[5]

Boston goalie Ed Johnston picked up the shutout for the victors. He had to work for it, stopping 26 Toronto shots. It seems incomprehensible today, but the 28-year-old Johnston was the only goalie who saw any action for Boston throughout the team's entire 70-game, 1963–64 NHL season.

The following night, the Bruins were back in action at Boston Garden. Their hot offense cooled off considerably as they scored just one goal in that game. It was a first-period power-play marker by Johnny Bucyk. Nevertheless, it was sufficient to earn Boston a hard-fought 1–1 tie versus the visiting Montreal Canadiens who were residing in second place in the NHL.

Toronto too had another game the night following the 11–0 contest. It was at Chicago Stadium. Don Simmons, who had allowed 22 goals in the four games when Johnny Bower was unavailable to play, was supposed to have been demoted to the minor leagues. However, his replacement, Al Millar of the Denver Invaders, ran into transportation difficulties when his United Airlines flight developed issues with its fuel pump. It was forced to land 333 miles away in Des Moines, Iowa, instead of at O'Hare International Airport. Millar never made it to the Windy City on time for Sunday's Toronto-Chicago game. The shell-shocked Simmons was forced into action for a fifth straight game—and, of course, shut out the NHL-leading Blackhawks, 2–0, making 27 saves in the process and generally looking terrific. Three of his stops were of the spectacular variety against Hawk sniper Bobby Hull. Chicago had soundly beaten the New York Rangers 6–1 the previous evening. Toronto bore little resemblance to the dismal squad from January 18. "The Leafs," said the Canadian Press report on the game, "were a most efficient defensive crew in front of Don Simmons, who was in the nets during Saturday's difficulties."[6] The *Calgary Herald*'s headline on its story documenting the weekend NHL action stated the obvious: "Leafs Show to Extremes."

A week later, on Sunday, January 26, Toronto and Boston renewed acquaintances. This time the venue was Boston Garden. The Bruins won again—and recorded another shutout. However, the score that night was more in keeping with a typical NHL game. It was only 2–0. Johnny Bower guarded the pipes for Toronto that night. Sandwiched between

Boston's two shutouts of Toronto was another shutout by Ed Johnston. The Bruins blanked Montreal 6–0 on January 25. For about a week, Boston looked to be an NHL powerhouse, but the illusion was fleeting.

Don Simmons would play in 21 games for Toronto in 1963–64. He toiled for both the Tulsa Oilers and Baltimore Clippers in the minor leagues over the next two seasons. He eventually returned to the NHL

Murray Oliver spent seven of his 17 NHL season as a Boston Bruin as a skillful playmaker. In 429 regular-season games with Boston, the crafty Oliver notched 116 goals and 216 assists. However, Oliver had the misfortune of playing on dismal Bruin clubs and never once saw Stanley Cup action with Boston (Weekend Magazine / Louis Jaques/ Library and Archives Canada / e002505676).

and played 20 games for the New York Rangers before retiring at age 37 in 1969. The shutout he recorded versus Chicago on January 19, 1964, was his twentieth—and last—as an NHL goaltender.

Boston won just eight more times in the 28 games remaining on their schedule. They finished the 1963–64 season in the league basement with a dismal 18–40–12 record. It was the fifth consecutive year the downtrodden Bruins failed to qualify for the Stanley Cup playoffs. They were last in the NHL in offense, scoring just 170 goals, an average of about 2.43 per game. Thus, the team's 11-goal outlier at Maple Leaf Gardens on January 18 represented 6.47 percent of its seasonal offensive output.

Conversely, the Toronto Maple Leafs finished the 1963–64 campaign in third place overall, 24 points superior to Boston. They won their third consecutive Stanley Cup that spring, ousting first-place Montreal in the playoff semifinals and Detroit in the finals. The Leafs' embarrassing 11–0 loss to Boston on January 18, 1964, not only equaled the worst loss in Toronto's history but was also the most lopsided regular-season defeat ever suffered by an eventual Stanley Cup champion to that point in NHL history. It was equaled on February 12, 1984, when the Hartford Whalers thumped the Edmonton Oilers by that same 11–0 margin.

Scoring Summary

First Period
- 0:53 BOS Gary Dornhoefer (assists: Johnny Bucyk, Murray Oliver)
- 6:20 BOS Andy Hebenton (assists: Orland Kurtenbach, Dean Prentice)
- 9:02 BOS Murray Oliver (assists: Johnny Bucyk, Leo Boivin)
- 9:28 BOS Dean Prentice (assist: Orland Kurtenbach)
- 14:51 BOS Andy Hebenton (assist: Dean Prentice)
- 19:54 BOS Dean Prentice (assist: Orland Kurtenbach)

Second Period
- 12:27 BOS Andy Hebenton (assists: Bobby Leiter, Dean Prentice)

Third Period
- 2:11 BOS Murray Oliver (assists: Johnny Bucyk, Ted Green)
- 6:17 BOS Dean Prentice (assist: Andy Hebenton)
- 7:04 BOS Johnny Bucyk (assists: Murray Oliver, Gary Dornhoefer)
- 15:47 BOS Jean-Guy Gendron (assists: Forbes Kennedy, Bob McCord)

11

April 2, 1969

*Playoff Brawl and Blowout—
Boston 10, Toronto 0*

For a team that had not won a Stanley Cup playoff game in ten long, frustrating years, on April 2, 1969, the Boston Bruins put that chunk of dismal history behind them as decisively as possible by routing the Toronto Maple Leafs 10–0. Among the many noteworthy things that happened that wild Wednesday night at Boston Garden was a four-goal performance by scoring superstar Phil Esposito to set a team record that has never been equaled, a brutal elbow to the head of Bobby Orr by Toronto's Pat Quinn that sent the Bruins' premier player to the hospital with a concussion and several fans into a violent frenzy, a masterful performance by Gerry Cheevers in the Boston goal—some observers maintained it was his best ever in a Bruin uniform—and there were fights galore. Were there ever! Fisticuffs were so prevalent that the next day's *Montreal Gazette* contained the following alliterative headline: "Bruins belt Leafs between brawls."

April 2 was the opening night of the first round of the 1969 Stanley Cup playoffs on four fronts. It was the second year since the league had doubled in size. It now had member clubs situated on both coasts of North America. Eight of the NHL's 12 teams began their quest for the Stanley Cup. In the East Division, the second-place Boston Bruins hosted the fourth-place Toronto Maple Leafs. Few neutral hockey observers gave Toronto much of a chance against the league's most colorful, rugged and talented bunch. Finishing a close second, just three points in arrears of the defending champion Montreal Canadiens in their division, the once unfashionable Bruins were obviously a team on the rise. They had achieved a club record 100 points in 1968–69. The Maple Leafs, on the other hand, were perceived as has-beens, a dynasty in decline, even though they had gotten 85 points from their 35–26–15 record in 76 games. Despite winning four Stanley Cups in the 1960s,

Toronto had certainly seen better days by the time the 1969 postseason rolled around. A Boston-Montreal semifinal seemed as inevitable as the sun setting in the west.

One thing that worried Bruins fans was the team's inability to play well in Toronto. They had gone 22 consecutive games without recording a win at Maple Leaf Gardens. Boston's last triumph there occurred on November 27, 1965, when Milt Schmidt was behind the Bruins' bench. Boston coach Harry Sinden dismissed the statistic as insignificant in the grand scheme of things. "I don't speak to the players about it," he told a Canadian Press reporter. "I'm sure they feel the way I do. It won't affect us at all. Anyway, it doesn't have a damned thing to do with the first two games."[1] (Games One and Two would be played at Boston Garden where the Bruins seldom lost.) Sports columnist Dink Carroll was not so sure. The *Montreal Gazette* scribe believed some of the Bruins were genuinely concerned about the so-called "Toronto jinx" and would have preferred a first-round playoff series versus the New York Rangers—who would be playing the Montreal Canadiens—rather than a matchup versus the Maple Leafs. Collectively speaking for his newspaper's entire sports staff, Carroll wrote, "We don't think the Boston-Toronto series will be a cakewalk for the Bruins."[2]

The Stanley Cup playoffs were still a bit of a novelty for Boston hockey fans in 1969. Having the home team expected to do great things was something only fans whose allegiance to the Bruins went back to the early 1940s could remember. The underdog Bruins reached the Stanley Cup finals in both 1957 and 1958, losing both times to the dominant Montreal Canadiens, a club in the midst of winning five consecutive Stanley Cups. The following year, a very capable Boston team lost in seven games to Toronto in a Stanley Cup semifinal. The once-proud club then entered an unprecedented down period in its illustrious history. The Bruins missed the playoffs in 1960, 1961, 1962 ... and so on. Boston would not again experience postseason hockey until the Expansion Era came in 1967–68. During the last home game of the 1966–67 season, even with sensational rookie Bobby Orr in their lineup, the Bruins were booed off the Garden ice in a listless 5–2 home loss to Toronto. "We're number six!" chanted the disillusioned patrons. A few tersely added the demeaning coda, "Next year we're number twelve!" After eight consecutive years of watching the Stanley Cup playoffs without the Bruins involved, Boston's hockey fans had earned the right to be a cynical bunch.

Things improved suddenly for Boston in 1967–68. The NHL'S Expansion Era clearly suited the Bruins well. So did some trades that reshaped the team. New acquisition Phil Esposito, formerly of the

Chicago Blackhawks, boldly predicted during the Bruins' training camp that his new team would certainly qualify for the playoffs in 1968, be a legitimate Stanley Cup threat the following year, and win it all in 1970. Jaded Boston sportswriters nodded politely but privately thought Esposito was off his rocker. But Boston's big #7 was true to his word. In the spring of 1968, the Bruins did qualify for the NHL playoffs as a third-place club. In a quarterfinal, however, they promptly dropped four straight games to the eventual Cup champion Montreal Canadiens without putting up too much resistance. Despite their undeniable improvement, Boston had still not won a playoff game since they edged Toronto, 5–4, at Maple Leaf Gardens on April 4, 1959.

Entering the 1969 playoffs, there was surprising news out of Boston on March 31. Longtime Bruins president Weston Adams, Sr., unexpectedly announced his retirement. He was replaced by his son, Weston Adams, Jr., who had been an executive vice-president on the club for many years. The retiring Adams noted in a hopeful tone that he believed the Bruins were on the right path to be competitive for years to come. In 1968–69 Boston had set a new NHL scoring record for goals in a season with 303 tallies, almost four per game. If that was not enough evidence to back up Adams' assertion, Game One versus Toronto the next night would provide ample proof that his Bruins were indeed poised to be an NHL powerhouse.

Game One provided many heroes for the partisan sellout crowd of 14,659 at Boston Garden to cheer and praise. "Jerry [sic] Cheevers' clutch goaltending and Phil Esposito's four-goal scoring spree carried the Boston Bruins to a brawl-filled, 10–0, near-record playoff victory over the Toronto Maple Leafs last night,"[3] declared a United Press International story, in which the Boston goalie's first name was misspelled. But there were several scoundrels in visiting white jerseys for the ticketholders to hiss at, too. By the conclusion of the third period, no Leaf was more reviled throughout New England than Toronto defenseman Pat Quinn.

"John Brian Patrick Quinn came out of the Maple Leafs dressing room last night at 11:30," reported Ray Fitzgerald of the *Boston Globe*. "Honestly, he didn't look like a villain. No horns marked his forehead, he didn't carry a pitchfork, and his ears weren't pointed. He looks like what he is—a darkly handsome Irishman who plays professional hockey for a living. He's a defenseman, and part of his job is to hit people."[4]

Fitzgerald was referring to an infamous hit on Bobby Orr when the Bruins were comfortably ahead of Toronto, 6–0, late in the second period. The UPI coverage of the game described the play and its crazy aftermath:

11. April 2, 1969

Defenseman Bobby Orr was knocked dizzy by a Pat Quinn elbow in the second period.

Orr was taken to hospital. X-rays were taken of his skull. Doctors ... ordered him held overnight for observation.

Several fans tried to get at [Quinn] in the penalty box. The entire Toronto squad came to [his] rescue by swinging their sticks.

Nine policemen escorted Quinn to the [visitors'] dressing room, arresting one young fan after he swung his program at [him].[5]

Orr was advancing the puck along the boards in the Boston zone when Quinn belted him with a brutal check in which he left his feet. Whether or not it was a legal hit by 1969's liberal standards for body contact—Quinn always maintained it was—is still passionately debated. Examining the play decades later on *Hockey Night in Canada*, television commentator Don Cherry bluntly opined, "Quinn would get 40 games for that now!"[6]

The spirited battling continued in the third period after a confrontation between Forbes Kennedy and Boston goaltender Gerry Cheevers escalated. It featured an unusual sight: All four goalies—both teams' starters and backups—were entangled in a full-scale, bench-clearing donnybrook. Referee John Ashley, a busy man, handed out 56 minutes in penalties from that skirmish alone. Kennedy, a former Bruin, was thrown out of the game.

During lulls in the fights, the Bruins were scoring goals in bunches, rolling up a 10–0 victory. It was their first playoff win since the days when the likes of Don McKenney, Jerry Toppazzini and Fleming Mackell were the top Bruin stars. Three minutes and 20 seconds into the first period, Boston had already scored twice, on goals by Phil Esposito (seven seconds into a Boston power play) and Johnny Bucyk. Esposito scored again at 14:01 to send the Bruins into the home dressing room with a 3–0 lead after 20 minutes.

The game became a rout in the second stanza, as Boston thrust four more daggers into the wounded Leaf carcass. It was 5–0 for the Bruins just past the halfway point of the period thanks to a second goal from the stick of veteran Johnny Bucyk and another from Derek Sanderson. Three-and-a-half minutes later, Phil Esposito "touched off a shower of hats and other articles"[7] with his third goal of the game, a power-play effort. Espo was not quite finished. His fourth goal of the contest came with just nine seconds remaining in the second period with the Bruins once more holding a man advantage. (Orr had been knocked senseless at the 18:03 mark.) No other Bruin had scored more than three goals in a playoff game before this night—and no one has achieved the feat in a Boston uniform since. With a period to play, Esposito had a very good chance to equal or better Maurice Richard's modern NHL record of five goals in a Stanley Cup playoff game, but he did not score again.

Three of Esposito's teammates added markers in the third period, however. They were Fred Stanfield, Derek Sanderson (again), and Ken Hodge. Esposito assisted on Hodge's goal—the Bruins; sixth power-play goal of the game. Boston ended up firing 51 shots at two Toronto goalies, Bruce Gamble and Johnny Bower. (Bower would replace the harried Gamble in the Toronto net when the third period began.) Despite the one-sided score favoring his team, Gerry Cheevers was far from idle guarding the Boston cage. The Maple Leafs fired 40 shots at him without finding a chink in his armor. Many of Cheevers' saves were both superb and timely, quashing any hopes of a Toronto comeback. Twenty-eight of the visitors' shots came in the game's first two periods when it was still a reasonably competitive contest. Cheevers' most important stop likely came in the very first minute of play when he thwarted a Brit Selby scoring opportunity that would have given Toronto a fast 1–0 advantage and perhaps changed the game's momentum.

Tom Fitzgerald of the *Boston Globe* was disgusted at how the game degenerated into brawls once the score got out of hand. He wrote, "Obviously the Bruins performed in consummate manner, even surpassing the expectations of their delirious followers." Fitzgerald continued,

> The Maple Leafs were a parody of a major league club. Since they were outplayed in such essentials as shooting, passing and skating, the Leafs resorted to the last refuge of the humiliated. They [became] a vengeful gang, dedicated to any consolation to be derived by provoking violence.
>
> They had ... avengers in Pat Quinn, [an], awkward young defenseman, and Forbes Kennedy, a knockabout forward ... to chop down their superiors in talent.[8]

In not so many words, Harry Sinden agreed with Fitzgerald. Sinden said he had seen nothing comparable since he accepted the Boston coaching job in May 1966. "We've had a lot of tough ones," he noted, "but none as bad as that in my time here."[9]

In the victorious Boston dressing room, Phil Esposito was downplaying his excellent night, claiming luck was responsible for many of the goals. Certainly, his power-play goal that opened the scoring 79 seconds into the first period was fortuitous, bouncing off his foot past luckless Bruce Gamble. The other three oozed quality. Francis Rosa of the *Globe* wrote,

> Esposito's third goal was magnificent, deliberate, almost in slow motion. There was a jam in front of the Toronto net. Esposito skated parallel to it,

going from left to right. Gamble went down and Esposito calmly lifted a backhand over him into the net. He did it so deliberately it looked as though you were watching it in stop action.[10]

Game One's unprecedented offensive outburst was important for Esposito as he had acquired a negative reputation as someone who did not perform well in the playoffs dating back to his days with the Chicago Blackhawks. Boston's scoring star was very defensive about the subject. He angrily told Rosa, "I never played in the playoffs for Chicago. I played in one period in four years. Then they benched me."[11] [Authors' note: Esposito was mistaken. In his four seasons with Chicago, he appeared in 29 playoff games and scored four goals.] During Boston's four-game loss to Montreal the previous spring, Esposito did not fare well. (In fairness, no Bruin did.) Montreal outclassed Boston. The Bruins scored eight goals in the four games; Espo scored none. Rosa claimed that Esposito's spectacular four-goal game against the Maple Leafs blew whatever negative playoff baggage Esposito may have had "all the way to Nome, Alaska."[12]

Phil Esposito also added a pair of assists in the Boston victory, giving him six points in a playoff game. That feat set a new Boston record. The mark has since been tied by Rick Middleton in 1983 and David Pastrnak in 2018, but it has never been surpassed.

Bobby Orr's health was cause for alarm in Boston. Clearly concussed, his status for Game Two—to be played the very next night—was questionable. Orr was officially listed as a possible participant by the Bruins. So was his defense partner Dallas Smith, who sustained a nasty gash on his forearm in the first period that required 13 stitches to mend. No Leaf was responsible for Smith's injury. It occurred when he collided with a piece of metal dangerously protruding from the protective glass.

The Bruins were under no illusions about what Game Two would probably entail. "I suppose [the Leafs will] try to play the same way," Phil Esposito proffered as he slowly changed into his civilian clothing. "So will we."[13]

Bobby Orr, Boston's most famous hospital patient, returned on Thursday for Game Two. He played a regular shift in the Bruins' easy 7–0 victory. Orr assisted on Johnny Bucky's first-period tally—which proved to be the game-winner. Cheevers got his second shutout in two days. Again, Toronto's starting goalie was not around for the finish. This time it was Johnny Bower who got the hook and was replaced by Bruce Gamble midway through the second period. The *Boston Globe* made much ado about the remarkable 17–0 aggregate score from the opening two games played at Boston Garden.

Typical of the NHL playoff schedule of the era, after just one day off for travel, Games Three and Four were contested in Toronto on Saturday and Sunday. Despite two dominant performances on home ice to begin the playoffs, one lingering question remained: Could Boston finally win at Maple Leaf Gardens and break the alleged "Toronto jinx." The hoodoo came to an end as the Bruins won 4–3 in Game Three. Toronto was never in front, although the game was level at 3–3 entering the third period. Derek Sanderson's goal at 2:52 broke the tie. Similarly, Boston won 3–2 in Game #4, never relinquishing the lead. Sanderson, having an excellent series, was the best Bruin on the ice, scoring twice for the visitors, giving him five scores in four games. Phil Esposito had the other Boston goal, raising his goal output to six in the four-game sweep.

After the game, longtime Toronto coach/general manager Punch Imlach was callously dismissed by his club despite having four Stanley Cups on his résumé. Leafs president Stafford Smythe allegedly gave his accomplished coach the ax two minutes after Game Four concluded. Imlach, however, insisted that no one from management formally told him he was fired—at least not in so many words. Imlach always maintained he heard the official news on his car radio while he was driving home. Harry Sinden was sympathetic about the demise of a fellow NHL coach. "When I get it, I certainly don't want to get it that way,"[14] he commented.

Calling Boston's 3–2 triumph "a solid victory," Tom Fitzgerald further penned in the *Boston Globe*, "[As in Game Three] the Toronto team once again was quite a contrast to the inept though desperately brawling gang Boston fans watched absorbing 10–0 and 7–0 humiliations in the Garden on Wednesday and Thursday."[15]

Although Toronto was officially vanquished after Game Four, the tone of Boston's triumph had been definitely set in Game One. After a decade of mostly being the NHL's doormats, the Boston Bruins rebranded themselves as a force to be reckoned with for the foreseeable future. It became perfectly clear to anyone who witnessed the 10–0 drubbing Boston inflicted on the Maple Leafs on April 2, 1969. The Bruins' recent dismal past was unchangeable, but their future was certainly a bright one.

Scoring Summary

First Period
- 1:19 BOS Phil Esposito (assists: Bobby Orr, Johnny Bucyk) PP
- 3:20 BOS Johnny Bucyk (assists: Phil Esposito, Ted Green) PP
- 14:01 BOS Phil Esposito (assists: Ken Hodge, Ron Murphy)

Second Period
- 7:22 BOS Johnny Bucyk (unassisted)
- 10:40 BOS Derek Sanderson (unassisted)
- 14:10 BOS Phil Esposito (assists: Ted Green, Ron Murphy) PP
- 19:51 BOS Phil Esposito (assists: Fred Stanfield, Ken Hodge) PP

Third Period
- 2:11 BOS Fred Stanfield (assists: John McKenzie, Johnny Bucyk) PP
- 4:34 BOS Derek Sanderson (assist: Ted Green)
- 12:47 BOS Ken Hodge (assists: Ed Westfall, Phil Esposito) PP

12

April 24, 1969
Bruins Fall to Habs in De Facto Cup Final

It had been about 14 hours since the last Boston Bruins hockey game of the 1968–69 season had concluded—and general manager Milt Schmidt still did not quite believe his team had been eliminated from the playoffs. Boston had just dropped its semifinal series to the Montreal Canadiens in six games, but Schmidt firmly believed that the nouveau riche Bruins—not the old-line Habs—should have gotten the East Division's berth in the championship round of the NHL's postseason. Speaking with veteran sports scribe Tom Fitzgerald, Schmidt bitterly grumbled, "Nobody can come into this office and tell me that the best team is in the Stanley Cup finals."[1] Few people in New England would have disagreed with the ex-Bruin star. After witnessing the terrifically entertaining series, most fair-minded neutral fans would have likely concurred with Schmidt, too.

Despite losing in a heartbreaking fashion, the Boston Bruins had achieved two intangible things instead of winning the Stanley Cup: They had shown the hockey world that they would likely be a force in the NHL for quite a few years. They had also shown that the league's new playoff system, in its second season of operation since the 1967 expansion, was a fiasco. It clearly deprived fans of seeing a great final. Now the best series was the semifinal featuring the surviving two clubs from the East Division.

In 1968–69 those teams were obviously Boston and Montreal. The quarterfinals played between the four East Division clubs proved what most NHL fans already knew: There were two elite teams in the NHL and the rest were also-rans of varying degrees. Montreal blew away the New York Rangers in four straight games. Boston handled the Toronto Maple Leafs in the same merciless way. This was the twenty-first consecutive Stanley Cup appearance for the reliable Habs, compared to just two for Boston. Montreal had been finalists in each of the last four seasons, winning the famous silver trophy in 1965, 1966 and 1968.

Montreal finished atop the NHL's East Division standings in 1968–69, edging out the Bruins 103 points to 100. Although the Boston lineup was significantly lighter in postseason experience than the defending Cup champions, they did possess a truly scary offense. The 1968–69 Bruins were the highest-scoring team in NHL history, scoring 303

Rugged John Ferguson, one of the NHL's toughest players in the Original Six era, had an excellent series versus the Bruins in the 1969 Stanley Cup playoffs. His key power play goal in Game One shifted the momentum of the first game of the East final (Jaques, Louis / Library and Archives Canada /e002343750).

goals in 76 games. Phil Esposito had accrued a whopping 126 points in regular-season play. Among those points were eight goals and two assists versus the Habs in eight contests in which the Bruins were 4–2–2. One of the two Montreal wins occurred on the second-last day of the schedule, a 5–3 triumph at the Forum on March 29. It was a key one. That result guaranteed the Habs would finish first overall and once again have home ice advantage in the playoffs, something they were certainly accustomed to possessing. Montreal had opened their last 15 playoff series at the Forum. Despite the Bruins being a younger and clearly ascending outfit, bookmakers put considerable stock in playoff experience. Accordingly, Montreal was listed as 3:2 betting favorites to take the series, largely because they would host Game Seven if the confrontation lasted that long.

The eagerly anticipated Bruins-Habs series opened at the Montreal Forum on Thursday, April 10. It would be played at a leisurely pace by Stanley Cup standards. To accommodate the demands of American television executives who wanted two Sunday afternoon telecasts guaranteed for the first and fourth matches—and a third matinee if a climactic seventh game was needed—11 days were set aside to play just the first four games of what was anticipated to be a lengthy and highly competitive battle. Writing in the *Montreal Gazette*, Pat Curran expressed the viewpoint of most serious hockey fans about what was at stake when the NHL's two foremost clubs clashed. "The best-of-seven round … has been billed as a semifinal," he noted, "but that's a laugh unless the expansion team performs a miracle in the East-West wrap-up."[2] Indeed, the other Stanley Cup semifinal, a matchup between the Los Angeles Kings and the St. Louis Blues, was largely perceived as little more than a curiosity. Neither team was thought to be much of a quality opponent for either Montreal or Boston.

Montreal's fiery John Ferguson, likely to avoid riling up the younger Bruins, rated Boston as the better of the two teams—at least publicly. "I'm looking for a close series, and a seventh game could mean a lot," he tactfully stated. Ferguson suggested the Habs' special teams might decide the outcome, reminding reporters that Montreal had scored five times in eight power-play opportunities versus New York while not conceding a single goal in the 12 instances when the Rangers possessed a man-advantage situation. "Bad penalties could really hurt [the Bruins] considering how well our power play has been going lately,"[3] he warned.

Before Game One, the Bruins flew from Boston on a private charter and were holed up in an unknown location somewhere just outside of Montreal in search of privacy. The big talking point in Boston was who would start in goal for the visiting Bruins in the opener. Coach Harry

12. April 24, 1969

Sinden chose 28-year-old Gerry Cheevers to guard the pipes instead of the more experienced Eddie Johnston, despite the former having had not an especially great result against the Habs in the previous spring's playoffs. Cheevers had allowed 15 goals in the Bruins' four-game loss in a 1968 Stanley Cup quarterfinal. "I've given it a lot of thought," Sinden told Curran, "not the least of which is the history of Johnston's work against Montreal. But Cheevers has had a great season. He played well against the Canadiens for two wins and two ties. He was terrific in our series versus Toronto."[4]

Game One lived up to fans' expectations. In what the *Boston Globe* described as "the most dramatic game the Bruins have played in years,"[5] Montreal won, 3–2, but it took a late comeback and an overtime goal by Ralph Backstrom 42 seconds into the fourth period to settle matters. It was Backstrom's first shot on goal all game. Boston defenseman Dallas Smith failed to clear a rebound properly. The fortuitous gaffe allowed Backstrom to lift the puck over the fallen Cheevers who had sprawled to make an initial save. Thoroughly frustrating for the Bruins and their supporters was that Boston was playing superbly and holding a 2–0 lead with only seven minutes left in the third period. (Derek Sanderson had scored both Boston goals; the second one came while the visitors were playing shorthanded.) However, a critical power-play marker by John Ferguson at 13:28, while Boston's Eddie Shack was serving an elbowing penalty, and a game-tying goal by Jean Béliveau at 19:04 with goalie Gump Worsley pulled for a sixth Montreal attacker, changed the game's momentum.

John Ahern wrote in the next day's *Boston Globe*, "Instead of holding that magnificent two-goal lead, the Bruins lost it all in the span of six minutes and 54 seconds, giving up three goals and losing 3–2. They found out first-hand why the Canadiens never are dead until the last bit of soil is patted down."[6]

"We beat them at about everything—except where it counts,"[7] insisted Boston's Ed Westfall, who had played an excellent game. "Actually, we played about 50 minutes of hockey," deadpanned Harry Sinden. "The game calls for 60."[8]

Three days later, the Bruins and Habs renewed acquaintances with a Sunday afternoon game for the benefit of CBS television. Again, Game Two required an overtime period. Again, Montreal emerged as the winner, this time by a 4–3 count. The winning goal was a power-play tally, at 4:55, scored by Mickey Redmond while Boston's Ted Green was serving a hooking penalty.

"There was some difference in the details and a slight variation in the timing, but the result was just about the same,"[9] penned Tom

Fitzgerald of the *Globe* in his account of Game Two at the Forum. Redmond's overtime power-play goal was a rarity in the 1960s NHL as referees tended to put their whistles away with so much at stake, but it seemed to be an accurate call, even to Boston scribes. Green had been sent off for what Fitzgerald deemed to be a necessary "tactical penalty to break up a Montreal scoring bid by Ralph Backstrom."[10] Green still had 36 seconds left to serve when Redmond found the target.

Veteran netminder Ed Johnston was the Boston goalie this time. He was making his Stanley Cup playoff debut at age 34. He played well, but it was all for naught in the end. Boston had broken a 2–2 deadlock on a Johnny Bucyk goal with less than six minutes remaining in the third period, but they could not run out the clock. Serge Savard got a tying tally with just 69 ticks left on the clock to force an extra period. Despite his team being in an unfavorable two-game hole, defiant Bruin coach Harry Sinden declared afterward, "They won't beat us again this year."[11]

With the clubs enjoying a lengthy break, the series moved to Boston Garden for the third and fourth games to be played on Thursday and Sunday. As promised by their coach, Game Three ended in a much-needed Boston victory, 5–0, as Gerry Cheevers notched his third playoff shutout of 1969. "The Bruins proved they weren't just whistling up their courage when they boasted they would come back and beat the Canadiens," stated Tom Fitzgerald in his *Globe* report. "They did just that last night."[12] Phil Esposito got two goals for the home team. Gump Worsley took the loss for the visiting Canadiens.

Before another matinee CBS television audience, the Bruins took Game Four to level the series. It was a closely contested 3–2 win. For the Habs, 23-year-old Rogatien (Rogie) Vachon started in goal as veteran netminder Gump Worsley was unable to play due to an injured hand. Bobby Orr got his first career Stanley Cup playoff goal against the bare-faced Vachon; it proved to be the decisive one. Unusually, two of Boston's three goals were scored while the home team was shorthanded. They came on tallies from the club's pair of esteemed penalty-killers, Ed Westfall and Derek Sanderson. Unfortunately for Sanderson, his goal came at a high price. He was injured on the play and was expected to miss at least two games. Orr's goal, which completed a nifty passing play, made the score 3–1 for Boston with just 1:47 remaining on the clock. However, Montreal had more late-game heroics stored in their arsenal. Coach Claude Ruel pulled Vachon for an extra attacker. As was becoming the norm, the move paid off as Montreal got within one goal, on a tally by Serge Savard, making the score 3–2 for Boston. The Habs got no closer, however. "The Orr goal stood up through the remaining pressurized seconds," wrote Tom Fitzgerald, "providing release for a great roar for the congregation of 14,659, saluting a victory which made the series all even at two games apiece."[13] The eventual outcome of this excellent and compelling playoff tussle was now anyone's guess.

Game Five, played on Tuesday, April 22, saw Montreal return to its familiar championship form. This time the Cup holders got off to an early lead and the Bruins had to assume the undesirable role of pursuers. After a closely contested 18 minutes of play with few scoring chances for either team, the Habs got three goals in short order by players not normally associated with offensive prowess. Defenseman Jacques Laperrière scored at 18:25 of the first period. (He had scored just five times in the regular season.) After 129 seconds of the second period, Boston found themselves staring at a three-goal deficit after Claude Provost and J.C. Tremblay—another Hab defenseman—added a pair of tallies. Boston responded with a huge bombardment of 26 shots in the second period alone. Ken Hodge made the game close by scoring twice for Boston three minutes apart in the middle of the frame. From that point onward, Rogie Vachon did not surrender another Boston goal. Claude Provost scored again in the third period to provide an unnecessary insurance buffer for the home team.

Two nights later, Boston and Montreal, both clubs worthy of all plaudits, contested Game Six at Boston Garden where the Bruins had seldom lost all year. (In 38 home games during the 1968–69 regular season, the Bruins were an outstanding 29–3–6. They were 4–0 in playoff games thus far at Boston Garden in 1969, with three of those wins being shutouts.) It was truly a terrific contest, deserving to be part of the real Stanley Cup final—not the de facto final.

With Derek Sanderson returning to the Boston lineup a game ahead of schedule, aging Ron Murphy got the Bruins off to a positive start at 2:29 of the first period, scoring his fourth goal of the 1969 playoffs on a backhand from close in on Rogie Vachon. Murphy had received an accurate pass from behind the net from Phil Esposito, who had stolen the puck from Montreal's Terry Harper. It was the final postseason goal Murphy would ever score. It also turned out to be the final goal scored by anyone in a Boston uniform in the 1968–69 season.

It had been a cleanly played series, but referee Art Skov had to deal with fisticuffs on two separate occasions in Game Six as players' nerves began to fray as the tension mounted. John Ferguson battled Don Awrey in the first period while in the second frame Derek Sanderson squared off against Henri Richard, an undersized Hab forward who seldom got involved in scraps. One Boston fan could not control himself. He leaned over the low protective glass and took a swing at the small Montreal player while he was engaged with Sanderson. Boston Garden security personnel swiftly dealt with the interloper.

Although Boston pumped 22 shots at Vachon in the middle frame, the score remained just 1–0 for the home team until early in the third period. At 1:05, Bruin defenseman Don Awrey was sent off the ice by Skov for cross-checking. Just five seconds later, Serge Savard, who was having an excellent series for Montreal, tied the game with a power-play tally on a low, hard shot from the blue line that eluded Gerry Cheevers, who was making his fifth start of the series for Boston. There was no further scoring in the period. Perhaps fittingly, for the third time in the series, the Habs and Bruins would require a fourth period—and perhaps longer—to decide a winner. For the first time since March 29, 1955, an overtime game would be played at Boston Garden.

The first 20 minutes of extra play decided nothing, but it was fun hockey to watch if one did not have a particular rooting interest in the outcome. However, the tension was almost unbearable for a fan of either team. Bud Collins eloquently wrote in his *Boston Globe* column, "Up and down the ice the Bruins and Canadiens surged, incredibly, beautifully, and roughly too, flashing their sticks murderously at Vachon and Cheevers, who repelled everything. Everything for four hours."[14]

Slightly past the halfway point of the first overtime period, Montreal was forced to deal with a minor penalty to John Ferguson, whom Skov whistled for a holding infraction. The visitors' penalty-killing unit did the job well. The Bruins failed to score and the contest continued into the night.

The end came on Friday morning, 13 minutes past midnight. Harshly for the home team, it was a goal scored against the run of play. The Bruins had been the dominant team in the second overtime period, but had failed to capitalize on several chances. The winning goal came when Montreal's Claude Provost correctly anticipated Don Awrey's attempt to clear the puck from the Boston zone around the boards. The Hab forward deftly intercepted it and then adroitly stepped aside from a charging Boston defender. Provost caught a glimpse of uncovered 37-year-old Jean Béliveau in the slot. "When I got the puck I had a little peek," Béliveau, Montreal's esteemed captain, said during the postgame celebration in the visitors' dressing room, "and I saw an opening by Cheevers' left side. I just let it go and I found the opening."[15] Béliveau's rising shot hit the top corner of the Boston net. The time of the goal was 11:28 of the fifth period. It was the popular Béliveau's 76th playoff goal in 16 NHL seasons. It was also the only overtime marker he ever scored for the Habs in his glorious Hall-of-Fame career.

"What can I say?" Cheevers asked rhetorically. "I saw the shot, but there just wasn't time [to react]. It was a very good shot."[16]

"The stunned Bruins have six months to think about how close they came to beating the Canadiens," wrote John Ahern in the following morning's *Boston Globe*. "They had innumerable chances, but Fate and Rogatien Vachon conspired against them."[17]

"The Montreal Canadiens are aging and last night they were tired," Ahern continued. "They could have cracked and they were expected to crack. But champions know how to win."[18]

The great Jean Béliveau scored just one playoff overtime goal in his illustrious 17-year career with the Montreal Canadiens: It came in Game Six of the 1969 Stanley Cup semifinal versus Boston—sealing a victory that sent the Habs to the Stanley Cup finals versus St. Louis for a second consecutive spring (Weekend Magazine / Louis Jaques / Library and Archives Canada / e002505688).

That seemed to be the prevailing wisdom in the various postmortems. To their credit, the defeated Bruins did not offer any alibis. They acknowledged their own shortcomings while generously applauding the victors' pluck. Mostly the vanquished home team credited the Habs' experience in Stanley Cup play as the single biggest difference determining which team won the series. "The old pros know how to do it," stated a sweat-soaked Johnny McKenzie, offering his thoughts on the outcome of Game Six as he pulled off his uniform. "They're like the old New York Yankees, the old Green Bay Packers. They know how to win. They got the chance. They accepted it. It makes no difference in what sport—baseball, football, hockey, rodeos. They are the same: champions."[19]

Boston's Ron Murphy, who had turned 36 two weeks earlier, had experience of the opposite kind. Eight years before, Murphy had been a member of the 1960–61 Chicago Blackhawks who upset the vaunted Canadiens in that season's Stanley Cup playoffs. One of those games was won by the Hawks in a triple-overtime thriller. He said he would always recall the jubilation of that night's dramatic victory, "but I'll remember this one too," he lamented. "[It's] the shock of it all, the way your heart stops when it happens. We're pounding away very well and then Jean Béliveau gets it. In three weeks it will be easier to take. But, God, it's going to be awful for a long time."[20]

Phil Esposito stormed into the Boston dressing room moments after Béliveau had notched the winner. He was thoroughly disappointed with the result in general and himself in particular. "It happened again!" he ranted to all and sundry. "I could have had at least two [goals] and I missed them. That makes it a million for me in the last two games. I had the chances and I couldn't do it. I guess all I can say is that the puck just didn't bounce for me."[21]

Esposito's equally frustrated teammate, Fred Stanfield, chimed in with an expanded version of the same tune. "We all had chances," he insisted. "No one was finishing off [scoring opportunities]. We could have had them—but look at the score."[22]

Boston coach Harry Sinden specifically pinpointed the moment where he thought the game had been squandered. "Look back to the second period where we had that two-man advantage for 46 seconds," he said. "We should have scored. We had every right to expect to score. We came up empty. That could be it right there."[23]

Further reflecting on the well-played series, Sinden added, "We had chances, lots of chances. Seldom did we have so many good chances to score [during the regular season] without capitalizing."[24] While talking about the tough loss to the assembled media, Sinden

12. April 24, 1969

was quietly approached by former Bruins president Weston Adams, Sr. Recently retired, Adams had dropped by the Bruins' dressing room to commiserate. "Harry, you didn't deserve that,"[25] Adams sympathetically told him.

Ken Hodge was perhaps the most embittered of the beaten Bruins—and he was not afraid to voice his displeasure at the outcome of the series. "They didn't deserve to win it; I know that," he concluded. "We outplayed them, and three of the six games they won in overtime. They don't deserve it, but there they are, still going. We're going home."[26]

Gerry Cheevers, never a good loser, said nothing to reporters for a long time before he finally opened up to a large collection of hockey scribes. He recalled the winning goal in short, terse language. "Provost put that pass on Béliveau's stick. He had it a split second. I couldn't move. No chance."[27] (Béliveau himself told reporters that Cheevers ought not to be faulted on the series-ending goal.) Giving credit where it was certainly due, Cheevers duly praised his youthful Montreal counterpart. "[Vachon] was super. How many stops did he have?"[28] he wondered aloud. The answer was 50 of 51, he was informed. Once Gump Worsley had been sidelined with his hand injury following Game Three, more than a couple of hockey writers had openly suggested that Rogie Vachon would be the Habs' weak spot that the high-scoring Bruins would be certain to exploit. He proved to be the complete opposite.

In the Friday evening edition of the *Boston Globe*, John Ahern thoughtfully summarized the big picture. He declared, "It was a hard [loss] to take for the Bruins and the fans, but everybody must agree it was one hell of a season. Too bad it didn't last two more weeks."[29]

Pat Curran of the *Montreal Gazette*, in his game report from Boston, mockingly referred to the upcoming Cup finals as the "expansion round" and predicted it would be a dud compared to the quality of hockey witnessed in the Montreal-Boston semifinal series. He wrote, "It won't be much of an encore after this meeting of the two best clubs in the NHL or last night's contest which left the Garden crowd limp with excitement."[30] Curran was absolutely correct in his assumption: In the official Stanley Cup finals, as was the case in 1968, Montreal romped past the St. Louis Blues in four straight games in what can only be described as a huge anticlimax.

Even before the first game of the championship round had been contested, Tom Fitzgerald of the *Boston Globe* candidly offered a similar opinion to Curran's, but he authored it in a more cosmopolitan context. Fitzgerald amusingly noted, "Montreal and Boston are the two best hockey teams in the world, barring dissent from Moscow."[31]

Scoring Summary

First Period
- 2:29 BOS Ron Murphy (assist: Phil Esposito)

Second Period
- No scoring

Third Period
- 1:10 MON Serge Savard (assist: Jean Béliveau) PP

First Overtime
- No Scoring

Second Overtime
- 12:28 MON Jean Béliveau (assist: Claude Provost)

13

April 26, 1970

*The Afternoon the Bruins
Really Won the 1970 Cup*

Any serious fan of the Boston Bruins recognizes May 10, 1970, as an important date in the club's history. The warm Mother's Day afternoon in Boston saw the Bruins win their fourth Stanley Cup—the team's first in 29 years—courtesy of Bobby Orr's iconic overtime goal versus the St. Louis Blues. What is often forgotten is that the 1970 Stanley Cup final was basically a coronation for the Bruins. Once the two finalists had been determined, few hockey followers doubted that Boston would triumph over the overmatched Blues. Game Four's overtime battle turned out to be the only closely contested game of the series. The "real final" had been settled precisely two weeks before when Boston won its semifinal series—the championship of the East Division—in what was perceived to be a mild upset over the Chicago Blackhawks. After that victory, a Stanley Cup championship was a foregone conclusion for the ascending crew from the Hub.

The bias was wholly understandable. Six new teams were added to the NHL for the 1967–68 season: St. Louis, Pittsburgh, Minnesota, Philadelphia, Los Angeles and Oakland. The league was split into two six-team divisions, East and West. Generously, the NHL placed all the newcomers into the West division with a playoff system that guaranteed one of them would advance to the Stanley Cup finals. The St. Louis Blues had been the West's representative in both 1968 and 1969—and failed to win a game in both years against the Montreal Canadiens. Not much was expected to change the next spring.

The 1969–70 NHL season, the East Division produced the tightest playoff race in NHL history. It was nearly as competitive in the West, too. Five of the six Original Six teams stayed within striking distance of each other all the way through the 76-game campaign. Only Toronto, the Stanley Cup champions from 1966 to 1967, were never seriously in the running for a playoff berth in the East. The other five teams were all extremely competitive. Never falling into a significant slump, Boston was perhaps the steadiest team of the bunch, although the Bruins had a terrible time beating fellow East Division clubs on the road. At Boston Garden, however, the Bruins were practically invincible. Chicago got off to a terrible start, dropping their first five games while Bobby Hull sat out in a contract dispute. Coach Billy Reay was nearly axed. However, the Blackhawks caught fire in November. Led by the returning Hull, a commitment to better defense, and a wonderful rookie goalie named Tony Esposito, Chicago became a top contender. The New York Rangers got off to a fabulous start but nearly threw it all away in a horrendous late-season slump. Detroit won their first two games of the year but fired coach Bill Gadsby anyway, replacing him with Sid Abel. In an up-and-down season, the Red Wings led by the aging but wonderful line of Frank Mahovlich, Gordie Howe and Alex Delvecchio, propelled the Red Wings to their first playoff berth in three seasons. The two-time defending Stanley Cup champion Montreal Canadiens seemed to be as solid as ever, but they got into the bad habit of blowing games. Late leads tended to vanish for the Habs far too frequently throughout the tightly fought campaign—and critical points were frittered away. A three-game losing streak cost Montreal a playoff spot in the last week of the regular-season. In the end, the East Division's postseason was without a Canadian-based team as the Maple Leafs and Canadiens both failed to make the top four. That had never happened before. For Montreal, it was the first time they were absent from the Stanley Cup playoffs since 1948.

When the final points were tallied, Chicago and Boston led the way in the East. Both had 99. The Blackhawks were awarded first-place on the basis of more wins. (It was a notable turnaround for Chicago. The previous season, the Blackhawks had finished dead last and missed the playoffs. The once vilified Billy Reay was suddenly the toast of Chicago.) Detroit finished alone in third spot with 95 points. New York and Montreal had both accrued 92 points and identical won-lost-tied records of 38–22–16, but the Rangers achieved fourth-place for scoring more goals than Montreal (246–244). It was that close. The Rangers' margin of victory was provided by a memorable nine-goal outburst on the final Sunday of the regular season at Madison Square Garden. It was a game where the visiting Detroit Red Wings had little to play for—and played accordingly.

The first all-American Stanley Cup tournament began on April 8 on four fronts. In the East, Detroit faced the Blackhawks with Chicago getting home ice advantage. It mattered little as Chicago won in a somewhat surprising four-game sweep. Remarkably, each game ended in the same score: 4–2 for the Hawks. (Such an oddity had never happened in the NHL playoffs before and has not happened since.) After four playoff games, Chicago looked like the front-runners to win their first Stanley Cup in nine years.

In the other East Division series, it took Boston six games to eliminate the feisty Rangers in a confrontation that set all sorts of records for individual and team penalty minutes. During the three games in New York City, the Bruins were greeted with banners that were not necessarily family-friendly. Boston's Johnny Bucyk recalled with disgust in his autobiography, "Some of the signs they had hung up on the walls of Madison Square Garden were shameful, totally disgraceful."[1] When the Rangers lost Game Six at home, 4–1, their angry supporters pelted the Bruins with garbage and dangerous missiles of every description when the final buzzer sounded, including large batteries and cans of shaving cream. They also attempted to set the arena's mezzanine on fire to demonstrate their collective frustration and, perhaps, their collective intelligence.

In the victorious Boston dressing room, a haven from the New York fans' malicious shenanigans, Bruins coach Harry Sinden was asked to handicap the East final. He declined, but New York coach/general manager Emile Francis, who dropped in to offer his congratulations to the winners, was more than willing to offer an opinion. "Sure, Chicago has to be favored. They've had a long rest and they're ready," he stated. "But they don't have Bobby Orr." To emphasize his point, Francis added this praiseful coda: "He's the greatest player in any game—ever. If we had him, no one would touch us."[2] In the Rangers' dressing room, the vanquished Jean Ratelle and goaltender Ed Giacomin were equally generous about the talents of the kid who had been the most responsible for ending their season. Ratelle summed up Orr in three words: "He is everything."[3] Giacomin offered four words: "He's more than that."[4]

The 22-year-old Orr had scored seven times against Francis' defeated Rangers, twice in Game Six, already surpassing the record number of goals by a defenseman in a single playoff year. The old mark had been five, set by Earl Siebert in 1938—and it had taken Siebert 10 games to attain it. Orr had eclipsed it in a single series. Orr's total was only one shy of the record for goals in a postseason series by any player, shared jointly by Gordie Howe, Bobby Hull, and retired Bruin Jerry Toppazzini.

In his fourth NHL season, Orr had become the face of a league that was trying to extend its appeal beyond its traditional markets. Polite, accommodating, modest to a fault, and possessing immense talent, no one had ever seen anyone quite like Robert Gordon Orr. A defenseman being a hockey team's offensive leader was something unheard of before Orr came along. By age 18, Orr was playing in the NHL and was named Rookie of the Year for 1966–67. Boston still missed qualifying for the playoffs for the eighth straight season, but the acquisition of Ken Hodge, Fred Stanfield and Phil Esposito from Chicago in the offseason gave the Bruins a solid foundation and a supporting cast for Orr that would pay dividends immediately.

CBS television began carrying NHL games on Sunday afternoons in 1969–70 in February, once the professional football season had wrapped up. Therefore, it was not surprising that the "real Stanley Cup final," as some writers preferred to call it, opened at Chicago Stadium on Sunday, April 19 with a day game for the benefit of American network TV. The Blackhawks were the better rested team, having had a week off since ousting Detroit, but the Bruins were seemingly the better prepared outfit. Using a combination of muscle and skill, Boston posted a convincing and surprisingly easy 6–3 win over the hometown Hawks. Boston fought off early Chicago pressure and counterpunched their way to a 3–0 lead by the midpoint of the game. Orr picked up two assists, but Phil Esposito was the Boston star. He scored a hattrick on his younger brother. In May, Tony Esposito would win the Calder Memorial Trophy—emblematic of the NHL's Rookie of the Year—by a large margin.

Two nights later, Boston won again at Chicago Stadium. This time the Bruins mostly eschewed the rough stuff and still won comfortably. Orr opened the scoring with a picturesque goal at 5:08 of the first period in which he was sent in alone on Tony Esposito. Boston again roared out to a 3–0 lead after two periods and won, 4–1. Most everyone in the hockey world had figured the Boston-Chicago series would be a competitive tilt, but the plucky Bruins had not followed the script. They were heading home, up two games to none, to a friendly locale where they seldom tasted defeat.

Game Three at Boston Garden was another Bruins triumph, 5–2. The Blackhawks held a 2–1 lead after 20 minutes, but surrendered three goals in the middle frame and never recovered. Boston's fourth goal was a Bobby Orr classic that has been shown on highlight reels for more than half a century. It was a power-play tally. Orr rushed the puck along the right boards into the Chicago zone. Three fearful Hawk defenders, like lemmings, mindlessly pursued Boston's #4 as he carried the disc behind the Hawks' goal. Orr made a simple pass in front of the net to an uncovered Phil Esposito who was standing alone to the right of his brother. Phil passed the puck to an equally unguarded Johnny Bucyk at the other side of the Chicago net for what Gary Ronberg of *Sports*

13. April 26, 1970

Illustrated described as "the easiest kind of goal."[5] That marker took the wind out of the Blackhawks' sails completely. An empty-net goal by Phil Esposito with 21 seconds left in the third period salted away another playoff victory for the home team, their fifth in a row. Boston was just a single win away from their first trip to the Stanley Cup finals in 12 years.

Game Four of the East Division final occurred on April 26. It was another CBS Sunday afternoon telecast. The network got lucky: It turned out to be the best game of the Boston-Chicago series by far, a thoroughly entertaining 60 minutes featuring numerous shifts in momentum and an abundance of talking points.

Clearly wanting to do away with the Hawks in the minimum number of games, the Bruins carried the play in the opening period. However, Tony Esposito was standing firm in the Chicago goal and beating back all of Boston's scoring threats. Even when the Bruins were playing shorthanded, they were a dangerous group, a point proved when youthful Don Marcotte scored on a Phil Esposito rebound in the 14th minute of play when Chicago had a man advantage. Boston was even more troublesome to the Blackhawks when they were on the power play. Johnny Bucyk scored with the Bruins a man up with exactly three minutes left in the first period. (Tony Esposito hotly maintained the puck had not crossed the goal line before he swept it away, charging at the three officials to passionately lodge his complaint. However, television replays showed the goal judge and referee Bill Friday were correct in awarding a score to Boston. Brother Phil amusingly signaled a goal, too.) Everything was going according to the Bruins' expectations as the two teams headed into the first intermission. Boston outshot Chicago 14–7 and led the game 2–0, but the score could have been perhaps 5–0 based on the many quality chances the Bruins failed to put past Tony Esposito.

The Esposito wearing the goalie equipment and the white visitors' jersey turned back more sustained Bruin assaults in the second period which allowed the game's momentum to shift dramatically. Totally against the run of play, Chicago took a 3–2 lead in the space of about eight minutes. Chicago's unexpected resurgence began after a timely slap shot by Keith Magnuson eluded Gerry Cheevers. It was something of an atonement for Magnuson, who had played poorly in Game Three and received a great deal of bad press about it. (Magnuson's goal was an aberration. The rugged defenseman had not scored the entire season before his well-placed shot sailed into the top of the Boston net past a surprised Cheevers. Magnuson made a point of collecting the puck as a souvenir.) Then Dennis Hull—Bobby's younger brother—scored a pair of pretty goals, especially his second tally where he deftly moved around Don Marcotte and beat Cheevers one-on-one. Suddenly, with 6:50

remaining in the second period, the assumed Bruin four-game series sweep was not entirely certain. A murmur of concern rippled throughout the 14,835 fans packed into cozy Boston Garden.

The Bruins responded quickly to the crisis, however. Exactly two and a half minutes after losing the lead, Boston leveled the score. Dallas Smith fed onrushing Fred Stanfield a pass at the red line. Stanfield moved across the Chicago blue line and unleashed a slap shot that appeared to catch Tony Esposito by surprise. The shot clanged off the inside of the goal post to Esposito's left and entered the net. After two exciting periods, the Bruins and Blackhawks were tied, 3–3.

With Chicago's Cliff Koroll serving a major high-sticking penalty, Boston failed to score on a five-minute power play that ran into the third period as Tony Esposito held firm. At the 4:10 mark of the third period, Chicago capitalized on their man-advantage situation. Rookie Bryan Campbell, also not known for his scoring exploits, knocked a rebound past Cheevers on a scrambly play to give his Hawks a 4–3 lead. Boston responded with wave after wave of attacks for more than ten minutes without success in an attempt to produce the tying goal. Tony Esposito superbly defended all of them, but the physical effort and mental strain were taking a toll on him. During one TV timeout, Esposito trudged to the visitors' bench for a sip of water. While there, he momentarily draped himself over the boards in utter exhaustion. Boston would fire 18 shots on goal in the third period to Chicago's six.

It was to be Boston's day, however. Ken Hodge subtly deflected Phil Esposito's centering pass past the tired Chicago netminder at 15:19, simultaneously energizing the partisan and emotional crowd while deflating the Blackhawks. The final momentum shift was palpable.

With overtime looming, the Bruins retook the lead in the final two minutes of regulation play. It was a bit of a sloppy goal. Stan Mikita uncharacteristically made an overly casual pass inside the Chicago blue line. It was neatly intercepted by John McKenzie. The undersized forward—who was surprisingly voted the most popular Bruin in a 1970 fan poll—fed a cross-ice pass to teammate Fred Stanfield. McKenzie moved forward and accepted a backhanded return pass. With traffic in front of the Chicago net obscuring Tony Esposito's view, McKenzie fired a shot that went over the crouching goalie's left shoulder and into the top of the net. The goal light flashed and Boston Garden went wild. There was just 1:41 remining in the third period.

Chicago coach Billy Reay pulled Esposito for a sixth attacker in the final minute of the game, but the Blackhawks could not produce the necessary tying goal. Johnny Bucyk nearly made the final score 6–4, but his shot at the open cage squarely hit the goal post. With a faceoff in the Chicago zone and only two seconds left on the clock, Tony Esposito returned to the ice. He made one final save—his 49th of the game—just before the horn sounded. A cute scene followed: Brother Phil affectionately patted Tony on his head before joining his teammates in celebrating the biggest Bruin win in more than a decade.

With Boston's semifinal triumph secure in the books, many hockey insiders were already conceding the Stanley Cup to the Bruins. Pat Curran of the *Montreal Gazette* was one of them. He wrote that Boston "had virtually clinched its first Stanley Cup in 29 years."[6] Smiling general manager Milt Schmidt was more cautious and diplomatic on the subject, but he was clearly thinking the same thing. Choosing his words carefully, the 52-year-old Bruin star from yesteryear told Curran, "It isn't here yet, but it's nice to have a pretty good shot at it."[7]

"The other guy was fantastic,"[8] declared Gerry Cheevers after the game. He was obviously referring to Chicago netminder Tony Esposito whose fine play under enormous fire in Game Four had won the respect of the most hardcore of Boston fans. Bobby Orr was quick to add his praise, too. "He was terrific all the time [the Hawks] were shorthanded on that major penalty," said Boston's famous #4. "You can't rap Tony. There was no knock on him in the series, anyway. [His teammates] only gave him six goals up until today, and you can't win many games that way."[9] The defeated Chicago goaltender was in no mood to received plaudits, however. "You never play good [sic] when you lose,"[10] he sadly stated.

Whom the Bruins were going to face in the legitimate Stanley Cup finals was still very much up in the air. While the Bruins were celebrating their sweep of the Blackhawks in Boston, the Pittsburgh Penguins and St. Louis Blues were eagerly preparing for the fourth game of the West Final that night at the Pittsburgh Civic Arena. The Blues held a 2–1 series edge after Game Three, but Pittsburgh leveled the series that night with a closely contested 2–1 victory with the home club's promising rookie Michel Brière providing the winning goal on a second-period breakaway. That result ensured the Blues and Pens would have to play a minimum of six games to decide the winner of their series, which meant the Cup finals would not begin until at least the following weekend. Thus, the Bruins could look forward to a long rest between games while the West Division's championship was being decided.

The Bruins would have a day off before resuming practices on Tuesday. Coach Harry Sinden was unsure of how the long gap between games would affect his team, a prospect that bothered him somewhat. "The rest should be good," he optimistically told Tom Fitzgerald of the *Boston Globe*, "but you have to wonder if a club might lose concentration. Also, when you're away from body contact for a while, it might be hard to pick it up again."[11]

Of course hockey writers posed the inevitable and obvious question to various happy Bruins reveling in their triumph over the Blackhawks: "Which team would you prefer to play in the Stanley Cup finals?" That query generally elicited answers along the lines of "I don't care" and "It doesn't really matter." However, a few jolly Bruins used the opportunity to put in their comedic two cents' worth. Goaltender Gerry Cheevers, a favorite of Boston sportswriters for his ever-present sense of humor, responded with "Hershey." (Presumably he was referring to the minor league Hershey Bears.) John McKenzie was even more creative with his reply. Sitting next to Cheevers, he expressed a deep desire for his Bruins to play the Nanton Palominos for the Stanley Cup. They were an obscure amateur team from McKenzie's hometown of Nanton, Alberta. The community had a population of about 2,000.

Bobby Orr, who had an undistinguished game, was asked by one visiting scribe if the playoff money he would receive really meant all that much to him since he was certainly well on his way to becoming a hockey millionaire. With an incredulous expression on his face, Orr promptly replied, "You must be kidding. This is for the Stanley Cup."[12]

Scoring Summary

First Period
- 13:14 BOS Don Marcotte (assists: Phil Esposito, Bobby Orr) SH
- 17:00 BOS Johnny Bucyk (assists: John McKenzie, Fred Stanfield) PP

Second Period
- 5:07 CHI Keith Magnuson (assist: Cliff Koroll)
- 9:20 CHI Dennis Hull (assists: Cliff Koroll, Stan Makita)
- 13:10 CHI Dennis Hull (assist: Chico Maki)
- 15:40 BOS Fred Stanfield (assist: Dallas Smith)

Third Period
- 4:10 CHI Bryan Campbell (assists: Keith Magnuson, Dennis Hull) PP
- 15:19 BOS Ken Hodge (assists: Phil Esposito, Wayne Cashman)
- 18:19 BOS John McKenzie (Assist: Fred Stanfield)

14

March 11, 1971

Phil Esposito Sets Single-Season Scoring Record

There was practically no drama at all attached to it. It was inevitable that the record would fall—and everyone knew it. Really, it was only a matter of when (and by how much) the new mark would surpass the old one. What was so certain? During the 1970–71 NHL regular season, Boston's Phil Esposito was on a such a prolific goal-scoring tear that it seemed as if only an act of God could stop him from eclipsing the previous best of 58 goals in a single season set by Bobby Hull of the Chicago Blackhawks just two seasons earlier.

The 29-year-old Esposito was a late bloomer when it came to hockey superstardom. As a member of the Chicago Blackhawks, he did not generate many headlines, although Esposito did score 71 goals in his final three seasons in a Chicago uniform. However, when Esposito was dealt to the Bruins in the summer of 1967 along with Ken Hodge and Fred Stanfield (for Pit Martin and Gilles Marotte in one of hockey's most lopsided deals), Boston general manager Milt Schmidt looked like a genius. Nobody foresaw that cellar-dwelling Boston had acquired the key tools to vault to the top of the league in a hurry. With youthful Bobby Orr dominating the game from the blue line as no one had done before, Esposito and his talented linemates were free to wreak havoc on opposing goaltenders. Espo donned the #7 jersey that had been Pit Martin's. He made his presence known quickly. In just his second game with the Bruins, Esposito had a spectacular four-goal night versus the Montreal Canadiens. They were the first batch of 459 goals Esposito would score as a Bruin. In 1968–69, Esposito became the first NHL player to score more than 100 points in a season. Espo surpassed the three-digit milestone with ease. He got 126 points that year and won the first of his five NHL scoring championships. In the seven seasons from 1968–69 to 1974–75, Esposito failed to finish atop the league's scoring race just twice. Both times he was beaten by teammate Bobby Orr.

Esposito was once described by *Hockey Night in Canada*'s Ron MacLean as "hockey's great slot machine." It was an apt description as Esposito routinely positioned himself in the area in front of the opposition's net for prime scoring opportunities. Strongly built, Espo was an extremely tough man to dislodge while patiently awaiting passes from his Bruin teammates. Esposito was blessed with a quick, accurate left-handed shot and excellent hand-eye coordination, too. He was especially adept at knocking pucks out of the air and redirecting shots from teammates. Goalies were often beaten before they realized Esposito had the puck in his possession. Esposito had 550 shots on goal in 1970–71—an enormous figure unmatched to this day. Critics of Esposito's offensive rampages were quick to point out that the 1967 expansion that doubled the size of the league from six to 12 teams had undeniably diluted the quality of the game and the value of goals. Indeed, 7–4 and 8–5 scores, rarities in pre-expansion days, were now common occurrences—especially from the Bruins who *averaged* a staggering 5.1 goals per game in 1970–71 playing most of their games versus the old, established NHL teams. (Boston was even an offensive threat when they were penalized, accruing the staggering sum of 26 shorthanded goals—a record.) Still, it was only Esposito who was accruing such lofty individual scoring statistics.

Five years earlier, the NHL's single-season goal-scoring record for one player was 54, set by Hull during the 1965–66 season, when the six-team league still existed and each club played a 70-game schedule. (Esposito and Hull were teammates that year.) In 1968–69, Hull upped the mark to 58 goals in a 76-game schedule for a Chicago team that somehow finished in last place in the East Division. Three games into 1970–71, Esposito had already notched five goals. Seldom would more than two games go by without an Esposito goal being added to the Boston ledger. Well before Christmas, hockey writers were predicting that Espo had a better than legitimate shot to set a new NHL scoring standard. Esposito had one advantage: the luxury of two extra games to surpass Hull. Furthermore, the league was now a watered-down 14-team loop, but these trivialities hardly mattered. Esposito kept rolling along, reaching the 50-goal plateau with remarkable ease on February 20 in a rare 5–4 Boston loss to Los Angeles. The rate of Espo's scoring declined slightly after that milestone was reached, but with nearly a month remaining on the Bruins' schedule, he was just one goal away from tying Hull's lofty mark.

On Wednesday, March 10, at the Oakland-Alameda Coliseum

14. March 11, 1971

Arena, a less-than-capacity crowd of 10,411 fans paid to witness Esposito's historic, record-tying 58th goal in the Bruins' 8–1 demolition of the lowly California Seals. Esposito had to score twice to get credit for one goal. His apparent 58th goal—a quick shot that eluded Seals goalie Gary Smith at 7:30 of the second period—was nullified when Boston's Wayne Cashman was penalized on the play for boarding by referee Ron Wicks. A scribe from the *Boston Globe* duly noted that "Esposito held his poise in the face of such a discouraging development."[1] Late in the second period, however, Esposito got one that Wicks allowed to stand. It was an atypical Espo score—not the usual sniper blast from the slot. Instead, Esposito took matters into his own hands. He stole a loose puck from behind the Seals' net and beat Smith with a wraparound shot. The goal, Boston's fourth of the second period, was an unassisted one.

It was pointed out in the next day's *Globe* that "Espo has something of an edge [over Hull] as he racked up his 58th goal in Boston's 66th game of the season."[2] Hull had scored his 58th in the 70th game of the 1968–69 campaign. Another melancholy journalist lamented the setting. "In Montreal or Toronto, or any of the traditional American hockey cities," he wrote, "fans would have been breaking down the doors to watch the game's biggest scoring record tied or even surpassed. But in Oakland, it was just another hockey game."[3] With a dozen games left on Boston's schedule and Esposito showing no signs of cooling down, Hull's record was certain to fall.

Although Esposito candidly told reporters that he preferred to break Hull's record in Boston where the feat would be more honored, his scoring blitz went on unabated. (All the while, Espo's fans back in the Hub were eagerly buying mildly sacrilegious bumper stickers declaring, "Jesus saves—but Esposito scores on the rebound!")

Indeed, the March 12 edition of the *Boston Globe* seemed to report on Esposito's new record with muted enthusiasm instead of the ballyhoo it truly merited. "Phil Esposito added two more records to his impressive collection last night," the newspaper declared, "as the Bruins ran over the Los Angeles Kings, 7–2." The article went on to explain the basics:

> With two goals and one assist, [Esposito] concluded the evening with figures of 60 goals, 68 assists, and 128 points.
> This gave Espo the new [NHL] high in goals, surpassing the mark of 58, formerly held by Bobby Hull, which the Boston star equaled the previous night in Oakland.
> The 128 points represented an increase of two over the all-time top of 126 which Esposito himself established in 1968–69.[4]

Los Angeles surprised Boston by opening the scoring early in the first period. At the 3:04 mark, Bob Pulford did his best Phil Esposito impersonation: He beat Boston goaltender Eddie Johnston on a rising 20-foot shot from the slot with his 15th goal of the campaign. He had been set up by an excellent pass from behind the Boston goal by teammate Mike Byers. For the time being, the home team was up 1–0. It was an aberration.

Esposito's record-breaking 59th goal of 1970–71 came about four minutes later. It did not possess much in the way of artistic beauty. The *Globe* scribe covering the game stated it "was not one of Phil's most glittering productions"—which was undoubtedly accurate—"but it did set off a celebration among the tall center and his colleagues."[5] Ken Hodge, stationed near the Kings' net, fed a pass backwards toward Boston defenseman Ted Green at the Los Angeles blue line. Green moved forward and attempted to launch a slapshot. However, his stick failed to connect cleanly with the puck which was not lying flat on the ice. The resulting 45-foot knuckle ball bounded toward Los Angeles goalie Denis DeJordy at about half speed, but Esposito was excellently positioned to deftly poke the puck between DeJordy's pads and into the net. "Teddy shoots low. I knew I could score if I got my stick on it,"[6] Esposito explained to reporters afterward. The historic goal leveled the score at 1–1. Johnny Bucyk got a power-play tally for Boston with just 12 seconds left in the first frame to give the visitors a 2–1 advantage and shift the game's momentum Boston's way.

With Boston holding a 3–1 lead, at 15:40 of the second period, Esposito reached the lofty 60-goal plateau when he converted passes from Dallas Smith and Ken Hodge. With the Bruins in complete control, 6–1, after two periods, DeJordy was mercifully yanked from the Los Angeles net by coach Larry Regan, a former Bruin. He was replaced by Jack Norris for the final 20 minutes. Norris did well; he allowed just one further Boston goal.

After the game, which Boston won by a typically lopsided 7–2 margin, a subdued Esposito modestly declared to the scribes within earshot, "Bobby Hull is still the greatest."[7] Despite no longer being teammates, Esposito and the popular Hull were good friends.

Esposito took his two-goal night as just another day at the office. When asked why he did not seem overly excited about breaking Hull's record, Esposito candidly told reporters,

> To be honest, I felt more pressure two years ago when I was [attempting to be] the first [player] to score more than 100 points. No one else had ever done it; I wanted to be the first. But I'm glad it's over. With 11 games left, I knew I'd get the record sooner or later, but I still wanted to get number 59 in 70 games so there wouldn't be an asterisk.[8]

14. March 11, 1971

Overshadowed by Esposito's feats were three other NHL single-season records that fell that same night—all of them to Boston's brilliant Bobby Orr. The great Orr quietly recorded three assists to raise his total to 88 for the season, eclipsing his own record set the previous year when he won the NHL scoring championship. Orr also raised his point total to 123 to establish a new seasonal mark for defensemen. Finally, Orr's 35th goal of the year—which made the score 6–1 for Boston—was a new league high for a player at his position.

The Esposito goals kept coming throughout the final three weeks of the regular season for Boston's fabulous #7. Versus Montreal in the Bruins' final game of the regular season on Sunday, April 4, Esposito concluded the Bruins' schedule with appropriate panache. He notched his seventh hattrick of the 1970–71 campaign—three more three-goal games than any other player had ever recorded in a single NHL season. (As a team, the Bruins had 14 hattricks that year.) The feat was appropriately witnessed by a raucous hometown crowd at Boston Garden. Esposito finished the season with nicely symmetric offensive statistics: 76 goals and 76 assists for 152 points, figures unapproached in the league until Wayne Gretzky came along a decade later. Boston general manager Milt Schmidt, who had been associated with the Bruins for 35 years, called Esposito's stellar year "a completely unimaginable feat."[9]

Lefty Reid, the curator of the Hockey Hall of Fame, was a busy man after the game, an easy 7–2 Boston victory. He diligently collected sticks from Esposito, Bobby Orr, Johnny Bucyk and Ken Hodge for the museum. All four Bruins had accrued 100 points during the 1970–71 season. Reid also asked Esposito to autograph the stick he had used to score his 76th goal. "I'm not sure I want to let this one go,"[10] Espo sternly informed him. The Boston superstar cracked a smile to indicate he was joking. The stick was dispatched with the other paraphernalia to Toronto to be part of a contemporary Bruins exhibit.

A touching moment occurred after Esposito had scored his 75th goal: The appreciative hometown fans saluted him with a prolonged standing ovation that both startled and humbled the recipient. Espo had already taken a seat on the Boston bench when the extensive, spontaneous cheering began and continued to grow, almost exponentially. Veteran reporter Francis Rosa, who had seen hundreds of NHL games during his long tenure with the *Boston Globe*, called it "one of the great moments in Garden history."[11]

"For the first time in my life I felt shy, embarrassed,"[12] the usually loquacious Esposito later told Rosa in the tumult of the Boston dressing room. Indeed, Esposito had quaintly attempted to hide his face in the crook of his left elbow for a moment or two when the cheering began.

The fans were not to be denied, though. With the applause reaching a deafening level, Esposito was forced to acknowledge it in some way. "Finally, Esposito stood up," Rosa wrote, "his tall body hunched forward as though he were huddling from a strong wind. He raised his left arm in a shy gesture and wiggled his fingers. And the chills ran up his spine."[13]

"During that ovation I just didn't know how to react," Esposito admitted. "It moved me a little bit, all right. The people here are just terrific."[14]

In 1970–71, so was Phil Esposito.

Scoring Summary

First Period
- 3:04 LAK Bob Pulford (assists: Mike Byers, Ross Lonsberry)
- 7:03 BOS Phil Esposito (assists: Ted Green, Ken Hodge)
- 19:48 BOS John Bucyk (assists: Bobby Orr, Phil Esposito) PP

Second Period
- 12:04 BOS Wayne Carleton (assist Bobby Orr, Mike Walton)
- 15:40 BOS Phil Esposito (assists: Dallas Smith, Ken Hodge)
- 16:24 BOS Ed Westfall (assist: Wayne Carleton)
- 17:49 BOS Bobby Orr (assists: John McKenzie, John Bucyk)

Third Period
- 6:11 BOS John Bucyk (assists: John McKenzie, Bobby Orr) PP
- 10:09 LAK Ralph Backstrom (assists Dale Hoganson, Larry Cahan)

15

February 23, 1972

*Bruins Rally from Five Goals
Down to Defeat Seals*

During the 1971–72 NHL season, a bettor probably could have gotten significantly long odds if he wagered that the mighty Boston Bruins would fall five goals in arrears in any game they played versus the lowly California Golden Seals. Those odds would have been even more generous if he added the important coda that the Bruins would end up winning that same game by two goals. As unlikely as those two scenarios were, they happened on Wednesday, February 23, 1972, as the real chance of a humiliating Boston defeat morphed into "one of the great comebacks" in franchise history. That's what Francis Rosa wrote in the next day's *Boston Globe*. He was well qualified to make such a statement, having covered the Bruins since the late 1940s.

The big news heading Into that night's game versus the struggling Seals was a five-player trade made between the two teams earlier that same day. Boston acquired the Seals' best overall and marketable player—mustachioed defenseman Carol Vadnais—someone who graced the cover of California's media guide even the following season! He did not come cheaply. Boston had to part with the very reliable Rick Smith, a defenseman who seldom contributed much offensive firepower, but one who did his job of thwarting opponents very competently.

Included in the Vadnais deal by the Bruins was a seldom-used forward named Reggie Leach who struggled to get adequate ice time on a Boston team loaded with goal scorers. Upon learning of the trade via a telephone call to his hotel room at 7:30 a.m., the crestfallen Leach told Ray Fitzgerald of the *Boston Globe* that he spent the next couple of hours simply lying on his bed, staring at the ceiling, trying to come to grips with the fact that he had suddenly lost a very good chance to play on a Stanley Cup winner. "I just let it sink in that I was no longer a Bruin," the 21-year-old said. "I know in the long run I'm going to be better off. I'll get a chance to play with the Seals."[1] (Leach would play for California until the end of 1973–74 campaign. He would be acquired by Philadelphia prior to the 1974–75 campaign. In his eight seasons with the Flyers, Leach became a scoring machine, notching 306 regular-season goals—including 61 in 1975–76, which still stands as a Philadelphia team record. Leach had scored just nine goals in 79 games as a Bruin.) On the reverse side, the 26-year-old Vadnais was thrilled by the development, suddenly having a chance to be part of a championship-caliber Boston team instead of toiling in virtual anonymity with the woeful Seals. The scuttlebutt from Oakland was that Vadnais had lost his enthusiasm for playing with the Golden Seals and had become too reckless in his play. An informal poll conducted by the *Boston Globe* found that a small sample of Bruin fans were split about 50/50 on liking or disliking the trade for Vadnais.

Two other fringe players were involved in the trade: Bob Stewart, a 21-year-old defenseman, who had played just eight games as a Bruin without making much of an impact; and Don O'Donoghue, a 22-year-old forward, who would never play a game for Boston or any other NHL team.

Smith and Leach would be in the lineup for the Golden Seals that night. Vadnais would suit up for Boston. Hockey writers noted that the Seals' roster now included six former Bruins. Perhaps it was not a coincidence as Gerry Young, the Bruins' former top scout, had been hired at the start of the 1971–72 season to be California's new general manager.

At the conclusion of the game, Boston coach Tom Johnson laughed at what transpired on the ice. "You can say what you want about an 8–6 hockey game," he told Francis Rosa, "but I liked it. It was pretty exciting."[2] Yes, it was.

Boston entered the game riding an impressive eight-game winning streak—including their first four contests of their current road trip. Coach Johnson was not shy about telling his formidable Bruins they were expected to win whenever they stepped onto the ice. Before the Bruins vacated Boston to play six games over the space of nine days as the visiting team, Johnson said to his squad that he fully expected them to get the maximum 12 points from those contests. In other words, he would only be satisfied with six wins. Boston victories in Philadelphia, Minnesota, Chicago and Vancouver put the Bruins on the right track to achieve Johnson's lofty goal. However, the game on February 23 against the Golden Seals at Oakland-Alameda County Coliseum Arena would be the Bruins' third in four nights, so fatigue combined with jet lag was a possibility. Still, on paper, the game was a mismatch. Boston was 44–8–9 in its 61 games contested thus far in 1971–72. The Seals were staggering at 18–29–14.

The game began as a nightmare scenario for new Bruin Carol Vadnais. Given a regular shift, but unfamiliar with the Bruins' defensive positioning and expectations, the newcomer looked lost on several occasions. By the time California had assumed a daunting 6–1 lead in the second period, Vadnais had been on the ice for five of the home team's goals. "We were all playing loosely on defense. He settled down in the third period and played much better," said Johnson in defense of Vadnais' shaky start. "He'll be okay. It will take him a little while to adjust to our style of hockey. And another thing: I think he's not in as good condition as our team is."[3]

The roster change seemed to inspire the home team greatly—at least for the first half of the contest. Francis Rosa noted in his game report for the *Boston Globe*, "The California Golden Seals came out flying, and with some former Bruins playing prominent roles, looked as if they would skate the Bruins out of the rink. That look began to fade late in the second period. In the third period, it was washed out completely."[4]

The first of the game's 14 goals occurred at 2:51. Future Bruin Dick Redmond was the marksman whose shot got by Boston goalie Eddie Johnston. One assist on the goal went to Wayne (Swoop) Carleton who had played on Boston's 1969–70 Stanley Cup-winning team. In fact, he was on the ice when Bobby Orr scored his famous overtime goal on Mother's Day. Carleton had been released by Boston after the 1970–71 season. Redmond also scored the home team's second goal, picking up a rebound 25 feet in front of the Boston net and scoring on a screened shot. This one was unassisted.

The Bruins looked like their usual selves for only brief times during the first period. One of those instances was when Fred Stanfield beat Gilles Meloche at 17:37 to narrow the Seals' lead to 2–1. California reassumed a two-goal edge with just eight seconds left in the first period on a goal by Gary Croteau. Reggie Leach picked up his first point as a Seal by getting the lone assist. California ended the first period holding a surprising 3–1 lead. Boston had been slightly unlucky in the game's first 20 minutes. Three times the Bruins had clanged pucks off goalposts. Fred Stanfield had also been stopped by Gilles Meloche on a penalty shot. (Penalty shots were seldom awarded at the time; Stanfield's was the first one taken by a Bruin in nearly five years!)

The Golden Seals seemed certain to post a rare victory over Boston when they erupted for three goals in the span of less than five minutes before the midway point of the second period. They came from the sticks of Wayne Carleton, Gary Croteau (again) and Craig Patrick. Rick Smith was credited with an assist on Carleton's goal. The home team retained its 6–1 advantage 34 minutes into the game. Then the tide started to turn. Whether it was caused by an angry bunch of Bruins fearful of being embarrassed by one of the NHL's doormats, overconfidence on the part of the Seals, fatigue settling on the California players who were clearly playing several notches above their norm, or any combination thereof, is anybody's guess. In the remaining six minutes of the middle frame, Boston scored twice (on goals by Wayne Cashman and Fred Stanfield) to whittle the Seals lead down to a more approachable 6–3. The 10,492 fans in attendance seemed to sense a dramatic change was in the air.

Between the second and third periods, coach Tom Johnson addressed his Bruins in their dressing room with tempered optimism. "I told them only that I thought we had a shot at winning. I told them we'd started to take over [the game] late in the second period and that we could win."[5]

It was not much of a pep talk, but Johnson's low-key speech had the desired effect. Boston launched a steady and formidable offensive assault in the third period. Its key proponents were the club's two best players: Bobby Orr and Phil Esposito. Orr narrowed the California lead to 6–4 with a goal at 2:52. About three minutes later, Orr assisted on Fred Stanfield's third goal of the game. It was now 6–5. The Seals were now wholly on the defensive. They managed to stave off the mighty Bruins for approximately nine minutes.

Phil Esposito's game-tying goal at 14:31 of the third period—his 53rd tally of the 1971–72 season—was picturesque. "It was a thing of beauty,"[6] wrote Rosa, and it showcased the creative facets of Esposito's wonderful scoring talents. It unfolded this way: Dallas Smith fed Esposito a pass to start a Boston breakout. Esposito then passed the puck to Ed Westfall who advanced over the blue line. The pass was slightly off the mark; it required some nifty footwork from Westfall to kick the puck onto the blade of his stick while maintaining his stride. Westfall then sent a perfect return pass to Esposito who had positioned himself near the left corner of the Seals' goal. A California defender had sprawled to cover the unguarded opening, so Esposito skillfully lifted the puck about a foot into the air above the prone man and deftly batted it home just under the crossbar. Remarkably, the topsy-turvy game was now deadlocked at 6–6. The momentum, however, was clearly on the side of the surging visitors.

One hundred and sixty seconds later, Esposito struck again,

15. February 23, 1972

notching the winning goal for Boston. This time he deflected a Wayne Cashman shot past weary Gilles Meloche. With 14 seconds left in the third period, and Meloche removed by Seals coach Vic Stasiuk for a sixth California attacker, Derek Sanderson salted the game away for the Bruins with an empty net goal—Boston's fifth goal of the third period, and their seventh consecutive score since trailing by five goals. Both teams' goaltenders, Meloche and Ed Johnston, played the entire game without being yanked despite the onslaught of pucks that eluded them. The Bruins had 37 shots on goal (including Sanderson's shot into the California empty net) compared to 33 for the Seals.

Curiously, none of the game's 14 goals came on a power play; all were scored at even strength. The only man advantage in the game favored the Seals, when Boston's Ed Westfall was whistled for hooking in the third period when the Seals were still on top, 6–5, and could have padded their lead.

Carol Vadnais did not record a point in his Bruin debut, but he was on the ice for three of his new team's goals, almost offsetting the five California goals he witnessed close up during the catastrophic first half of the game. Thus, he finished the night with a minus-two. Vadnais' mind may have been occupied with more mundane but necessary tasks—such as how to get his and his wife's personal belongings literally from one end of America to the other. The couple had been married just eight months. "We still have wedding gifts we haven't unpacked yet,"[7] the distracted Vadnais told Kevin Walsh of the *Globe*.

Quietly Bobby Orr accrued a goal and four assists for the winners. It was a typical Orr night. He was plus-five. Mike Walton and Ed Westfall were also singled out by Francis Rosa as being unsung heroes for their hard work in the noteworthy Boston comeback victory.

With the Bruins seemingly poised for an unstoppable cakewalk to the Stanley Cup, veteran *Globe* writer Harold Kaese took a tongue-in-cheek approach in examining the trade that brought Carol Vadnais to Boston. He amusingly penned,

> It was high time for the Bruins to strengthen themselves. Were they going to be satisfied with a .795 [winning] percentage and eight games lost out of 61 played? They weren't leading the league in goals scored, were they? They weren't winning the Vezina Trophy, were they? They hadn't yet won 30 games in a row, had they? Carol Vadnais ought to correct all that. The new defenseman will make the Bruins a solid team.[8]

Three nights later, Boston edged the Los Angeles Kings at the Great Western Forum, 5–4, to complete the perfect road trip that coach Tom Johnson had sought. The Bruins jumped out to a 3–0 first-period advantage over the Kings. Boston never trailed in that game.

Scoring Summary

First Period
- 2:51 CGS Dick Redmond (assists: Wayne Carleton, Bert Marshall)
- 13:22 CGS Dick Redmond (unassisted)
- 17:37 BOS Fred Stanfield (assist: John McKenzie)
- 19:52 CGS Gary Croteau (assist: Reggie Leach)

Second Period
- 3:58 CGS Wayne Carleton (assist: Rick Smith)
- 7:34 CGS Gary Croteau (assists Joey Johnston, Paul Shmyr)
- 8:53 CGS Craig Patrick (assists: Marshall Johnston, Garry Jarrett)
- 14:36 BOS Wayne Cashman (assists: Bobby Orr, Mike Walton)
- 17:15 BOS Fred Stanfield (assist: Bobby Orr)

Third Period
- 2:52 BOS Bobby Orr (assist: Ed Westfall)
- 5:59 BOS Fred Stanfield (assists: Bobby Orr, Don Awrey)
- 14:31 BOS Phil Esposito (assists: Ed Westfall, Dallas Smith)
- 17:11 BOS Phil Esposito (assists: Wayne Cashman, Dallas Smith)
- 19:46 BOS Derek Sanderson (assists: Ed Westfall, Bobby Orr) EN

16

April 30, 1972
The One That Nearly Got Away

The two best teams in the NHL, the Boston Bruins and New York Rangers, began their highly anticipated best-of-seven Stanley Cup finals on Sunday, April 30, 1972. It sounds odd, but Boston may have won the series by winning that first game at Boston Garden by a 6–5 score—but they just as easily could have lost it that same night had they not reversed the game's dramatically shifting momentum.

To fully understand the importance of what happened in Game One of the 1972 Stanley Cup finals, one needs to possess a strong grasp of some very negative Bruin history. Two years previous, in the spring of 1970, Boston won its first Stanley Cup in 29 years. Their first-round playoff opponents were the New York Rangers, who battled the Bruins—both figuratively and literally—for six bruising and bloody games that set new postseason records for combined penalty minutes. Years later Phil Esposito told a reporter that he quietly figured whichever team was still standing after the Bruins-Rangers quarterfinal would likely win the Stanley Cup. Boston emerged victorious in six games—but the seeds of a very competitive Bruins-Rangers rivalry had been revived after a long period of dormancy.

The following spring, the powerful Bruins, led by the record-smashing scoring exploits of Phil Esposito, the overall brilliance of Bobby Orr, and a strong cast of superb supporting players, made a mockery of the rest of the NHL with a 57–14–7 record for 121 points. The Bruins were such overwhelming favorites to win the Stanley Cup again that scarcely any unbiased hockey observer could see any other logical outcome to the 1971 playoffs. Yet the unthinkable happened: After winning the first game of their quarterfinal versus a very capable Montreal team, 3–1, Boston roared out to a 5–1 lead halfway through Game Two. Years later, in an interview with *Sports Illustrated*, Boston broadcaster Fred Kusick recalled that victory in that game—and the series—seemed so certain that he spent part of the first intermission discussing Boston's potential opponents in the Stanley Cup semifinals. Incredibly, the roof caved in on the home team. Montreal scored six consecutive goals to turn the series upside down with a 7–5 triumph that sent shockwaves throughout the NHL. Their confidence severely shaken, the Bruins dropped Game Three in Montreal, as well. Boston momentarily righted whatever was ailing them by winning the next two games of the series comfortably. However, a bad 8–3 loss in Montreal in Game Six set up something few fans figured would be necessary: a decisive seventh game at Boston Garden on April 18. In front of a continental television audience that Sunday afternoon, the home team grabbed an early 1–0 lead over the visiting Habs, but eventually lost the game, 4–2. It remains one of the most shocking postseason results in the history of North American professional sports. Most everyone realized, in retrospect, that Boston's epic collapse in Game Two was responsible for the team's eventual demise.

In 1971–72, the Bruins continued their regular-season dominance, again winning the NHL's East Division with 119 points, but close on their tails were the ascending New York Rangers with 109. Boston romped through the first two rounds of the 1972 Stanley Cup playoffs, dropping just one game against plucky Toronto and then blowing away the overmatched St. Louis Blues in the semis. They were out to prove that their loss to Montreal the previous spring was entirely a freak occurrence. Certainly, there would be no horrendous collapse this time.

The New York Rangers were almost as dominant as Boston was in cruising their way to the 1972 Stanley Cup finals. They ousted Montreal, the defending Cup champions who had 108 points, in a six-game quarterfinal and then swiftly eliminated the Chicago Blackhawks, champions of the NHL's West Division, in four straight games. With the Bruins and Rangers as the last teams standing, the Stanley Cup finals unquestionably had star appeal with the league's top two teams vying for the title. Based on the 1971–72 regular season, the Bruins looked like solid favorites. In six games, Boston had won five and New York just one. The Rangers' lone victory seemed like ancient history to Boston fans. It occurred back on October 10. The Bruins had also outscored the Rangers in those clashes by a wide ratio—25:8—including an 8–1 pasting at Boston Garden on December 16. In the teams' last five matchups, all won by Boston, New York, had not scored more than one goal.

Because the Bruins had posted the better regular-season record, the first two games of Stanley Cup finals would be played at Boston Garden, along with Game Five and Seven, if necessary. Game One was scheduled for Sunday, April 30.

16. April 30, 1972

Boston wanted to send a message to the Rangers that they would do everything within their power—fair or foul—to win the opener. Ted Blackman, covering the Cup finals for the *Montreal Gazette*, noted,

> It appeared [that Bruin coach Tom] Johnson had ordered his troops to take no prisoners. From 0:38 of the first period, when [Boston's] John McKenzie left an elbow print on Gene Carr's expression, until 10:46 of the second when Ken Hodge completed his hattrick, the Rangers had 20/20 hearing.
>
> The first period resembled.... Gordie Howe's defensive career: Elbows. Sprinkled adequately among the flying forearms were body checks that cut down Rod Gilbert and Bobby Rousseau.[1]

Be that as it may, New York's Dale Rolfe let the Boston fans know that the underdog Rangers would be putting up a fight. With each team having a man in the penalty box, Rolfe scored at 3:52 of the first period, beating Boston goalie Gerry Cheevers from just inside the blue line, to give the visitors a quick 1–0 lead.

New York's advantage did not last long. Fred Stanfield got the Bruins level at 5:07 as he converted a pass from John McKenzie. Ken Hodge put Boston ahead 2–1 about ten minutes later. "It was a typical Bruins raid," reported Tim Burke of the *Montreal Gazette*. "Hodge seemed to be one of a dozen white-yellow-and-black jerseys scrambling over [Ed] Giacomin for a Don Awrey rebound."[2]

By the time the first period ended, Boston held a strong 4–1 edge. The third and fourth goals by the home team were both scored while Boston was shorthanded. In fact, both came on the same Bruins penalty—an Awrey elbowing infraction. The first one, described as a masterpiece by one hockey writer, came off the stick of Derek Sanderson, Boston's superb penalty killer. Sanderson was playing his first game for Boston since being injured on April 12. Ken Hodge scored the other one on a sequence in which Ranger goalie Ed Giacomin lost his stick, giving him two tallies in the opening 20 minutes. "[Giacomin] didn't have much of a chance on that one," Hodge compassionately said afterward. "I think [Ranger defenseman] Jim Neilson had him partially screened."[3] In a truly funny incident following the goal, Hodge briefly hugged Neilson, mistaking the surprised Ranger for linemate Phil Esposito. Boston could have remarkably scored four shorthanded goals while killing the Awrey minor penalty. When play resumed, Giacomin stopped Bobby Orr on a breakaway and, moments afterward, he thwarted Phil Esposito on another clear-cut chance.

Nevertheless, the usually reliable Giacomin seemed quite shaky and nervous in his first Stanley Cup finals assignment. (Giacomin was a surprise Game One starter. Gilles Villemure, one year younger than Giacomin, had been excellent guarding the pipes versus Chicago in the semifinals. However, New York, coach/general manager Emile Francis opted for his favorite netminder instead of staying with the goalie who had the hot hand.) Momentum clearly belonged to Boston when the opening period concluded. Garden fans were already celebrating an anticipated win. A few were taunting the visitors from New York. "Bring back St. Louis!" one heckler gleefully shouted at the Ranger bench. "We want some competition!" Boston had outscored the Blues 28–8 in their semifinal series.

During the first intermission on *Hockey Night in Canada*'s English-language telecast, veteran Toronto goaltender Jacques Plante, arguably the best NHL netminder of all time, questioned Francis' choice of Giacomin to start Game One for the Rangers rather than going with Villemure. Plante opined that Giacomin went down far too quickly which left him vulnerable on high shots. Plante's comments proved to be prophetic.

In the second period, the script continued as the favorites figured it would. Boston got a fifth goal at 10:46. Ken Hodge recorded his hattrick with assists coming from Phil Esposito and Bobby Orr. Hodge pounced on a rebound that bounced favorably off the boards directly to the Boston forward. With slightly less than 30 minutes remaining in regulation time, the outcome of Game One seemed to have been decided.

The Rangers were not so sure about it, however. At 11:54, Rod Gilbert scored on a power play (with assists going to linemates Vic Hadfield and Jean Ratelle) to whittle the Boston lead down to a less daunting 5–2. That was how the second period ended. However, the Bruins began a steady parade to the penalty box for what Ted Blackman of the *Montreal Gazette* described as "non-bullying infractions."[4] The home team drew five consecutive penalties from referee Bill Friday at one point.

The shift in momentum in the third period came without any warning whatsoever. Boston's three-goal advantage vanished in the space of less than seven and a half minutes as the visitors took complete charge of the game. "We stopped forechecking,"[5] Don Awrey later concisely explained.

Vic Hadfield got New York's third goal on a slapshot that seemed to take Gerry Cheevers by surprise. It occurred at 1:56 while Derek Sanderson was sitting out a hooking penalty. At 7:48 Walt Tkaczuk scored an unassisted goal on another slapshot after stealing the puck from Derek Sanderson in the faceoff circle. Boston Garden suddenly became quiet as the fans sensed a repeat of the infamous 1971 Montreal debacle in which Boston had carelessly frittered away a similar 5–1 lead. Their fears were well founded. The Rangers tied the game, 5–5, shortly thereafter as Ted Irvine outworked two Bruins to gain control of a loose puck. His

16. April 30, 1972

pass set up Bruce MacGregor whose shot beat Gerry Cheevers 9:17 into the third period. It was now anyone's game, but fickle momentum now appeared to favor the team wearing the blue shirts.

Phil Esposito missed seeing the majority of the impressive New York comeback. He left the game with Boston ahead 5–2 to get five stitches applied to the top of his nose after it violently collided with Jim Neilson's skull. When Esposito was told that the Rangers had tied the score, he assumed the messenger was joking—until he returned to the Boston bench and glanced at the Garden's scoreboard.

Ed Giacomin's game improved noticeably once the score was level. He made spectacular saves on both Johnny Bucyk and Fred Stanfield. Late in the game, Bobby Rousseau failed on an excellent opportunity to put the Rangers into a 6–5 lead. He was sent in alone on Cheevers, but he fired the puck wide of the Boston net.

Scribe Harold Kaese humorously summed up the growing angst experienced by the typical Bruin fan in the next day's *Boston Globe* by writing, "When the Rangers scored four consecutive goals to tie the game, 5–5, those Bruin followers who had not fainted in their seats started guessing the name of the man who would win it for them. If anyone named Ace Bailey, it would have to be his fiancée."[6] Indeed, Boston's winning goal came from that unlikely source.

Not long after Rousseau's miss, the tiebreaking goal came. Against the run of play, it went to Boston. Mike Walton fed an accurate pass to Garnet (Ace) Bailey, a seldom-used Bruin forward who had recently been converted to a center. Bailey deftly skated around Brad Park who misjudged his check. He moved in alone on Giacomin and proceeded to follow the Bruins' scouting report on the Ranger goalie. Bailey waited out Giacomin who went down. Bailey coolly lifted the puck over him and into the upper half of the net. The time of the goal was 17:44.

Harold Kaese lauded the usually unheralded Bailey, writing, "Bailey … is no midget, no creampuff, no shooter of blank cartridges. He is a relatively obscure player who has produced a mighty feat."[7] Bailey, no relation to Toronto's Irvin (Ace) Bailey whose NHL career was cut short in 1933 by Eddie Shore, had scored nine goals for Boston in 73 games during the 1971–72 season.

"I just flipped it over him, a backhand" the blond-haired, 23-year-old from Lloydminster, Saskatchewan, happily recalled. "I practice that move a lot, but it's seldom [I] get the chance to use it in a game."[8] A picture of Bailey's shot denting the twine behind Giacomin graced the front page of the *Boston Globe* the next day. It was the biggest moment in Bailey's NHL playing career. Twenty-nine years later, on September 11, 2001, while working as the head of pro scouting for the Los Angeles

Kings, Bailey was a passenger on hijacked United Airlines Flight #175 that slammed into the World Trade Center.

Predictably, Emile Francis pulled Ed Giacomin from the Ranger net for a sixth attacker in the final minute of the third period in a last-ditch attempt to level the score. It nearly paid off. Vic Hadfield had the best chance to tie the game. He rattled a shot off the goalpost, but it stayed out of the Boston net. The Bruins eked out a 6–5 win that was not glorious, but it was certainly a needed gut-check for the Stanley Cup favorites. They had not fallen apart as they had in the previous season's quarterfinal round versus the Habs.

When asked if the Bruins' 7–5 loss to Montreal in 1971 had entered his mind or the minds of his teammates when the Rangers began to rally, Boston's Ed Westfall honestly replied with a wry smile on his face, "It made us think a little."[9]

"We almost had a replay of history," Ted Blackman accurately stated in his *Montreal Gazette* column the next day, "but the Bruins blew a 5–1 lead and survived. They gave up more goals to New York in one playoff game than they did in all of their five victories over the Rangers during the regular season."[10]

New York defenseman Brad Park—widely regarded as the second-best player at his position in the NHL, behind only Bobby Orr—saw a moral victory in his team's slim defeat in Game One. He noted, "When [the Bruins] were ahead 5–1, I said to myself, 'Hell, this is like one of those hee-haw industrial leaguers.' It could just have easily been the other way around. But it can only help us to know that we can score on Cheevers. We hadn't been able to do a thing on him all season."[11] Park was correct. Cheevers had indeed been the Rangers' bugaboo in 1971–72, allowing just seven goals in the five regular-season games he had started against New York.

Emile Francis concurred with Park. "We made a hell of a comeback," he told reporters. "They just happened to get one at the right time."[12] Ken Hodge in the sullen but victorious Boston dressing room stated the obvious. He bluntly stated, "Let's face it: We lucked out on this one."[13]

Bobby Orr had an unusually mediocre game by his high standards. He certainly did not have a poor outing, but he was not a standout performer, either—a rarity for the 24-year-old in 1972. Recent Boston acquisition Carol Vadnais' passive defensive play was harshly criticized by many writers, however. "Did you like the way Vadnais stepped aside to give Dale Rolfe clear shooting on the Rangers' opening goal?"[14] Blackman asked rhetorically. The acerbic scribe also noted that Orr was not named one of Game One's three stars. Blackman somewhat harshly declared that when the Boston superstar fails to play a leading role, his Bruins were akin to "the Swedish all-stars ... with elbows."[15]

Two nights later, on Tuesday, May 2, the Bruins took Game Two in Boston by a 2–1 score. It was a tightly fought contest in which the Rangers felt they had gotten the short end of a few calls by referee Art Skov. Both of Boston's goals came on the power play; the second one, scored by Ken Hodge, came late in the third period with two Rangers sitting in the penalty box. Derek Sanderson candidly told the press afterwards that the questionable tripping penalty called by Skov on New York's Walt Tkaczuk that put the Rangers two men down was indeed an undeserved one. Gilles Villemure was New York's goalie this time. The general consensus among hockey observers was that things did not bode well for the Rangers considering they had played very well in Boston twice but still came up short in those two attempts.

When the Series shifted to New York, the Rangers played excellently, upping their performance level in Game Three to win 5–2. Boston, however, fought back and won Game Four at Madison Square Garden, 3–2, to take a 3–1 lead in the series. The confident Bruins headed back to Boston fully expecting to win Game Five on May 9 and give the home fans a good look at the Stanley Cup. It was not to be. Former Montreal star Bobby Rousseau scored a pair of third-period goals for the Rangers to change a 2–1 deficit into a dramatic 3–2 New York victory. The series was surprisingly returning to New York City for Game Six.

After enduring the disappointing loss in Game Five, Phil Esposito confidently told reporters there would be no Game Seven; Boston would take care of its unfinished business and defeat the Rangers in their home building two nights hence. That is precisely what happened. On Thursday, May 11, Boston won, 3–0. Gerry Cheevers played well, making some key early saves, and got a well-earned shutout. Wayne Cashman scored the final two goals for the victors. The feisty forward did a taunting, celebratory jig after his second tally (and Boston's third) was partially stopped by Gilles Villemure but had just enough momentum to trickle over the goal line. As in 1970, Bobby Orr scored the Stanley Cup-winning goal and was named the winner of the Conn Smythe Trophy as playoff MVP. Veteran Johnny Bucyk, Boston's all-time scoring leader who had endured the club's darkest days, accepted Lord Stanley's trophy from NHL president Clarence Campbell at center ice. It was the fifth such triumph in Bruin history and the second in three seasons. He skated around Madison Square Garden proudly holding the Cup aloft. Most of the disappointed New York crowd had already left the building by that point. It was a sight that would not be repeated for Bruin fans for 39 long years.

For four members of the Bruins, May 11, 1972 marked their last game in their familiar black and gold Boston jerseys—at least for a while. Ed Westfall would be lost in the 1972 NHL expansion draft to the newly formed New York Islanders. John McKenzie, miffed over not being protected from the draft, fled in a huff to the Philadelphia Blazers of the new World Hockey Association, never to return to the NHL. Gerry Cheevers and Derek Sanderson, lured by bigger money than the

Talented Bobby Rousseau is best remembered for his nine seasons with the Montreal Canadiens, but he was the hero for the New York Rangers in Game Five of the 1972 Stanley Cup finals, scoring twice in the third period to propel New York to a 3–2 comeback victory over the Bruins at Boston Garden (Jaques, Louis/Library and Archives Canada/e002343749).

frugal Bruins were prepared to pay them, signed WHA contracts too. For a time, Sanderson was the highest paid athlete in North American team sports. Both he and Cheevers would eventually return to Boston, however.

Game One had clearly been the key match of the 1972 Stanley Cup finals: Boston salvaging a 6–5 win with Ace Bailey's late goal quite likely rescuing their season and preventing a second consecutive postseason catastrophe from occurring. "Geez, it must be disappointing for the Rangers," Derek Sanderson theorized in discussing the conclusion of the series opener, "to come all the way back like that and then lose it." Then Sanderson thoughtfully paused for a moment to look at the situation from the victors' point of view. "But if they'd won it, what do you think that would have done to us?"[16]

Scoring Summary

First Period
- 3:52 NYR Dale Rolfe (assists: Rod Gilbert, Brad Park)
- 5:07 BOS Fred Stanfield (assist: John McKenzie)
- 15:48 BOS Ken Hodge (assists: Phil Esposito, Mike Walton)
- 17:29 BOS Derek Sanderson (assist: Ed Westfall) SH
- 18:14 BOS Ken Hodge (assist: Phil Esposito) SH

Second Period
- 10:46 BOS Ken Hodge (assists: Phil Esposito, Bobby Orr)
- 11:54 NYR Rod Gilbert (assists: Vic Hadfield and Jean Ratelle) PP

Third Period
- 1:56 NYR Vic Hadfield (assists: Walt Tkaczuk, Rod Gilbert) PP
- 7:48 NYR Walt Tkaczuk (unassisted)
- 9:17 NYR Bruce MacGregor (assists: Ted Irvine, Pete Stemkowski)
- 17:44 BOS Ace Bailey (assists: Mike Walton, Ed Westfall)

17

December 30, 1973
Chris Oddleifson's Four-Goal Game

In the century-long history of the Boston Bruins, no Bruin has ever managed to score five goals in a regular-season or playoff contest. However, there have been more than two dozen instances where someone on the club scored four goals in a single game. Starting with Harry Oliver's four-goal effort versus Chicago on January 11, 1927, most of the players who have enjoyed these huge offensive nights for Boston have had reputations as prolific scorers and, accordingly, are well known among Bruins fans. These players include the likes of Cooney Weiland, Johnny Bucyk, Phil Esposito, and Patrice Bergeron. One very notable exception occurred on December 30, 1973, when the Bruins, in easily defeating the California Golden Seals 8–1 in Oakland, got four goals from the most unlikely of sources: Chris Oddleifson. In his truncated career with Boston, Oddleifson only managed to find the back of the net a grand total of ten times.

Chris Oddleifson was born in Brandon, Manitoba, on September 7, 1950. After enjoying an outstanding 1969–70 season with the junior Winnipeg Jets of the Western Canada Hockey League in which he accrued 95 points and led the circuit in assists, Oddleifson, a center, was chosen 10th overall in the NHL's 1970 amateur draft. The team that selected him was the Oakland Seals—soon to be rebranded as the California Golden Seals. Not afraid to engage in the rougher aspects of hockey, Oddleifson also racked up a significant sum of 243 penalty minutes in his final season of amateur play in Winnipeg.

Oddleifson was assigned to the minors by the Seals and never played a single game for that franchise. He was dealt to the Bruins on November 17, 1971. He and Rich LeDuc came to Boston in exchange for Ivan Boldirev. The deal did not generate very much excitement or discussion in the hockey world.

During the 1972–73 season, Oddleifson made his NHL debut for

Boston. He got into six games for the Bruins, but he did not score any goals nor did he record any assists for the club. The following season, 1973–74, Oddleifson earned a regular spot on the Bruins. It was quite a feat considering how solid the Boston lineup was in the early 1970s. Still classified as a rookie, Oddleifson fared moderately well in a Boston uniform. On opening night, October 10, he scored a goal in the Bruins' 6–4 victory over Vancouver at Boston Garden. It was his first NHL tally. On October 25, Oddleifson enjoyed a two-goal outburst in Boston's 9–4 home win over Buffalo. Entering Boston's final game of 1973, Oddleifson had scored twice more to up his goal total to five. John Powers of the *Boston Globe* was unimpressed, however. "Oddleifson has not exactly been terrorizing enemy netminders this year,"[1] he noted. The last contest of the calendar year for the Bruins would be far from home in the remote NHL backwater of California. No one could have possibly foreseen that Oddleifson, who would play center that night as a result of a sudden Boston lineup shift and wear jersey #22, would nearly double his seasonal goal output to date.

Remarkably, Oddleifson's four goals versus California came consecutively—interrupted only by the lone Seals tally of the game by Walt McKechnie. "It started to click with 24 seconds remaining in the first period," wrote John Powers in the next day's *Boston Globe*, "just as it was supposed to. The puck began coming out of the corner directly in front and onto the stick of Chris Oddleifson, who zipped it past Seals goaltender Bob Champoux, just as he was supposed to."[2] That goal gave the Bruins a daunting 3–0 lead as they headed back to their dressing room for the first intermission. Gregg Sheppard and Johnny Bucyk had scored earlier in the first period for the visitors.

Oddleifson would later tell Powers, "That's how we worked on it during the drills. The fast shot from the slot. We had it going pretty well in practice."[3]

Boston upped its lead to 4–0 by scoring the only goal of the second period. Oddleifson's second goal, at 8:38, came on a well-executed breakaway, thanks to an accurate pass from the stick of Darryl Edestrand. Bobby Orr got an assist on the goal, too.

Twice more in the third period Oddleifson scored on the exact same play that resulted in his first goal—by deftly positioning himself in front of the Seals' net and accepting a perfect pass from Terry O'Reilly. They were his third and fourth markers of the contest. By the time Oddleifson had cooled off, the score was 6–1 in favor of Boston with 8:02 left on the clock and the outcome clearly beyond doubt. Later, Boston added two more goals just 20 seconds apart (by Ken Hodge and Wayne Cashman) to complete the thorough 8–1 shellacking of the Seals. Oddleifson did not figure in either of those goals.

The 10,850 fans in attendance at Oakland-Alameda County Coliseum Arena—the largest turnout of the 1973–74 season for a Seals home date—could scarcely believe that one of Boston's lesser lights was singlehandedly turning the game into a rout. After the fourth goal, even the home team's fans stood and applauded Oddleifson's outstanding achievement. Seals coach Fred Glover could be seen shaking his head in bewilderment at the wholly unexpected development. Glover had been the coach who had instigated trading minor-leaguer Oddleifson to the Bruins two years earlier.

"Oddleifson has a much better shot than he had in the minors a few years ago," Glover conceded. As Oddleifson was more of a playmaker than a marksman, Glover insisted, "He never shot then."[4]

"I'm overwhelmed," Oddleifson told reporters in the victorious visitors' dressing room. "I've never scored this many goals in a game before." (Obviously, this was true at the NHL level. Presumably, Oddleifson meant at any level of organized hockey.) Realizing that he had been perceived as a bit of a disappointment as a Bruin, Oddleifson added, "I'm glad to get the chance to show what I can do. I'm grateful to both Don Marcotte and Terry O'Reilly for what they did. [My linemates] deserve as much credit as I do."[5]

The line of Oddleifson, Marcotte and O'Reilly "was a combination that seemed to come out of nowhere,"[6] wrote *Globe* scribe John Powers the next day. Coach Bep Guidolin shook up his lines after Boston lost in Los Angeles on December 29. The Kings had topped Boston, 4–1, and the score was almost flattering to the listless Bruins that night.

Before the Bruins took to the ice the following night versus the Seals, Guidolin quickly and boldly made wholesale changes. He hoped to improve the overall scoring balance of the team. Specifically, Guidolin believed that greater scoring punch needed to be generated by the Bruins' second, third and fourth lines. Accordingly, he decided to experiment beginning with the December 30 game. The creation of a Marcotte-Oddleifson-O'Reilly line was probably the least noteworthy result of the tweaking Guidolin did between the Kings and Seals games. (Breaking up the all-powerful Phil Esposito line raised the most eyebrows among Boston's hockey reporters.) Still, declared the *Globe*, "It was a combination that Guidolin arrived at almost by the process of elimination, but he may think twice about breaking it up."[7]

"What came out of it was an Oddleifson who played like a man possessed," wrote a *Globe* correspondent who did not merit a byline. "He started scoring at 19:36 of the first period. When he finished halfway through the third, he had tied the Bruin record for most goals in a game with four, and Boston had won an 8–1 laugher over the crumbling

California Seals."[8] Indeed, the Seals' record after 34 games was a miserable 7–23–4. Bob Champoux endured the entire 60 minutes in goal for the home team without relief. According to the UPI hockey report in the next day's *Pittsburgh Press*, Bruin goaltender Ross Brooks had his bid for a shutout end when Walt McKechnie's 30-foot slapshot took "an errant bounce" at 8:35 of the third period. (McKechnie would later play one unproductive season with Boston.) Remarkably, all eight Bruin goals were of the even-strength variety, as was McKechnie's for California. Perennial NHL scoring champion Phil Esposito surprisingly failed to get a single point—a rare occurrence in 1973–74. Meanwhile, promising youngster Terry O'Reilly assisted on four Boston goals, faring slightly better than Bobby Orr who quietly picked up three helpers.

All glory is fleeting, however. In the cutthroat world of professional team sports, past achievements—no matter how remarkable they might be—really account for nothing. On February 7, 1974, Boston hosted the St. Louis Blues. The home team won the rough affair that Thursday night, 5–3. Immediately after the game, Chris Oddleifson and Fred O'Donnell were both approached by Boston general manager Harry Sinden. They were brusquely told they had just been traded to Vancouver in a deal that would see Bobby Schmautz move from the Canucks to the Bruins. Both had played well in Boston's victory that night: Oddleifson had gotten an assist on Boston's fifth goal; O'Donnell had recorded two assists on the night.

It had been rumored for quite a while that the Bruins were aggressively pursuing Schmautz—and many of the fringe players on the Boston lineup feared being traded from a solid Stanley Cup contender to a mediocre Canucks club that was almost certainly going to miss the playoffs. Tom Fitzgerald wrote in the February 8 edition of the *Boston Globe*, "Chris and Freddie definitely weren't very happy, which you might have expected, but some other young men on the Bruins' list were breathing deeply in relief."[9] Indeed, an Associated Press news photograph showed a grim-faced Oddleifson leaving Boston Garden with his head down. It had been just 39 days since Oddleifson had registered his magnificent four-goal game against the California Golden Seals. The 23-year-old, however, had scored just once in the interim, in a 6–2 loss in Toronto on February 2.

Oddleifson got three goals for Vancouver during the final 21 games of the 1973–74 season. Indeed, the Canucks did not qualify for the Stanley Cup playoffs that spring. They were not even in the running, finishing a distant 27 points out of a berth in seventh place in the eight-team East Division. Oddleifson would spend the remaining seven and a half seasons of his NHL career with the Canucks, playing in 469 games and scoring 85 goals. (His best seasonal output for Vancouver was 17 goals in 1977–78. His best single-game goal total for the Canucks was a hat-trick versus Atlanta on December 6, 1974.) Combined with the ten goals Oddleifson notched for Boston, his overall NHL total was 95. In other words, Oddleifson accounted for about 4.2 percent of his career goals in a span of approximately thirty-two and a half minutes one glorious and spectacular evening in Oakland as 1973 was coming to an end.

A dozen years after his last NHL game, Oddleifson was inducted into the Manitoba Hockey Hall of Fame in 1993. Fellow Bruins Mel Hill and Sugar Jim Henry are also honorees.

Despite the passage of time, Oddleifson is often asked to give his recollections of his remarkable feat. In a 2007 interview for a Vancouver Canucks fan website, the middle-aged Oddleifson said he has retained one negative lingering memory from the day after his famous four-goal game for the Boston Bruins on December 30, 1973, when the team's overnight flight arrived back in the Hub. He ruefully admitted, "You know what really bugged me, though? In one [Boston] newspaper the next morning, the headline read, 'Esposito held off scoresheet.'"[10]

Scoring Summary

First Period
- 4:04 BOS Gregg Sheppard (assists: Terry O'Reilly, Bobby Orr)
- 5:36 BOS John Bucyk (assist: Ken Hodge)
- 19:36 BOS Chris Oddleifson (assists: Terry O'Reilly, Bobby Orr)

Second Period
- 8:38 BOS Chris Oddleifson (assists: Darryl Edestrand, Bobby Orr)

Third Period
- 5:25 BOS Chris Oddleifson (assists: Terry O'Reilly, Don Marcotte)
- 8:35 CGS Walt McKechnie (assist: Joey Johnston)
- 11:58 BOS Chris Oddleifson (assists: Terry O'Reilly, Don Marcotte)
- 14:46 BOS Ken Hodge (assists: Dallas Smith, Gary Doak)
- 15:06 BOS Wayne Cashman (assist: Derek Sanderson)

18

October 7, 1976
Rick Middleton's Debut Hattrick

When Rick Middleton began his NHL career with the New York Rangers in 1974, he was regarded as a selfish, one-dimensional player who forsook the defensive elements of the game to solely pursue lofty offensive numbers. By the time his career ended in 1988, Middleton was one of the finest defensive-minded forwards in hockey—but he also remained one of the NHL's most prolific scorers.

Although Middleton had been a first-round draft pick for New York in 1973—the fourteenth selection overall—the Rangers did not figure they were losing too much when they dealt the stocky, 5'10" Middleton to the Boston Bruins in exchange for Ken Hodge on May 26, 1976. In fact, the Rangers figured they had thoroughly fleeced the Bruins out of one of their greatest players ever.

Hodge *had* been a great star for Boston, having scored 289 regular-season goals in nine seasons. However, when speaking about Hodge, the emphasis was on the past tense. His best years were behind him. Hodge had scored 25 goals in 1975–76, but serious Bruins fans knew his days with the club were likely numbered. First, Hodge did not get along especially well with third-year coach Don Cherry. Moreover, the spectators at Boston Garden were starting to heckle the 6'3" Hodge about his passive style of play which was largely perceived to lack typical Bruin-esque aggressiveness. Also, Hodge, at age 32, was almost a full decade older than the ascending Middleton and, unbeknownst to him, he had just one full year left in his fading NHL career.

After spending a year in the minors with the Providence Reds, Middleton had recorded very respectable numbers (46 goals and 44 assists) in his two NHL seasons with the Rangers. Nevertheless, he was considered to have been a bit of a disappointment. Defensively he was a ghastly minus-39 in 1975–76, a season in which the Rangers missed the playoffs for the first time in a decade. Middleton had also missed a sizable portion of his rookie season after suffering an ankle fracture. Worst of all, Middleton had developed the reputation as something of a reckless partier. New York coach Ron Stewart, who preceded John Ferguson, often benched Middleton when he was healthy. Thus, the Bruins' acquisition of Middleton was a bit of a gamble.

"Bruins trade Hodge to Rangers" shouted a front-page headline in the May 27, 1976, edition of the *Boston Globe*. (In a much smaller font, written below was, "Get right winger Rick Middleton.") Seeing Hodge's departure from the Bruins as inevitable, *Globe* sportswriter Ray Fitzgerald humorously commented, "The trading of Ken Hodge was first rumored in 1917, shortly after the National Hockey League was organized."[1] Hodge publicly announced he was pleased by the deal, which gave him the chance to be reunited with Phil Esposito, who had been dealt to the Rangers by Boston in November 1975. Another *Globe* scribe, Tom Fitzgerald (who was no relation to Ray), claimed, "Yesterday's trade almost certainly was influenced to some degree by Esposito, the man who was not only Hodge's center, but a close friend."[2] Esposito and Hodge reputedly celebrated the deal by having dinner together with mutual Boston friends. "We are delighted to acquire a player of Kenny's stature and ability,"[3] Rangers coach-general manager John Ferguson told the media.

Middleton expressed some surprise about the deal even though he had heard rumors about it from friends in his hometown of Toronto—where it had been discussed on a radio program. "When I officially heard about it from Ferguson, it was still a shock," he said. Middleton then added, "Now that I've had time to think about it, I'm quite happy. Boston has a very good club. Boston is a good hockey city, and I played for a year in Providence, so I know about New England."[4] Ultimately, the worries about the trade among Bruin supporters proved to be completely unwarranted. Boston got the better of the Hodge-for-Middleton deal—by far. In acquiring Middleton, the Bruins picked up a gritty, entertaining, wonderfully team-minded player who would score nearly 900 regular-season points over a dozen seasons, acquire the apt nickname "Nifty," and become a huge fan favorite.

Boston coach Don Cherry was concerned about the one-dimensional play that Middleton had displayed thus far in his NHL career, but he thought it was an issue that could be corrected in short order. "You can teach anybody about backchecking," Cherry insisted. "You can't teach them how to score. Middleton has that good touch close to the net that we lacked last season."[5] In subsequent years Cherry liked to joke that he had to introduce Middleton to Boston's goalies when he first became a Bruin because, true to his past exploits, he did not see much of them in his goal-scoring pursuits.

Middleton himself was fully aware of his defensive shortcomings and he knew things had to change if he were to succeed as a Bruin. "I didn't have a good plus-minus this [1975–76] season," he told the *Globe*, stating the obvious. "But I improved a lot later in the season when I was playing on a line with Phil Esposito and Pat Hickey."[6]

Boston's first game of the 1976–77 season was a home contest versus the Minnesota North Stars on Thursday, October 7—a team that had remarkably never won a game at Boston Garden since joining the NHL as one of the six 1967 expansion clubs. (They had accrued five ties and 20 losses in 25 previous attempts.) The North Stars already had one game under their belts, losing to the New York Rangers, 6–5, at Madison Square Garden the night before. Ken Hodge got one assist for the home team in his Ranger debut.

Despite having a quality team that reached the Stanley Cup semifinals in 1975–76 (falling to Philadelphia in five games), the Bruins were enmeshed in a losing public-relations battle. Disenchanted fans were upset that their beloved Bobby Orr had been allowed to play out his option and leave Boston for a huge contract with the Chicago Blackhawks. The incomparable Orr was basically a public institution in Boston, and his departure struck a nerve with many Bruin fans who blamed the team for not doing enough to entice him to stay in the Hub. Many Orr admirers vowed to stay away from Boston Garden in protest—and many did so for much of the regular season and playoffs.

Accordingly, on October 7, there were several thousand empty seats, a sight utterly unthinkable just a couple of seasons before when Bruin tickets were treasured commodities. The Bruins and North Stars battled in front of the smallest Opening Night crowd in Boston in a quarter century. This was somewhat ironic. During the summer, as a measure to make it more fan-friendly, Boston Garden had undergone upgrades to hide its signs of aging. It was the worst turnout at any Boston home game since February 9, 1969, when a severe blizzard kept the turnstile count below 8,000 for a game versus Philadelphia. One creative fan who did show up hung a punny banner with an angry message aimed at the club's ownership. It read, "The Jacobs brothers sold us down the river without an Orr." As things turned out, the vexed boycotters missed out on witnessing the Boston premiere of flashy new right winger Rick Middleton. It was a spectacular one.

"There were only 9,221 first-nighters at the Garden last night and maybe they caught the debut of a rising young star," optimistically stated Francis Rosa in the opening paragraph of his report on the Bruins' 6–2 victory over Minnesota for the *Boston Globe*. "His name is Rick

Middleton. His age is 22. His number is 16. Remember all of these, for he is a scorer."[7]

Rosa informed his readers that the lopsided final outcome was not representative of the game as a whole. "Don't be deceived by the score," he wrote. "It wasn't that much of a romp. It was a 3–2 game with 4½ minutes to play—which tells you the two goalies [Minnesota's] Pete LoPresti and Gerry Cheevers were playing a pretty strong game."[8]

The Bruins opened the scoring that Thursday night on a goal by 22-year-old defenseman Ray Maluta, a player known to only the most hardcore of Bruin fans. Maluta, a native of Flin Flon, Manitoba, was playing in just his third NHL game; he would only appear in 25. His shot that beat Pete LoPresti in the North Stars' net at 13:16 of the first period accounted for 50 percent of his career NHL goals. Maluta moved in from his position on the blue line to pounce on a juicy rebound that was invitingly sitting for him near the right faceoff circle. His accurate drive found the back of the net. When the goal light went on, Maluta went into a celebratory dance. "I was a little excited,"[9] he sheepishly admitted to reporters after the game. (Thirty-three years later, Maluta would coach the American men's sledge hockey team to the world championship in 2009.) Johnny Bucyk—who ended up scoring 543 more goals as a Bruin than Maluta did—picked up the only assist on Maluta's tally. It was his first of three helpers on the night. The first period ended with the home team holding a narrow 1–0 edge.

Rick Middleton scored the first of his 402 career goals for Boston at the 15:21 mark of the second period, briefly doubling the Bruins' advantage to 2–0. Assists came courtesy of Jean Ratelle and Johnny Bucyk. Middleton had been left unguarded while Bucyk controlled the puck in the left corner of the Minnesota zone. Ratelle saw Middleton was by himself in front of LoPresti and shouted at Bucyk. The Boston captain calmly sent the newcomer a perfect pass. Middleton ripped it home.

The North Stars fought back with their first score of the night with just ten seconds left to play in the second period that caused the home supporters to collectively groan. The goal was an unassisted one notched by Tim Young. Young had just returned to the ice after sitting out a minor penalty for hooking. It was a long, hopeful drive that deflected off Gerry Cheevers' glove with enough momentum to cross the goal line. The veteran Boston goalie had not expected the shot—and freely admitted that was the case. "I was sound asleep," he told Francis Rosa. "It took something like that to wake me up."[10] In a hard-fought contest, Boston's narrow 2–1 lead seemed to be about right as the two teams headed off the ice for the second intermission.

If the North Stars thought Young's goal was a harbinger of a change in momentum, they were clearly a mistaken bunch. Just 20 seconds into the third period, Jean Ratelle restored Boston's two-goal advantage with a shot that passed through LoPresti's pads and into the Minnesota net. The always modest Ratelle gave most of the credit to Johnny Bucyk for his excellent pass that created the scoring chance.

At the 10-minute mark of the final period, Minnesota again narrowed their deficit to a single goal. Dean Talafous knocked home a rebound from a scramble in front of Cheevers. With doubt creeping into the game's outcome, the new fellow wearing #16 on the back of his Boston uniform took charge of the game to ensure another Bruin victory at the Garden over the luckless North Stars.

About five and a half minutes after Talafous' goal, Middleton and Don Marcotte advanced into the Minnesota zone. Middleton had the puck on his stick. He intended to pass it to his onrushing teammate, but fate intervened. Middleton said afterward, "I looked up to pass to Marcotte and I lost control of the puck. By the time I got it under control, I was in too close [to the Minnesota net], so I just shot it. I'm surprised I beat LoPresti on the short side because he has such a good glove hand."[11] Boston's lead had been extended to 4–2 with 4:24 left in the game. Assists went to Gregg Sheppard and goaltender Gerry Cheevers. Amusingly, one game into the 1976–77 season, Cheevers had more points than either Brad Park or Wayne Cashman.

Less than three minutes later, Middleton got his hattrick, putting the game out of reach for the visitors. His third goal was a pretty display of scorer's talent. A fine pass by Don Marcotte sent Middleton alone on LoPresti. The North Star goalie bit on Middleton's fake shot. The Boston right winger then deftly skated around the fooled goaltender. Displaying an artist's understated touch, Middleton calmly backhanded the puck into the gaping, vacant net. The small but vocal Boston Garden crowd roared its approval. One spectator's hat was gleefully flung onto the ice surface to commemorate Middleton's three-goal feat. "He [Middleton] just might be the scoring star every team needs,"[12] Francis Rosa suggested in his game summary for the *Globe*. Perhaps the trade that sent Ken Hodge to Broadway was a good deal for the Bruins after all.

Bobby Schmautz finished things off with the sixth Boston goal of the evening with just 11 seconds remaining on the Garden's clock. Jean Ratelle's assist gave him three points on Opening Night.

Of course, Middleton was absolutely thrilled by how his first game as a Bruin unfolded. "I don't know quite how to describe it," he pondered. "I wasn't nervous before the game so much as apprehensive. I couldn't help thinking that a loss in this game would be just about all we'd need in view of everything else." Middleton, adroit with the words he chose, was alluding to the awkward and contentious Bobby Orr situation without specifically mentioning it. "Anyway, [the fans] got a good view of this club tonight,"[13] he added. That same night, Orr scored a second-period goal and had two assists for Chicago in the Blackhawks' 6–4 win over the Blues in St. Louis. It was Orr's debut game for his new club.

As for the solitary chapeau tossed from the seats, Middleton reflected on another multiple-goal evening when he was a Ranger. "I don't remember if there were any hats when I scored four goals [in one game] in New York two years ago. But then, not many guys wear hats nowadays, do they?"[14]

Not surprisingly, Middleton was named the game's first star by the Boston media. It was an auspicious start for someone who, over the next dozen years, would become one of the greatest players in the history of the Boston Bruins. Interestingly, Middleton's terrific Opening Night in 1976 accounted for 15 percent of his goal total for the entire season as he finished the 1976–77 season with 20 tallies. In retrospect, it was a poor output for Nifty. Middleton steadily improved on that modest figure for the next five years, culminating with a 51-goal season in 1981–82. The following campaign Middleton's goal total dropped slightly to 49.

Don (Grapes) Cherry slowly converted Middleton into a fine defensive player without affecting his scoring touch in the slightest. It was an education that Middleton fully appreciated. Years later he gratefully noted,

> Don changed my whole philosophy about hockey. I became a complete player because of Don. I always knew how to carry the puck and play offensive hockey, but Grapes taught me how to be in the right position and I wouldn't waste any steps. It's amazing how things worked out when I learned how to do it his way. Even by backchecking I got a lot of offensive opportunities.[15]

Of course, with the benefit of hindsight, today's New York Rangers supporters can accurately gauge the Hodge-for-Middleton deal. In November 2018, hockey historian George Grimm wrote,

> It's a universally accepted truth among Ranger fans that the worst trade in team history was made on May 26, 1976 when John Ferguson sent 23-year-old Rick Middleton to the Boston Bruins for Ken Hodge, nine years his senior. So when the Bruins announced they would be retiring Middleton's #16 sweater … it was like rubbing salt in an old wound. At last check, neither the Bruins nor the Rangers have any plans on retiring Hodge's sweater.[16]

18. October 7, 1976

Scoring Summary

First Period
- 13:16 BOS Ray Maluta (assist: Johnny Bucyk)

Second Period
- 15:21 BOS Rick Middleton (assists: Jean Ratelle, Johnny Bucyk)
- 19:50 MIN Tim Young (unassisted)

Third Period
- 0:20 BOS Jean Ratelle (assist: Johnny Bucyk)
- 10:00 MIN Dean Talafous (assists: Pierre Jarry, Tim Young)
- 15:36 BOS Rick Middleton (assists: Gregg Sheppard, Gerry Cheevers)
- 18:21 BOS Rick Middleton (assist: Don Marcotte)
- 19:49 BOS Bobby Schmautz (assist: Jean Ratelle)

19

December 23, 1979
Bruins Battle Ranger Fans

The 1970s are often characterized as a rough-and-tumble era in NHL history. Therefore, what happened in New York City on December 23, 1979, as the decade was approaching its end seemed almost fitting. On the morning after the events of the infamous "Shoe Brawl" between the New York Rangers and the Boston Bruins, both the *New York Daily News* and the *Boston Globe* featured the same photograph on their respective front pages. "A stick save—and a beauty," exclaimed the *Daily News*' punny caption. The more reserved *Globe* proclaimed, "Skater vs. Spectator." They were both referring to one small segment of a much broader wild incident: Bruins tough guy Terry O'Reilly taking on New Jersey businessman and Ranger fan John Kaptain amidst the padded seats at Madison Square Garden. To the best of anyone's recollection, nothing like it had ever been seen before in an NHL arena.

The Bruins, under new coach Fred Creighton, entered the Sunday night matchup at Madison Square Garden with one of the best records in the league (19–9–5), although they had been stumbling through a disappointing 3–6–2 skein over their past 11 games. Injuries to Brad Park, Don Marcotte, Jean Ratelle and Wayne Cashman were taking their toll on the aging club. The Rangers were a disappointing group thus far in 1979–80, middling just above the .500 mark with 16 wins, 15 losses and five ties. Despite their mediocre overall record, the Rangers had been playing rather well of late, posting seven wins and three ties in their last 11 games. Both teams had a negative shared experience in 1979. Each had fallen to the powerhouse Montreal Canadiens in the previous season's playoffs. Boston had famously lost a hard fought seven-game semifinal while the Rangers bowed out in the Stanley Cup finals in just five games. It was the first of four scheduled meetings between the Original Six rivals during the 1979–80 season. All signs pointed to a spirited engagement.

The game itself was a fairly typical NHL contest for the most part. Mario Marois of L'Ancienne-Lorette, Quebec, opened the scoring for the home team at 9:47 of the first period. Don Maloney and Phil Esposito drew assists. Marois' goal was the only puck to cross either team's goal line during the first period. Five minor penalties were assessed by referee Gregg Madill during the opening stanza, three to the Rangers and two to the Bruins. There was nothing to indicate that the contest would go down in infamy because of postgame craziness.

Boston tied the game just 83 seconds into the middle period with the ever-consistent Rick Middleton beating Ranger goalie John Davidson. Rick Smith and recent call-up Craig MacTavish were credited with assists. New York responded quickly with a power-play marker from the stick of Don Murdoch that beat veteran Boston goalie Gerry Cheevers at 3:46. Late in the frame, Anders Hedberg completed the second-period offense with a goal at 18:06, assisted by fellow Swede Ulf Nilsson, to give the hometown crew a 3–1 lead going into the final period. Six more minor penalties were called, three per team. Still, despite the 11 minor penalties and the escalating tension between the two longtime rivals, there was no way anyone could foresee what would transpire once the final buzzer sounded.

Ulf Nilsson drew a costly tripping penalty just 29 seconds into the final period that put the Rangers two men shorthanded. It was an ideal way start the final stanza for Fred Creighton's crew. Boston was quick to capitalize on a power-play goal by Terry O'Reilly, who scored at 1:09 from the left side of the crease. Just 64 seconds later, 5'5" Bobby Lalonde, who had the distinction of being the shortest player in the NHL at the time, brought the Bruins level at 3–3 with a well-placed backhand shot while the Rangers were still down one player. Promising rookie defenseman Raymond Bourque had assists on both goals. The game's momentum had clearly shifted to the team wearing the black jerseys. Stan Jonathan put the visitors ahead, 4–3, with referee Madill's hand in the air to signal a delayed penalty on New York with Gerry Cheevers pulled from the Boston net, several passes eventually set up Jonathan, who beat Davidson with a 25-foot wrist shot that sailed into the cage under his glove hand. It completed a fine Boston comeback with just under six and a half minutes showing on Madison Square Garden's scoreboard clock.

Upset that their two-goal lead had become a one-goal deficit, but still undaunted, the Rangers mounted a desperate offensive flurry. It was to no avail, however, as the Bruins retained their lead until the clock showed all zeroes. The game featured a somewhat frantic finish, though. New York coach Fred Shero had pulled goalie John Davidson for a sixth attacker to put added pressure on the Bruins defense in an attempt to earn a tie. At one point, Boston netminder Gerry Cheevers boldly tried to fire the puck into the Rangers' empty net—something rare at the time for a goalie to attempt—but his shot lacked steam. It was easily sent back into Boston territory. Moments later, New York's Ron Greschner made a skillful save with his team's net still empty to allow the Rangers to make one final push for an equalizer.

Remarkably, the Bruins suffered a major defensive breakdown with just a few seconds remaining to play. Phil Esposito got a clear breakaway on the Boston goal, but Gerry Cheevers stymied his former teammate with a sprawling save to his right to end the game with a dramatic flair. Shortly after the buzzer sounded, Cheevers skated from his net and lightly tapped Esposito from behind with his stick to console him. Espo was not placated by the act of sympathy. He violently broke his stick on the ice, clearly upset at missing a game-tying goal. Esposito left the ice in an obvious huff. The horn had sounded to end the third period, but the action, it turned out, was far from over. It was later revealed that someone in the crowd had tossed a tennis ball onto the ice during Esposito's breakaway. It had distracted Esposito and likely lessened his chances to tie the game.

Boston defenseman Mike Milbury later reflected on the odd incident.

> The game was tight. We had a one-goal lead with just seconds to go. Esposito somehow wound up on a breakaway and [Gerry] Cheevers stoned him. And during the breakaway somebody actually threw a tennis ball in front of Esposito from the stands. It was Madison Square Garden, so I don't know if it was a Bruins fan or some guy who was just lit. Anyway, [Esposito] missed the shot.[1]

Both teams now decided the time was ripe to settle a few lingering grudges. Ranger netminder John Davidson was irate. Earlier in the game, Bruins left winger John Wensink had gone into the New York goal area and had gotten both skate blades up on the prostrate Davidson's chest, according to television commentary on the Rangers broadcast. With tension rising, Bruins forward Al Secord sucker-punched Ulf Nilsson, telling him it was "an eye for an eye"[2] as Nilsson had allegedly done the same thing to Secord earlier in the game. Minor scuffles amongst the players occurred as a growing mob of players drew close to one side of the rink. That was when a Ranger fan, later identified as 29-year-old John Kaptain, stupidly decided to get involved. "That's the way a pretty good hockey game between the Bruins and Rangers was shoved into the background,"[3] wrote Francis Rosa in the next day's *Boston Globe*.

Kaptain reached over the low protective glass that ran alongside the right side of the Boston zone. He brazenly struck Stan Jonathan in the head with a rolled-up program, drawing blood from the startled Bruin, deftly plucked the hockey stick from Jonathan's grasp, and swung it around his own head in celebration! Terry O'Reilly, known for his tough demeanor—he would ultimately rack up the most penalty minutes in Bruins franchise history with 2,095—promptly scaled the unimposing barricade and wrestled the stick away from Kaptain.

That was far from the end of the postgame hullaballoo, however. Seeing O'Reilly entangled with Kaptain, eventually 18 Bruin players, coach Fred Creighton, and general manager Harry Sinden would venture into the stands. It was not to spread Christmas cheer. It was to defend one of their own from harm. The players also intended to take on any and all Ranger supporters and hooligans who chose to become involved in the melee. With punches flying everywhere, Kaptain was able to escape the clutches of O'Reilly. He scurried up a few rows of seats until Peter McNab and Mike Milbury—still wearing skates, of course—chased after him and successfully brought him to the ground to inflict something akin to Bruin-style frontier justice. It was at this moment that Milbury removed one of Kaptain's shoes and whacked him solidly with it! Television coverage shows the shoe being passing to another fan, despite some media reports and Milbury's persistent claim that he had cavalierly flung it onto the ice. During all this excitement, Phil Esposito began to wonder why he was sitting alone in the Rangers' dressing room. Curious, he made his way back onto the ice, joining his fellow teammates as they coolly watched the bizarre spectacle in the stands unfold.

Similarly, Mike Milbury had gone into the visitors' dressing room where only Gerry Cheevers was seated. Milbury was quick to question why no other Bruins were present. Cheevers told him there was some sort of vague ruckus back on the ice. Milbury returned, saw O'Reilly besieged in the stands, charged into the fray, and earned himself a unique place in Bruins lore.

The sight of Peter McNab rushing into the seats with mayhem on his mind was almost unbelievable to Bruin fans. McNab, despite being a big man, seldom got involved in rough stuff. He had accrued only four penalty minutes the previous season. Stan Jonathan would later joke, "Peter was usually the guy who'd pick up our gloves for us after a fight."[4]

Jonathan, who scored Boston's game-winning goal and became the target of John Kaptain's wrath, recalled the events from the moment he was struck by the program. "It felt like a helluva good jolt and I didn't know where it came from," he recalled. "I put my stick up as a reflex action and the guy grabbed it. Then the rest of [our] guys went up [into the stands]."[5]

Kaptain's excuse for igniting the sordid incident was a specious one. He told reporters he was merely coming to the defense of his brother! "I'm not saying I'm right in hitting [Jonathan]," he confessed. "I don't even know if I hit the right player. But my brother got hit by one of the [Bruins] first."[6]

O'Reilly, the first Bruin to climb the glass and venture into the crowd, felt he had to protect his teammate from violent New York interlopers. He had his alibi ready. He stated, "There was no way he was going to strike one of my teammates and steal his stick, wield it like a weapon, and then disappear into the crowd, and go to a local bar with a souvenir and a great story." O'Reilly knew what he was doing had put him in a precarious position. "As soon as I got him into a bearhug, I felt like I was being pummeled by multiple people," he said, "All I could do was cover up."[7]

Feisty Don Cherry, who had coached the Bruins from 1974 to 1979 and was now employed as the bench boss of the Colorado Rockies, was promptly contacted for his thoughts about what had happened at Madison Square Garden. He commented, "Never in my life did I see Terry O'Reilly covering up during a fight." Cherry also mentioned he was glad to see the usually peaceful McNab acting out of character and being a willing participant in the scuffle to protect a teammate. "I was quite proud of him,"[8] Cherry admitted.

Colgate-educated Mike Milbury, the Bruin who famously removed Kaptain's shoe and gleefully beat him with it, had this to say regarding what had occurred when he had hold of the man who would become the most famous (or infamous) New York Ranger fan in North America:

> I grabbed his shoe, took a little tug on it, and then sort of double-pumped. I don't know if I hesitated for a minute because I thought I'd be vilified for the next 30 years, but I gave him a cuff across the leg, and then I did what I thought was probably the most egregious thing of all: I threw his shoe on the ice.[9]

New York's Dave Maloney would be the last player off the ice. Along with his team having blown a two-goal lead against the Bruins, Maloney was also incensed about the game's officiating. Gregg Madill, usually rated among the worst NHL referees in polls official and unofficial by both players and coaches, was involved in a heated and very animated postgame argument with the Ranger captain. Maloney, a Kitchener, Ontario, native, complained that Madill had sworn at him and accused New York's Swedish players of diving to draw undeserved penalties on Ranger opponents. Maloney smashed his stick onto the ice in frustration and was immediately slapped with a game misconduct well after the contest had concluded.

Not long after hostilities had ceased in the stands, John Kaptain and his party—which included his brother, his father and a family friend—were all arrested and charged with disorderly conduct. "The Bruins did not want to press charges, so the Garden did,"[10] wrote Francis Rosa. They would ultimately be dropped. In return, the Kaptains agreed not to file charges against any of the Boston players.

Catherine Kaptain, the mother of John and his brother, happened to tune in to an evening news broadcast and was flabbergasted to witness her son being beaten with his own shoe during the postgame antics. Already convinced that hockey was a senseless and violent pastime, she recalled screaming at her television set, "They're beating up my babies!"[11]

Actor Denis Leary, a fanatical Boston sports fan, happily weighed in on the matter. He stated that anyone who believed "that two tickets and four plastic cups of beer entitled you to antagonize men who beat the living headlights out of each other for a living deserves to have his keister kicked." He added, "That's what I call thinning the herd."[12]

Boston Globe sportswriter Kevin Paul Dupont said the Bruins fighting in the stands was nothing like he had seen before, yet he offered this piece of prognostication: "I think if the guy had just given the stick back to O'Reilly, it would have been over. Knowing O'Reilly, he then would have told the dude to stay there after peace was made and he would have sent a stick boy over with an autographed stick."[13]

Commenting further about the brotherhood of the Big Bad Bruins, the eloquent Dupont wrote years later that he found the ethos of the situation to be its most endearing aspect.

> O'Reilly over the boards, and without hesitation, everyone to follow ... even McNab, who had no stomach for a fight ... and Milbury smacking the guy with his own shoe. Endearing because that was their brand. Sounds so corny today, that all-for-one attitude. But they lived by it. In the end, a few of them paid a heavy price. But it was real, woven into their belief of how a team should play and how teammates support one another.[14]

It took a month for a thorough investigation to conclude before NHL president John Ziegler doled out the punishments to Boston's battling Bruins. For being the first player to charge into the crowd, O'Reilly received an eight-game suspension. McNab and Milbury would each miss six games. The threesome was each fined $500 while all the other Bruins who ended up skirmishing amongst the Ranger fans were fined various amounts. Goaltender Gerry Cheevers escaped punishment altogether as he was noticeably absent from the violence. He wanted nothing whatsoever to do with the incident. Later he jokingly quipped, "I was already on my second beer."[15] Paul Mooney, the president of the Bruins, witnessed the events vastly differently than Ziegler, going so far as to praise his team with the following statement: "We do not accept his findings, and we are very proud of our players and the way they conducted themselves under very difficult circumstances."[16]

Terry O'Reilly felt similarly justified in his decision to venture into the crowd to seek what he perceived as justice. "Under the same circumstances, I don't think I'd go through a process of sorting through the rules and regulations and legal consequences," he thoughtfully said. "I think I'd jump over the glass and grab the guy again."[17]

Ziegler would take no punitive action against the Rangers or referee Gregg Madill despite the latter ignoring a trip and a retaliation, two actions that indirectly led to the on-ice brouhaha after the final horn and the subsequent mess in the seats.

As the years went by, Milbury would acknowledge the seriousness of the "shoe brawl" and how it could have been perceived by the masses. "None of us wanted to be in the toothless Neanderthal grouping," he said. "In the greater public's view, it re-emphasized [negative] stereotypes of hockey players."[18]

Some good came from such a disastrous night to the NHL's image. Not long afterwards, the league made the sensible decision to greatly raise the height of the glass between the ice surface and the paying customers to the level where today's hockey fans would expect it to be.

John Kaptain can no longer share his reminiscences of the famous conflict. He died suddenly on September 9, 1999, at the young age of 49. A minor celebrity in the Big Apple because of what occurred on December 23, 1979—at least among hockey fans—his passing was newsworthy in New York City. His cause of death was reported as an apparent heart attack. His father, Manny, would pass away 14 years later, two months shy of his 88th birthday. Manny never went to another hockey game at Madison Square Garden after the infamous Sunday night when his son had to walk home with one shoe on and one shoe off.

Scoring Summary

First Period
- 9:47 NYR Mario Marois (assists: Don Maloney, Phil Esposito)

Second Period
- 1:23 BOS Rick Middleton (assists: Rick Smith, Craig MacTavish)
- 3:46 NYR Don Murdoch (assists: Steve Vickers, Carol Vadnais) PP
- 18:06 NYR Anders Hedberg (assist: Ulf Nilsson)

19. December 23, 1979

Third Period
- 1:09 BOS Terry O'Reilly (assist: Peter McNab, Ray Bourque) PP
- 2:13 BOS Bobby Lalonde (assist: Ray Bourque) PP
- 13:36 BOS Stan Jonathan (assists: Bobby Lalonde, Peter McNab)

20

February 26, 1981
Boston's Biggest Brawl

Anyone who follows hockey, even casually, knows that penalties are not an uncommon occurrence at any level of the game. That is especially true in NHL play. Rare is the game in which neither team endures at least a few minutes in the sin bin. However, on February 26, 1981, history would be made as the Boston Bruins played host to the Minnesota North Stars. The two teams would go on to set several league records, including the most penalties assigned in a period (67) and the most penalty minutes for a game (406).

By late February 1981, Minnesota was a team on the rise in the NHL. Their steady ascension could be observed a year earlier. They were coming off a rather successful 1979–80 campaign which saw them surprisingly advance to the Stanley Cup semifinals for the first time since the early 1970s, ousting Montreal along the way. They lost in five games to the Philadelphia Flyers in the semifinals. Boston seemed headed in the other direction. The Bruins had lost in the Stanley Cup finals in 1977 and 1978 and the semifinals in 1979. Sticking to their regress chart, Boston was eliminated in the quarterfinals of the 1980 postseason, falling in five closely fought games to the New York Islanders, three of which were decided in overtime. That spring the Islanders would eventually go on to win their first of four consecutive Stanley Cups. Boston hired their recently retired goalie, Gerry Cheevers, to coach the team in 1980–81. The club got off to a truly awful start; after 12 games the Bruins were 2–9–1. "When I played, hockey was my life" the always amusing Cheevers quipped. "This could be death after life."[1] Boston had managed to turn things around by late February. The Bruins were three games above .500 when the Minnesota North Stars came to Boston Garden in an unusually feisty mood.

On Thursday, February 26, 1981, the North Stars were entering an environment they considered to be hostile territory. They had good reason to feel this way. Since entering the NHL in 1967, Minnesota had yet to win a single contest at Boston Garden! It was a horrendous dry streak that encompassed 34 games in which the North Stars were 0–27–7. Furthermore, there was a distinct possibility of a Minnesota-Boston matchup in the first round of the postseason. The North Stars also had some negative baggage they were trying to unload. Throughout much of the NHL—and especially in Boston—they were perceived as pushovers who were easily intimidated. Accordingly, the visitors arrived in the Hub intending to send a clear message to their intimidating hosts: Rough stuff would be welcome. During the pregame warmups, Minnesota right winger Tom Younghans skated by linesman Gord Broseker and uttered this amusing but somewhat dire statement: "I hope you and Kevin [Collins] went to the gym today."[2] It would be a long night for the pair of veteran linesmen who would indeed expend a great deal of time and energy that evening breaking up fights.

If anyone could be held responsible for the carnage that ensued on this given night, fingers would have to be pointed at Glen Sonmor, Minnesota's bench boss. Younghans recalled,

> I remember at the [pregame] team meal, while we were having dessert, Sonmor addressed us all. He started matching guys up: Jack Carlson and Stan Jonathan, Bobby Smith and Steve Kasper. He told us we were just as tough, but they [the Bruins] play together. He emphasized how important it was to react. If someone breathed on you, or looked at you cross-eyed, it was important to set the stage.[3]

The North Stars took their coach's aggressive advice to heart. It took all of seven seconds for one of Sonmor's volatile matchups to clash for the first penalties of the game. Bobby Smith found Steve Kasper and promptly dropped his gloves to the ice. Smith himself was promptly dropped to the ice too with the much larger Bruin on top of him. Once the two combatants had been separated, Broseker led the chirping Smith away to the penalty box. Smith had a wide smile on his face the entire time. There was a ripple effect on the Minnesota bench, however, much to the delight of the North Star players and Sonmor. Steve Payne went after Boston right winger Keith Crowder and a second fight ensued. After those penalties had been assessed, there were already a total of 60 minutes handed out to just four players. Payne earned the lion's share. He was slapped with 29 penalty minutes, including two ten-minute misconducts, a five-minute fighting major, and two unsportsmanlike conduct penalties at two minutes each. Bobby Smith, who initiated the brouhaha, found himself with only a fighting major plus a two-minute minor for high sticking. On the Bruins side of the ledger, Kasper received a fighting major and two minutes for high sticking, while Crowder earned a ten-minute misconduct, a fighting major, and two minutes for unsportsmanlike conduct. Clearly, it was merely a harbinger of the type of game to be expected.

At 2:53 of the first period, Steve Christoff of the North Stars and Mike Milbury of the Bruins received offsetting high sticking minors, a rather mild moment in the game. Surely the message Minnesota had intended to send to the Bruins was received as just 42 seconds later Boston's rugged right winger, Terry O'Reilly, would earn two minutes for slashing and matching five-minute fighting majors for his scuffle with Minnesota left winger Jack Carlson. Fans craving more penalties only had to wait another 53 seconds to see Boston's Brad McCrimmon earn two minutes in the home team's penalty box for a hooking infraction. Fewer than five minutes had run off the clock at Boston Garden and already 78 minutes in penalties had been assigned. There was more of that sort of thing to come—plenty more.

The first period proceeded peaceably, at least for a brief time, with only sporadic punitive action from referee Dave Newell. Minnesota's Craig Hartsburg was tagged with a relatively pedestrian penalty at 5:42, a two-minute sentence for holding. Similarly, just twenty seconds later, his teammate, Greg Smith, got his name into the referee's official game summary with a routine hooking minor. However, at 8:06, the players were battling again at full force. This time the initial pugilists were Minnesota's Tom Younghans who tangled with Boston's Mike Milbury behind the home team's net. As linesmen Collins and Broseker were busily dealing with them, Boston's Mike Gillis engaged in fisticuffs with Minnesota's Craig Hartsburg. These spirited altercations resulted in identical five-minute majors for both Younghans and Millbury, while Gillis and Hartsburg earned additional ten-minute misconduct penalties to go with their fighting majors. Boston would also earn two minutes for a nonviolent infraction for too many men on the ice, giving the visitors a power play.

Just 52 seconds later, general roughhousing erupted again as both teams mixed it up again with flying fists. This time it was Boston's Brad McCrimmon duking it out with Minnesota's Greg Smith who would receive 15 minutes of penalties capped off with a game misconduct. McCrimmon's bout with Smith apparently left him unsated. He then went after Minnesota's Gordie Roberts in another tussle. When things were settled, at least for the moment, McCrimmon received a whopping 32 minutes of penalties, including a game misconduct.

If things were not bad enough already, they were certainly about to get worse as the benches cleared and a full-on melee ensued. Even the goalies, Gilles Meloche for Minnesota and Rogie Vachon for Boston, got in on the action. When the dust had settled, another 205 minutes of penalties had been issued by Newell, raising the game's running total to 336 minutes. Remarkably. Fewer than nine minutes into the contest, the North Stars and Bruins had combined to record the fourth-greatest penalty-minute total in a single NHL game! That dubious distinction had been set two years earlier. On March 11, 1979, the Philadelphia Flyers and Los Angeles Kings had accrued 380 penalty minutes through an assortment of battles large and small and other infractions aplenty. The first fight in that game occurred after just 20 seconds had elapsed.

Years later, embattled linesman Gord Broseker had this recollection about the penalty-filled first period of the North Stars-Bruins tilt:

> Back then, you had to put another player in the box if a guy got a misconduct. We went over to the coaches and said we couldn't put all those guys in the box because we won't have any players. This is the rule, but we're going to waive it or else we'll have to cancel the game.[4]

When play finally did manage to resume, the North Stars still enjoyed their man advantage. However, it was Boston who would capitalize on the situation. The Bruins opened the scoring on a shorthanded goal by defenseman Mike O'Connell at 9:56.

The rest of the first stanza saw a rare interlude of détente between the batting clubs. Only three more minor penalties were assigned before the Garden's horn sounded. Minnesota's Brad Maxwell got an interference penalty at 12:44 while teammate Ron Zanussi was penalized for slashing at 14:02. Boston would take advantage of the Zanussi penalty to go up 2–0 as pacifistic veteran Jean Ratelle notched his eleventh goal of the season. Ray Bourque and Rick Middleton were credited with assists on Ratelle's score. (For Middleton, it was his second of the game.) Boston added to the penalty parade as Steve Kasper was whistled for hooking at 16:36.

If fans thought the opening 20 minutes took an extraordinarily long time to complete, they were not mistaken. Moving at a snail's pace due to all the donnybrooks, it took an astounding 91 minutes to play and saw a pair of new NHL records established for general thuggery: The mark for the most penalties in one period by one team was now held by Minnesota with 34. The record for the most penalties in one period by both teams was now 67.

The second period would be relatively quiet by comparison, but it was not without several more players getting involved in mayhem of some sort. In the hockey aspect of the game, Minnesota's Mike Polich, an American-born player, cut Boston's lead in half with his fifth goal of the season, on a nifty backhand. It occurred during the longest stretch of the game without a penalty. Assists went to Bobby Smith and Dino Ciccarelli. Including the final three minutes and 24 seconds of the first period and the first nine minutes of the second, it would be a restful 12 minutes and 24 seconds of relatively easy refereeing for Dave Newell and his two weary linesmen colleagues. However, Minnesota's Brad Maxwell and Boston's Wayne Cashman got into a dustup, earning each man a five-minute fighting major. Maxwell also was tagged with an additional two minutes for high sticking. Confusion on the North Stars bench resulted in the visitors' own minor penalty for too many men on the ice. Boston had another man-advantage opportunity.

Boston would deliver on the subsequent power play. Defenseman Ray Bourque, in his second season of what would be a terrific NHL career, recorded his 21st goal of 1980–81. It came just 13 seconds into the Boston man advantage. Brad Park, no slouch himself, picked up the lone assist on the Bourque score. Boston's one-goal lead was now two. A little more than three minutes later Boston's Dick Redmond would earn two minutes in the home team's sin bin for a cross-checking violation. At 17:13, Rick Middleton—normally a mild-mannered Bruin—engaged in a rare bout with Ron Zanussi. With 18 seconds left in the second period North Star defenseman Paul Shmyr and Boston's Steve Kasper decided to test the accuracy of their punching. Each man got a five-minute penalty from referee Newell. With still one period to play, the two teams had already combined to establish new NHL records for total penalty minutes in one game. Just how high (or low) the bar would be set was still to be determined, however.

An issue that complicated matters was the geography of Boston Garden. The hallway to the visitors' dressing room came right off Boston's bench, so each North Star kicked out of the game had to walk right by the entire Bruins team. At one point in the game, brawling players filled the hallway along with fans, security officials and even an unfortunate TV cameraman who found himself stuck in the middle of the fracas.

When the third period got underway, the patrons at Boston Garden witnessed a whole 95 seconds go by before more penalties were being meted out by Newell. Boston's Bobby Lalonde and Minnesota's Steve Christoff each earned a pair of minutes in the box for roughing, while Christoff would receive an additional five for fighting a more significant skirmish with Bruin right winger Dwight Foster.

Boston's Mike O'Connell was banished from the ice for two minutes for a hooking penalty at 4:48, sending Minnesota to the power play. Again, the Bruins turned the setback into something positive. Boston scored another shorthanded marker. This time it was Rick Middleton with his 34th of the season unassisted at 5:15 giving Boston a commanding 4–1 lead. About a minute later, Middleton would put the game away with another goal, concluding the game's scoring while Boston was still killing O'Connell's penalty. (Shorthanded goals were a Middleton specialty. By the time he retired in 1988, Middleton had eclipsed Derek Sanderson's career mark for Boston. With 25, he possessed the Bruin record himself for more than three decades until Brad Marchand came along.) Jean Ratelle earned the only assist on Middleton's 35th tally of 1980–81. Sadly, Middleton's excellent four-point performance would play second fiddle to the game's big story—the unrelenting fisticuffs.

Although the scoring was finished at Boston Garden, the penalties were not. Boston left winger Don Marcotte received a tripping minor at 9:38. Bobby Lalonde and Steve Christoff concluded the evening's boxing matches at 18:52. Both men got fighting majors. It would be the final bout of the record-setting contest.

By the time the final bell had sounded at the Garden, Minnesota, was penalized a record 211 minutes. The North Stars accrued 18 minor infractions, 13 majors, four 10-minute misconducts and seven game misconducts. Boston did their share of dirty work, too. The Bruins were saddled with 195 penalty minutes. The home team's contribution pushed the game's total penalty minutes to an NHL record 406. The headline in the next day's *Boston Globe* summed things up succinctly: "Bruins win a record war, 5–1." (The record lasted 23 years until March 5, 2004, when the Ottawa Senators and Philadelphia Flyers combined for 419 penalty minutes.) Minnesota would finish the season with 1,624 penalty minutes, making the 211 earned on February 26 nearly 13 percent of the North Stars' total for the season. The 195 penalty minutes racked up by Boston equated to a paltry 10.6 percent of theirs. For those fans interested in hockey statistics rather than scuffles, all five of Boston's goals came via their special teams. The Bruins had three shorthanded goals on the night—a true rarity. Their other two markers came on power plays.

In games where fighting gets out of hand, officials are required to file reports on the goings-on to NHL headquarters—and there was certainly plenty to cover in the February 26, 1981, contest that featured so many penalties and ejections. Gord Broseker recalled his lengthy postgame paperwork duties. "It was two or three in the morning before I went to bed," he remembered. "I'm not saying I didn't have a couple beers while I wrote those reports, but I definitely had a couple after."[5]

The fighting in Boston Garden was not restricted to the 60 minutes on the ice. Minnesota coach Glenn Sonmor (almost 52 years old) and Boston coach Gerry Cheevers (age 40) very nearly came to blows after the game in the infamous shared hallway. Sonmor reputedly told a scribe from the *Minneapolis Star Tribune* that if Cheevers wanted to discuss things further, he could find Sonmor the following week when the two teams met again, this time at the Met Center in Bloomington. (That game, played on March 4, featured surprisingly few major penalties for fighting—just four. It ended in a 3–3 tie.) One irritated Bruin fan took matters into his own hands and attacked Sonmor after the game. The twosome's fight required speedy intervention by Boston policemen to halt it. A photograph that ran in the *Tribune* showed Sonmor, in mid-windup, throwing a punch at his assailant.

When asked by a journalist if he was proud of how team had performed on the night, Sonmor was quite candid. "Proud? You're right I'm proud," he declared. "We made a stand." He voluntarily added, "We're through taking the cheap shots. We're going to react immediately., and as often as necessary."[6]

The Boston players and the local media saw things a little bit differently than Sonmor did. Francis Rosa of the *Globe* wrote, "The North Stars came into the Garden with a pretty obvious plan—intimidate the Bruins and don't back down. [But the home team] destroyed the Minnesota North Stars' dream of winning a game in Boston as sure as the Bruins destroyed the North Stars' plan of aggressive hockey. Nobody will outmuscle the Bruins very often in the Garden."[7]

"I guess that was their plan," surmised Mike O'Connell. "Three shorthanded goals was the answer."[8] Fellow Bruin defenseman Dick Redmond concurred. "If that was their game plan," Redmond noted, "they were wrong."[9]

Sonmor gladly and unapologetically explained the actions of his North Stars, noting, "You can't go out there and take it all the time. The league says they'll stop these cheap shots, but they never do it. The Bruins brag about it. They found out tonight we wouldn't take it."[10]

Cheevers was asked by a reporter if the violent aspects of the game may have turned off some potential fans from fully embracing the sport. The Bruins' first-year coach objected to the adjective contained within the scribe's question. "Violent?" he asked with a level of incredulity. "It might be violence in tennis or bowling, but not in hockey."[11]

The 5–1 loss to the Bruins extended Minnesota's streak of futility at Boston Garden to 35 games over a span of 14 years. Both teams qualified for the postseason and, as fate would have it, they faced each other in the first round of the playoffs. Minnesota picked the ideal time to end the franchise's horrible dry spell on Boston ice. The Bruins' defense seemed to be absent as the North Stars won the first two games in Boston (5–4 in overtime; and 9–6). They also took the third contest in

Bloomington, 6–4, to complete an unexpected sweep of the best-of-five preliminary round series. The suddenly formidable North Stars surprisingly advanced all the way to the Stanley Cup finals in 1981 where they lost in five games to the defending champion New York Islanders. The Bruins-North Stars clash that April was the only time the two teams ever confronted each other in a playoff series.

One attendee at the first Minnesota-Boston playoff game on April 8 was Kevin McHale, who was concluding his rookie NBA season with the Boston Celtics. The 23-year-old McHale was born in Hibbing, Minnesota, and had grown up as a passionate North Stars fan. McHale roughly learned that his status as a notable professional athlete for a Boston-based team did not grant him the privilege of openly cheering against the Bruins at Boston Garden. "I'm working in Boston now," he told a reporter from the *Minneapolis Star Tribune* who had spotted the basketball player among the Garden spectators. "I'm a North Stars fan all the way. I was clapping [for Minnesota] and somebody doused me with a beer from upstairs. I thought, 'So what? It was worth it.'"[12]

Scoring Summary

First Period
- 9:56 BOS Mike O'Connell (assist: Rick Middleton) SH
- 15:31 BOS Jean Ratelle (assists: Ray Bourque, Rick Middleton) PP

Second Period
- 6:31 MIN Mike Polich (assists: Bobby Smith, Dino Ciccarelli)
- 9:13 BOS Ray Bourque (assist: Brad Park) PP

Third Period
- 5:15 BOS Rick Middleton (unassisted) SH
- 6:17 BOS Rick Middleton (assist: Jean Ratelle) SH

21

May 8, 1988
Doughnut-Gate

Perhaps the most embarrassing debacle the National Hockey League ever had to contend with occurred in the spring of 1988. One intense Stanley Cup playoff series featured a coach being suspended for allegedly accosting a referee, his maverick team defying the NHL, a wildcat officials' strike, and a league president who, inexplicably, was nowhere to be found. The entire sordid episode came to be humorously known as "Doughnut-Gate."

In 1988, the New Jersey Devils were making their first playoff appearance in franchise history. They were an outfit that originally saw the light of day as the Kansas City Scouts in 1974–75. After two calamitous seasons in Missouri, the club shifted to Denver where it operated as the Colorado Rockies until 1981–82. Poor results and fan apathy caused the club to move again, this time to New Jersey for the 1982–83 season. It took an unlikely run of five dramatic wins at the end of the 1987–88 season—including a 4–3 overtime triumph over Chicago on the last day of the season—for New Jersey to even qualify for the postseason. Once they got there, however, they clearly seemed to be a team of destiny. A six-game win over the New York Islanders in the Patrick Division semifinals and a seven-game win over Washington in the divisional finals got them a meeting with the Adams Division champion Boston Bruins in the Wales Conference finals, also known as the Stanley Cup semifinals.

Boston was enjoying some overdue playoff success. Although the Bruins had qualified for the Stanley Cup playoffs for the twenty-first consecutive season in 1988, they had not won a playoff series since 1983. In each of the previous four years, Boston had been ousted in the first round by their eternal nemeses, the Montreal Canadiens. There was a new confidence growing in the club, however. Boston beat Buffalo in six games and Montreal in five to get to the conference finals against an ascending team they never expected to encounter—the New Jersey Devils.

Boston, the favorites, won the opener, 5–3 at home on May 2. Two nights later, the Devils surprised the Bruins with a 3–2 overtime win at the Garden to even the series. (Doug Brown scored the winner for the visitors.) It had been a fairly routine series to that point as the locale changed from Boston to New Jersey for the third and fourth contests in the best-of-seven series.

The trouble began on Friday, May 6, 1988, during Game Three. In the first period, 32-year-old referee Don Koharski angered Devils coach Jim Schoenfeld by penalizing Kirk Muller and Pat Verbeek simultaneously at 19:30. By the 2:18 mark of the second period, the Bruins tallied three quick goals on their way to an easy 6–1 win in the penalty-filled contest to take a 2–1 series lead.

The home team did not accept the result of the game well. When the third period ended, Schoenfeld verbally berated Koharski and pursued him down the runway toward the officials' dressing room to yell at him some more. Thirty years later, Schoenfeld remembered the incident this way in an interview with the *New York Post*:

> I felt we were being screwed, so I waited for Don as he came off the ice. I'm not irate.... I just want to ask him, "What's going on?" But he gets heated and I get heated. Things kind of escalate and they reach the tipping point.
>
> The corridor is crowded. There's really no room, and there's a commotion going on. He kind of stumbles and his skate hits the concrete. The rest lives in infamy.[1]

Footage shot by a local TV news crew (from WABC) plainly showed that Koharski appeared to stumble off the carpet on his own, but the referee immediately accused Schoenfeld of shoving him.

"You're through!" shouted an upset Koharski. "You'll never coach another game in this league!"

"You're crazy—you fell, you fat pig!" replied Schoenfeld. "Have another doughnut!"[2]

Koharski, who was considered among the NHL's best referees in 1988 despite being slightly overweight, promptly reported the alleged shoving incident to league headquarters. NHL vice-president Brian O'Neill—who typically handled all league disciplinary matters—handed Schoenfeld an immediate one-game suspension with the possibility and likelihood of more to come.

The food angle of the story seemed to amuse hockey fans. One business saw the possibility of advertising gold in it. Throughout Massachusetts and other parts of New England, stores from a prominent doughnut chain began promoting a timely new special: 13 doughnuts for the price of a dozen. Its print adverts humorously insisted, "Referee Koharski isn't the only person who should have another doughnut."[3] Meanwhile, several hundred miles away, at the home of Jim Schoenfeld's parents in Cambridge, Ontario, pranksters littered their front lawn with whole doughnuts and doughnut holes for several days running.

Schoenfeld adamantly denied shoving Koharski, although it was undeniable that he had pursued Koharski to the officials' room to continue the argument. The Devils' management fully backed his assertion that Koharski had stumbled and that their coach was absolutely blameless. They wanted to appeal his suspension to NHL president John Ziegler. The trouble was, nobody was quite sure where to find Ziegler. Rumors had the prexy being everywhere from Bermuda to Moscow. (The *Toronto Star* published an unsubstantiated report that Ziegler was in New York City attempting to free his son from a religious cult!) Whatever the case, the NHL's credibility took a severe beating. Passionate hockey fans were amazed that an NHL president could be AWOL during the Stanley Cup playoffs.

With Ziegler apparently unavailable to personally review the Schoenfeld-Koharski incident, Devils general manager Lou Lamoriello contacted Judge J.F. Madden of New Jersey's Superior Court. Lamoriello persuaded the judge to issue a temporary restraining order which, in effect, circumvented O'Neill's mandate and postponed Schoenfeld's suspension. He would be behind the bench, as usual, for Game Four on Sunday, May 8. Lamoriello, with apparent sincerity, told the media, "I am very sorry we were forced to seek legal action outside of the league's jurisdiction, but we did seek every internal redress possible."[4]

Now the NHL officials were outraged. They were predictably angry that a "rent-a-judge" had overturned a league ruling regarding an alleged assault on one of their own. This was unheard of in professional hockey. To show their support for Koharski, referee Dave Newell and linesmen Ray Scapinello and Gord Broseker packed up their gear and left Brendan Byrne Arena—just moments before they were to work Game Four. By coincidence, Newell, age 43, was also the sitting president of the National Hockey League Officials' Association (NHLOA).

John McCauley, a superb referee in his day before an eye injury caused by a punch from an angry, drunken fan ended his on-ice career in 1979, was the NHL's supervisor of officials in 1988. He explained to the media, "The NHL game officials made a personal decision that they could not perform their duties given the circumstances of Devils coach Jim Schoenfeld being behind the bench."[5] The 1988 Stanley Cup playoffs had certainly exposed some nasty rifts between the NHLOA and the league's supervisors of officials. During the Boston-Buffalo playoff series, former NHL ref Bryan Lewis, now an underling of McCauley's, was vilified by Newell for describing a penalty whistled against Boston's Glen Wesley by referee Kerry Fraser as "a horseshit call."[6]

Suddenly without officials for a crucial game, the contest was delayed nearly an hour while the NHL's bigwigs huddled to decide what to do next. William W. Wirtz, head of the NHL's Board of Governors, ordered the game had to be played that night regardless of who officiated it. Three local amateur referees, all accredited by the Amateur Hockey Association of the United States (AHAUS), were tracked down inside the arena and given rapid advancement as on-ice officials for a Stanley Cup semifinal game. Referee Paul McInnis, 38, the manager of an arena in Yonkers, New York, was given the only striped shirt that could be readily found. It bore the AHAUS logo. With no proper referee's trousers, McInnis had to don sweatpants bearing the team colors of New Jersey. The two linesmen, Jim Sullivan, 38, and Vin Godleski, 40, were each employed part time as NHL penalty timekeepers (one for the Devils and one for the New York Islanders). They embarrassingly wore gaudy yellow warm-up jerseys borrowed from the home team. (By the first intermission, striped shirts had been secured for the twosome.) The game had not even started and the three on-ice officials were already a conspicuous lot.

For a while, the Bruins pondered whether they should take a walk too. They were not at fault, they argued. Why should they have to put up with substandard officiating? Wirtz informed Boston coach Terry O'Reilly his team either played or forfeited the game. Boston played with a notable lack of vigor and lost, 3–1. At least the *Boston Globe* got a punny headline out of it the next day: "Bruins hit an official snag."

As in Game Three, there were plenty of penalties whistled, but most of them were of the offsetting variety. Many hockey writers sensed that referee McInnis was reluctant to give either team a man-advantage situation. New Jersey scored twice, 45 seconds apart, in the first period on goals by David Maley and Pat Verbeek to assume a lead they would never relinquish. Cam Neely got a power-play goal for Boston in the second period to narrow the deficit to 2–1, but the visitors got no closer. Tom Kurvers scored for the Devils at the 4:04 mark of the final period to salt things away for the home side. There was no further scoring. The 3–1 New Jersey win leveled the series at two games apiece.

Game Four's officiating got mixed reviews. "Neither team could complain very much about the job the substitute officials did," wrote Austin Murphy of *Sports Illustrated* with a tinge of sarcasm. "Okay, they almost lost control of the game in the second period when three fights broke out simultaneously. They also missed a couple of dozen offsides, and McInnis pretty much put his whistle away in the third period."[7]

Bruins general manager Harry Sinden was more complimentary. He said, "The margin between officials we plucked out of the stands and officials we pay a great deal of money to was incredibly minimal."[8] Terry O'Reilly disagreed. "This game was a cross between football and Irish rugby," he declared. "It's a shame we have to suffer for a problem created by the New Jersey coaching staff and exaggerated by the officials."[9]

Francis Rosa of the *Boston Globe* figured that both teams suffered equally. He wrote, "Both teams played under the same handicap of the amateur officials, who did a decent job, but at the same time were in over their heads."[10] Rosa did concede that the Devils seemed to be aware about the potential of the officials' walkout well in advance of the Bruins, which perhaps gave them a psychological edge. Indeed, New Jersey, abruptly stopped its pregame warmup several minutes before the Bruins were even aware that there might me something imperiling the game.

Boston's Rick Middleton, winding down a superb 14-year NHL career in search of an elusive Stanley Cup title, was almost at a loss for words when asked to describe the situation. "Just when you thought you've seen everything in this league ... it's a shame,"[11] he said.

When later asked if he could have and should have vetoed the replacement officials, Harry Sinden told Michael Madden of the *Globe*, "Maybe I could have, but I never would have done it. For me, the primary thing, the responsibility we have, is to play the game. We did—and we seem to be the innocent victims here." Madden opined that Sinden "looked like a sad, beaten man. For the NHL is Sinden's love, and this was a lost night for the sport and the league."[12]

Others were more ably articulating their feelings, and what they were saying about absentee John Ziegler and the NHL in general was not pleasant. "The league made a laughingstock of a sold-out playoff game [that aired] on U.S. and Canadian television, with one team two wins from competing for the league's precious—but now undeniably devalued—Stanley Cup,"[13] Austin Murphy declared.

In a scathing editorial in *Sports Illustrated*, E.M. Swift wrote, "Calling John Ziegler. Has anyone out there seen John Ziegler, the puppet president of the National Hockey League? We have an important message for you: Resign. Quit. Your sport is a leaderless joke."[14]

After a proper hearing was held by the NHL, Jim Shoenfeld's one-game suspension was upheld for Game Five in Boston on May 10. It was not for the alleged shove which plainly did not occur, but for abusive behavior and demeaning language toward an on-ice official. Lou

Lamiorello made his NHL coaching debut by assuming Shoenfeld's spot behind the Devils' bench. Regular NHL officials returned to the ice to call the game. Boston won Game #5 in a rout, 7–1. New Jersey rallied one more time to take Game Six, but the Bruins eventually ousted the Devils in seven games. Thus, Terry O'Reilly's battlers earned a trip to the Stanley Cup finals for the first time since Don Cherry's lunch pail gang—featuring O'Reilly—had managed the feat back in 1978. However, the Bruins lost decisively in the championship round to the last Edmonton Oiler team to feature Wayne Gretzky on its roster.

The ridiculous Doughnut-Gate situation still overshadowed everything that followed it, especially in hockey-mad Canada. On *Sports Page*, a TSN panel show, moderator John Wells asked with incredulity, "Can you imagine this happening if [authoritarian former NHL president] Clarence Campbell were alive?"

Jim Hunt of the *Toronto Sun* quickly replied, "I can't imagine this happening if John Ziegler were alive!"[15]

Scoring Summary

First Period
- 10:47 NJ David Maley (assists: Claude Loiselle, Doug Sulliman)
- 11:32 NJ Pat Verbeek (unassisted)

Second Period
- 12:31 BOS Cam Neely (assists: Craig Janney, Bob Joyce) PP

Third Period
- 4:04 NJ Tom Kurvers (assists: Brendan Shanahan, John MacLean)

22

October 16, 1988
Cam Neely's Seven-Point Game

Boston Bruin coach Terry O'Reilly needed to shake up his team. They were suffering through a mini-slump, having dropped the first two contests of a five-game road swing. Entering their game in Chicago on Sunday, October 16, 1988, O'Reilly, a chess enthusiast, reorganized the pieces of his team, juggled his lines and tried a new opening. Defenseman Garry Galley was back in the Boston lineup after being a healthy scratch the night before in Minnesota. Boston's lines had players moved in and out of them. The pleasant result of the tinkering for the visiting Bruins was an enormous offensive turnaround and a record-tying night for Cam Neely, who was fast becoming the face of the entire Boston franchise.

The previous season, 1987–88, had seen the Bruins battle their way to the Stanley Cup finals for the first time in a decade. Playoff victories over Buffalo, Montreal (for the first time since 1943), and New Jersey took the team to the championship round for the first time since the spring of 1978 when O'Reilly was one of the key Boston cogs as a rugged player. In the finals, Boston lost to the last Edmonton Oilers team to feature Wayne Gretzky, but the stage was apparently set for the Bruins to be a very formidable Cup contender into the 1990s. Boston began the 1988–89 season looking like potential championship challengers. On Opening Night at Boston Garden on October 6, the Bruins edged the Toronto Maple Leafs by a 2–1 score. Cam Neely got a goal and an assist for Boston. Defenseman Ray Bourque was pleased with the outcome. He told Francis Rosa of the *Boston Globe*, "We wanted to win this opening game, and we wanted to establish ourselves as a good home team. We did both."[1] A pair of home and away wins over the Hartford Whalers, 6–2 and 3–1, quickly followed, giving the Bruins a perfect 3–0 start for the campaign. Everything seemed to be clicking.

The club then began a five-game road trip to western NHL locales that did not begin well at all. On Wednesday, October 12, Boston lost badly to the Kings in Los Angeles, 6–1. Boston fell apart in the last stanza, allowing five third-period goals. Newly acquired Wayne Gretzky starred in the Kings' impressive victory, scoring a shorthanded goal to lead his team's comeback. Rosa admiringly wrote, "Gretzky isn't a disease, he's an epidemic. He has turned the Los Angeles Kings into the Edmonton Oilers of the United States."[2]

Three nights later they fell to the North Stars in Minnesota in another one-sided affair. This time the score was 5–1. Rosa aptly described the Bruins' play that Saturday night as "erratic." He further commented on the two dismal games the Bruins had played to begin the first road trip of the season, "The Bruins left their game in Boston Garden, which is a terrible place to leave it when you're traveling—and unraveling—through the West."[3] Boston had led the game 1–0 on Bob Joyce's first-period goal, but Minnesota scored twice in 84 second to erase the Bruins' slim advantage and take the lead themselves before the first 20 minutes expired. The North Stars had not won a game in 1988–89 before the Bruins arrived in Bloomington.

Certainly, coach Terry O'Reilly had cause for concern as the Bruins, now a shaky 3–2 after five contests, rushed off to Chicago Stadium for their sixth game of the season to be played the very next night. "We have to be a lot sharper mentally," he told Rosa. Remaining outwardly confident, O'Reilly nevertheless predicted, "We don't have much time to regroup, but we'll bounce back."[4] Cam Neely certainly did.

Cam Neely is so solidly linked with the Boston Bruins that it is easy to forget he started his NHL career elsewhere. The Bruins acquired Neely in an offseason trade with Vancouver in June 1986. In exchange, Boston sent Barry Pederson to the Canucks. The transaction was controversial in Boston for a while as Pederson was routinely found among Boston's top scorers. In Pederson's first three full seasons in the NHL, his goal totals those years were terrific: 44, 46 and 39. Overall he notched 166 goals for Boston in regular-season play and another 22 in the postseason. Pederson was just 25 years old when the 1985–86 season ended. However, there was a specter of doubt lingering over him. In the summer of 1984, a benign tumor was removed from Pederson's right shoulder. It was not a simple operation; the procedure required that part of the muscle be removed. Pederson missed three-quarters of the next season, only appearing in 22 of Boston's games to conclude the 1984–85 campaign. In those, he scored just four goals. Although Pederson rebounded with 29 goals in the 1985–86 season, he clearly did not possess the form he had had before his surgery. Pederson became expendable. Left unsigned by the Bruins, Vancouver picked him up. Since Pederson was classified as a restricted free agent, under NHL rules the Canucks had to provide compensation to Boston. It came in the form of underused Cam Neely *and* a first-round draft pick in 1987. The deal was finalized on June 6, 1986—which, by coincidence, happened to be Neely's 21st birthday.

In his three seasons as a Canuck, Neely had been a bit of a bust on Canada's west coast considering he was the ninth-player selected overall in the 1983 NHL entry draft. He had scored just 14 goals for Vancouver in 1985–86 and was perceived by coach Tom Watt as a lackadaisical defensive player. His ice time with the Canucks was reduced. However, the Bruins liked Neely's size (6'1", 215 pounds) and aggressively offensive style of play. The club hoped Neely might be another tough forward in the mold of Wayne Cashman or Terry O'Reilly who had yet to fulfill his potential, but could if he were given the opportunity. Neely fit right in to Boston's way of playing. Blessed with a quick and accurate shot, Neely scored twice in the team's second game of 1986–87 and 36 goals overall in his first year as a Bruin. Not surprisingly, he immediately became a fan favorite in Boston. Neely's Wikipedia biography says after relocating to Boston, he "became the archetype of the power forward." This is undeniably true.

Chicago entered the October 16 game with a 1–3–1 record, having both scored and allowed 25 goals in their first five games. The latter statistic bothered newly installed coach Mike Keenan, who had stressed solid defensive play when he coached the Philadelphia Flyers to two Stanley Cup finals. In an interview with the *Globe*'s Francis Rosa, Keenan said he intended to instill fundamentals and a better work ethic into his charges, calling it an ongoing and continuous process. The results of that night's match would prove there was indeed plenty of work needed to be done by Keenan to improve the Blackhawks.

The Bruins stepped onto the Chicago Stadium ice that Sunday night "equipped with squad-wide concentration and intensity,"[5] according to Francis Rosa. They hardly seemed like the blasé bunch who had sleepwalked their way to two uninspiring losses in their first ventures away from Boston Garden. Defenseman Glen Wesley got the opening goal for Boston, collecting a Ken Linseman pass, and scoring on a 30-foot shot past young goaltender Jimmy Waite. Chicago rallied, however, scoring twice on goals by Steve Larmer and Rick Vaive, to take a very temporary 2–1 lead. Vaive's goal came on a Chicago power play. Undaunted, Boston tied the score just 24 second later and retook the lead, 3–2, by the end of the first period. The Bruins had scored more goals in 20 minutes in Chicago than they had managed in two hours in Los Angeles and Minnesota in their prior two games. Scoring for the visitors were Linseman and Bob Joyce. Neely assisted on Joyce's tally, feeding him an excellent pass from behind the Chicago net. Boston goalie Andy Moog made a wonderful save in the final minute of the period, blocking a Denis Savard wrist shot, to preserve the slim Boston advantage.

One key factor in the game was referee Bob Hall who, in the second period, was suddenly in the mood to send players from both teams to the sin bin for the slightest transgression. Francis Rosa panned Hall's performance, describing the middle 20 minutes as "a fiasco of penalties."[6] Chicago rookie Mike Hudson leveled the score for the home team early in the second period. It was the last time Moog would be beaten. The Bruins then embarked on a "40-minute attack binge,"[7] noted Rosa, that saw them hold a 7–3 lead at the end of the second period thanks to an unchecked outburst of four goals in a span of about 16 minutes.

Keith Crowder got the Bruins back into the lead, 4–3, by lifting a loose puck over the sprawled and helpless Blackhawks netminder. Then it was Neely's turn to add to the Boston scoring parade. Working his way to the slot, Neely, in typical fashion, fought off a check by Chicago's Mike Eagles, deftly regained his balance, and fired a 20-foot shot past Waite. Boston's Michael Thelvén upped the score to 6–3 about three minutes later. With the Bruins working on a power play, Thelvén was at the right place at the right time to knock home Cam Neely's rebound from about 10 feet to the right of Waite. Referee Hall continued to whistle penalties aplenty. With Boston enjoying a two-man advantage, Neely struck again to make it a 7–3 game. Positioned in the slot, Neely knocked down an airborne puck with his hand and quickly ripped it past Waite. The rout was on—but Waite would suffer no more once the siren sounded to end the middle frame. Chicago coach Mike Keenan mercifully yanked his 19-year-old rookie netminder from the game and replaced him with Darren Pang for the third period.

That change in goaltending personnel did not stop the Bruins from attaining double-digits on the Chicago Stadium scoreboard. They scored three more times in the final 20 minutes as the Blackhawks' resistance seemed to collapse on several occasions. Neely figured in all three. He got his third marker to make the score 8–3, another shot from the slot, 15 feet in front of Pang. It was another Boston power-play goal. As Neely returned to the Boston bench, his Bruins teammates jokingly serenaded him with a chant of "Steroids!

Steroids!" as the dubious drug scandals of the recent 1988 Seoul Olympic Games were still very much a hot topic in the sports world. Neely's reaction was a bemused smirk.

Steve Kasper recorded the final two goals for Boston in the third period. Neely's assist on Boston's tenth goal got him a spot in the Boston record books. "Everybody wanted to get in on the action,"[8] wrote Francis Rosa in the next day's *Boston Globe*. Five of Boston's tallies came while Chicago was playing shorthanded. "The Bruins had a .500 night, five-for-ten with the man advantage,"[9] quipped Rosa. On the other side of the coin, the Blackhawks tied a negative team record by allowing five power play goals in a single game. Edmonton had done the same thing to the Hawks on November 26, 1980. Remarkably, that game versus the Oilers was another 10–3 Chicago defeat.

The hattrick was Neely's sixth in his NHL career, all had occurred while clad in a Boston uniform. His seven-point game equaled a club record. It was the fourth time a Bruin had attained that many points in a single regular-season contest. The other three men to do it were Phil Esposito, Bobby Orr and Barry Pederson, the man whom Neely had replaced in 1986. Neely's feat—and the Bruins' seven-goal victory—did not even get top billing on the front page of the *Boston Globe*'s Monday sports section. It nearly did not make the first page at all. Reports on the dramatic Dodgers-A's World Series and the New England-Cincinnati NFL game pushed the Bruins-Blackhawks tilt to the very bottom of the page. Moreover, in another NHL contest, Mario Lemieux had a spectacular eight-point game the night before versus St. Louis, so Neely's marvelous effort in Chicago had not quite measured up to what the Pittsburgh Penguins superstar had accomplished on October 15.

In his report for the *Globe*, Rosa credited the coach and his bold lineup shuffling for Boston's big win over the Blackhawks. "With new lines and the same old drive that characterized [Boston's] first three games," he penned, "Terry O'Reilly—almost in the manner of Red Sox manager Joe Morgan—used his whole squad to get the Bruins out of a little mental slump that was threatening to turn the road trip into a mess. Now they can look forward to three days in romantic, exotic Winnipeg with a 1–2 record on this five-game road trip."[10]

Boston's 10–3 victory over the Chicago Blackhawks was the 4,118th regular-season game in the club's history, annals that date back to the 1924–25 NHL campaign. It was the 27th time that the Bruins had achieved a double-digit score. As of March 2022, in the nearly 2,600 subsequent games the Bruins have played since October 16, 1988, they have yet to do it again.

Scoring Summary

First Period
- 3:38 BOS Glen Wesley (assists: Ken Linseman, Michael Thelvén)
- 10:50 CHI Steve Larmer (assists: Denis Savard, Doug Wilson)
- 14:54 CHI Rick Vaive (assists: Denis Savard, Keith Brown) PP
- 15:18 BOS Ken Linseman (assists: Garry Galley, Michael Thelvén) PP
- 16:17 BOS Bob Joyce (assists: Cam Neely, Craig Janney)

Second Period
- 2:28 CHI Hudson (assists: Dave Manson, Trent Yawney)
- 4:35 BOS Keith Crowder (assists: Ken Linseman, Garry Galley) PP
- 13:49 BOS Cam Neeley (assists: Glen Wesley, Craig Janney)
- 16:10 BOS Michael Thelvén (assists: Cam Neeley, Glenn Wesley) PP
- 17:33 BOS Cam Neely (assists: Glen Wesley, Ray Bourque) PP

Third Period
- 7:30 BOS Cam Neely (assists Craig Janney, Bob Joyce) PP
- 8:54 BOS Steve Kasper (assists: Cam Neely, Randy Burridge)
- 12:04 BOS Steve Kasper (assists: Cam Neely, Glen Wesley)

23

April 11, 1990

Four Goals in Third Period
to Salvage Playoff Series

When the 1989–90 NHL regular season had concluded, the Boston Bruins had compiled the best record of any team in the circuit with an excellent 46–25–9 mark over 80 games. The team's 101 points made the Bruins the only club in the 21-team league to accrue a three-figure total, although two of Boston's Adams Division rivals, Buffalo and Montreal, were close behind with point totals in the nineties. Under the NHL's playoff format of the time, the first two rounds were contested within a team's own division. This meant the Bruins had a best-of-seven clash with the nearby Hartford Whalers to begin postseason play. Without a remarkable comeback in Game Four, it may have been Boston's last playoff series of 1990.

The Hartford Whalers were one of four teams left afloat amongst the flotsam of the World Hockey Association, a rival pro league that unsuccessfully challenged the NHL for seven financially turbulent seasons from 1972 to 1973 through 1978–79. The Whalers—who were known as the New England Whalers in their WHA days—were absorbed into the NHL in 1979 along with the Quebec Nordiques, Winnipeg Jets, and Edmonton Oilers. At the Bruins' insistence, the Whalers were rebranded as the Hartford Whalers when they joined the NHL. As an NHL entity, the Whalers largely ended up being New England's other hockey team. Nevertheless, geography naturally dictated that the two teams would develop some sort of rivalry. It was not until the 1989–90 season, however, that the teams would face one another in the Stanley Cup playoffs. The series turned out to be a doozy.

Hartford entered their Adams Division semifinal with Boston as decided underdogs. Despite being 40:1 preseason long shots to win the Stanley Cup, the Whalers were no slouches. During the regular-season they had fought to a decent 38–33–9 record for 85 points, not too far in arrears of the three juggernaut teams ahead of them in the divisional standings. They had a strong core of quality veteran players, such as Kevin Dineen, Ron Francis, Pat Verbeek and Dave Babych, who could cause trouble for any NHL opponent on any given night. From the perspective of fair-minded Bruin fans, the Whalers were a worthy adversary, not one to be taken lightly. In their eight regular-season meetings versus "the Whale," Boston had won four games, lost three times and tied one, outscoring their unfashionable neighbors only by a 27:22 ratio. Hartford inconveniently chose the first round of the Stanley Cup playoffs to give the Bruins even greater competition when it counted the most.

The series began in Boston Garden on Thursday, April 5. By the 6:19 mark of the second period, the visitors had jumped out to a significant 3–0 lead, a sizable advantage that the home team could not overcome. It came against the run of play and the norms seen during the regular season when Boston had posted the best defensive record in the NHL. Réjean (Reggie) Lemelin, the hero of the Bruins' 1988 playoff series versus Montreal, had an uncustomary poor night in the Boston goal. He allowed the initial Hartford marker on the first shot he faced, and allowed four goals on eight shots. Hartford only managed 17 shots in the entire game. Meanwhile, Boston fired 36 at Hartford netminder Peter Sidorkiewicz, who played a terrific game under constant pressure from the Bruins. With two Whalers in the penalty box, Boston made it a close contest with a last-minute goal by Dave Poulin to excite the home crowd, but Hartford hung on to take the opener, 4–3. "We got some breaks,"[1] commented Hartford's Ron Francis after the win. Kevin Paul Dupont was highly critical of the home team's outing to start the postseason. He caustically wrote in the next day's *Boston Globe*, "The Bruins opened the 1990 Stanley Cup playoffs last night with their worst skate forward and their goaltending suspect. Home wasn't homey, it was downright homely."[2]

Two nights later at the Garden, Boston was a much-improved club and evened the series at a game apiece, but it was not an easy task for the home team. The game was a tightly contested affair whose outcome was a 3–1 win in which every Boston goal was scored when the home side possessed a man advantage. Andy Moog was terrific. The winning Boston goalie stopped 25 of 26 Hartford shots aimed at his cage. Kevin Paul Dupont had a much more optimistic view of Game Two compared to his distinctly negative impressions of the Bruins' efforts in Game One. This time he penned in recipe form,

One part goalie. One part power play. One part penalty killing. And cook for 40 minutes with Ray Bourque.

Led by power-play goals from Bourque, Garry Galley and Bobby

Carpenter, along with some sparkling/sensational goaltending from Andy Moog, the Bruins moved one-sixteenth of the way toward their first Stanley Cup since 1972. If all of the postseason was a power play, the Bruins could feel fine about their pursuit of the other fifteen-sixteenths.[3]

Although they had dropped Game Two and the series was returning to Hartford deadlocked, the Whalers were a satisfied group knowing they were at least matching the Bruins' level of hockey and sometimes surpassing it.

The Whalers continued their surprising play in Game Three at the Hartford Civic Center on April 9, winning 5–3. Kevin Dineen salted the game away for the home side with an empty-net goal with just 18 seconds left on the clock. (Boston fans at the arena and on television witnessed the peculiar and slightly disconcerting sight of Bobby Orr, the greatest Bruin ever, watching the game from the Whalers' VIP box as a special guest of general manager Ed Johnston, Boston's former goalie from the 1960s and 1970s. Orr, now 42 years old, still maintained a close friendship with his ex-teammate and even went as far to join the Whalers' Board of Directors to provide occasional help whenever the 54-year-old Johnston asked for it.) Boston had played Game Three without perennial all-star defenseman Ray Bourque in their lineup; he was nursing an injured left hip. Bourque was a gametime scratch after enduring a painful morning practice. Now holding an unexpected two-games-to-one edge over the Bruins, the Whalers had an abundance of confidence heading into Game Four on Wednesday, April 11. Although he conceded that Boston had a stronger lineup on paper, Orr sensed the Bruins might be in serious trouble. "This Hartford team has come a long way," he told a hockey reporter from the *Pittsburgh Press*. "They're a better team now than they were at the beginning of the season. The Bruins are going to have to play well to beat them."[4] Kevin Paul Dupont concurred. He wrote, "The Bruins lost their best player in the morning, and then didn't give their best effort in the evening. Suddenly things are getting ugly."[5]

Orr's assessment seemed to be spot on when Game Four began. With Ray Bourque still unable to suit up for the Bruins, Hartford seized the initiative and had a 1–0 lead after just 78 seconds of play thanks to a weird, unassisted goal credited to Dean Evason. Andy Moog had played goal for Boston in Game Three not especially well, so coach Mike Milbury opted to give Game One starter Reggie Lemelin another try. Lemelin and Moog had shared the netminding duties in Boston fairly evenly all season, each producing his fair share of strong results. Such goaltending steadiness was conspicuously absent so far in the series. The first Hartford goal was a clear indication. Reggie Lemelin made a poor clearing pass of a loose puck. It went horizontally, rebounding off the boards to his left. Evason pounced on it and made a strong but wild pass toward the slot. It struck the foot of Boston defenseman Jim Wiemer and went through Lemelin's legs for an unexpected Hartford score. It was not a good omen for the Bruins or their suddenly shaky goalie. "The Bruins can ill afford that,"[6] said 71-year-old Fred Cusick in his television commentary for NESN.

Evason's fluky tally was the only scoring play of the first 20 minutes. Hartford struck early in the second period too, at the 2:04 mark. Brad Shaw, a rookie defenseman, scored on a long backhand to conclude a sequence of events in the Boston zone in which defenseman Bob Beers was twice flattened by hard Whaler checks. Again, the 35-year-old Lemelin did not look sharp. It was the first shot he had faced in the period. About two and a half minutes later, the Bruins responded positively to narrow their deficit to 2–1. Dave Christian finished off the visitors' scoring play on a three-on-one breakout into the Hartford zone. Craig Janney's feed to Christian was perfect. "Ah, that boy can pass the puck!"[7] gushed NESN analyst Derek Sanderson, who was noted for the same skill in his glory days playing for Boston in the most recent Stanley Cup years.

At 7:02, Hartford regained their two-goal edge as the result of sustained pressure paying off. Five tired Bruins were desperately seeking a line change, but the Whalers' persistence would not allow it. Kevin Dineen eventually fired a low drive past Lemelin from near the faceoff spot to the goaltender's right. "The Hartford attack was relentless,"[8] noted Fred Cusick. Derek Sanderson preferred to label it as sloppy hockey from the Bruins. It was a 3–1 game only for a short time. Eighty-seven seconds later the home team upped the score to 4–1 on a breakaway goal by the unheralded Yvon Corriveau. Lemelin moved out of his goal and committed himself too early. The speedy, 23-year-old journeyman deftly maneuvered around the Bruin goalie and slid the puck into the gaping net. It was Hartford's nineteenth shot of the game. Favored Boston falling behind three games to one to the underdogs in the series was now a very real possibility. "This is an uphill climb," bemoaned Derek Sanderson over the NESN airwaves. With the game less than half over he wrongly declared, "It's pretty much insurmountable at this point."[9]

Boston continued to fight back in a game where Kerry Fraser basically put away his whistle. There were several instances where players on both teams were improperly impeded—or dumped outright—that were ignored by the NHL's most noticeably coiffed referee. Each team would only enjoy one abbreviated, 24-second power play all game. Those calls came from Fraser in the first period. At 10:24 of the second stanza, the Bruins managed to get a goal back on a play in which Hartford goaltender Peter Sidorkiewicz was screened. A wrist shot by Glen Wesley from 10 feet inside the blue line got past the Whaler netminder. Sidorkiewicz's body language indicated he had no idea the puck had sailed past him and was spinning inside his net. The large contingent of traveling Bruins supporters cheered their men in black and gold, but Hartford still held a 4–2 lead in a game that was steadily becoming less and less defensive-oriented.

Sidorkiewicz twice made excellent saves to retain the home's team's two-goal lead. About six minutes after Wesley's tally, the Whalers once again assumed a three-goal edge. This time a bad giveaway by Jim Wiemer ended up directly on the stick of Hartford captain Ron Francis. Wasting no time, his wrist shot beat Lemelin to his right side. Having a 5–2 lead with just one period to play indicated strongly that it would be the Whalers' night yet again. Derek Sanderson proffered that the Whalers, as series underdogs, were playing as if they had nothing to lose—and achieving great results because of that casual, devil-may-care attitude. "The Whalers are playing fine defensive hockey,"[10] noted Sanderson moments after the third period began. He further stated that Hartford was catching the lion's share of the game's breaks.

Boston coach Mike Milbury opted to switch goaltenders for the final 20 minutes. Reggie Lemelin was benched. Andy Moog, the losing Boston goal in Game Three two nights before, entered the contest in relief. If the personnel move was designed to shake up the Bruins, the ploy worked quite well. Just 88 seconds after play resumed, Dave Poulin's redirection hit the goalpost, but he batted his own rebound past Sidorkiewicz for an unassisted goal. Quickly the score became a more manageable 5–3 for the visitors—and there were still eighteen and a half minutes left on the Civic Center's clock.

That amount of time proved to be more than sufficient for the more offensive-minded Bruins. The Whalers collectively began to become more tentative while Boston became the more assertive and aggressive team. At precisely the 7:00 mark, Boston's rookie defenseman Bob Beers scored his first NHL goal on a pretty play. Craig Janney crossed the Hartford blue line with teammate Cam Neely. Four Whalers focused their attention on the high-scoring Neely while totally ignoring Beers who entered the Hartford zone unimpeded at the far side of the ice. Janney fed Beers another one of his superb passes. Beers' high shot caught part of Sidorkiewicz, but the puck carried enough momentum to flutter into the net. The once insurmountable Hartford lead had dwindled to a surmountable 5–4.

The key point in the game occurred just 70 seconds later. Hartford botched a three-on-one situation in the Boston zone with a weak pass that was intercepted. The Bruins promptly launched a counterattack. It looked like it was going to amount to naught, but the suddenly omnipresent Bob Beers kept the play alive by stopping a Hartford clearing pass just inside the Whalers' blue line. Under pressure, Beers knocked the puck forward to teammate Randy Burridge. His quick pass to Dave Poulin was followed by a quicker cross-ice pass to Dave Christian who was standing alone in the faceoff circle to the right of Peter Sidorkiewicz. Christian one-timed a slap shot past the Hartford goalie who had no chance to make the save. It was a thoroughly picturesque tying goal. At the 8:10 mark of the third period, the Hartford lead was gone. The score stood at 5–5 as the Bruin fans inside the Hartford Civic Center became considerably louder.

The fourth and fifth Boston goals were appealing to the eyes for their highlight-reel quality. Their sixth, however, was a rather ugly tally—but it proved to be the most important score of the night, perhaps of the club's entire 1989–90 season. Dave Poulin, who had been acquired by Boston in a midseason trade with Philadelphia for gritty Ken Linseman, got his second goal of the night on a strange play. In the neutral zone, Cam Neely spotted an onrushing Randy Burridge and fed him an accurate pass just before he and Poulin entered the Hartford zone. Poulin skated toward the Hartford net while Burridge moved with the puck toward the slot. His backhand shot was partially deflected and moved slowly along the ice toward Whaler goalie Peter Sidorkiewicz. It should have been a very easy puck for the goaltender to handle, but suddenly Poulin became a factor. While Poulin was being hampered by Hartford defender Ulf Samuelsson, the puck struck his skate and changed direction ever so slightly. Sidorkiewicz, appeared to lose sight of it as Poulin, Samuelsson and the puck approached the net simultaneously. Although he had been knocked to his knees by the hulking Swedish defenseman, Poulin rapped the puck past Sidorkiewicz. "I have no idea how it went in,"[11] Poulin would later confess. Kerry Fraser emphatically signaled the go-ahead goal for Boston with 1:44 left on the scoreboard clock. Against long odds, Boston was in the lead for the first time all night.

The Whalers, despite pulling Sidorkiewicz for a sixth attacker in the final minute of play, failed to mount a serious scoring threat. Cam Neely missed putting the game away for the visitors when he shot wide of the empty net with just 18 seconds to play while being manhandled. (Again, Kerry Fraser took no heed of the infraction and let play continue.) Nevertheless, Boston held on for a 6–5 victory. Coach Mike

Milbury was visibly overjoyed by the turn of events. Smiling broadly, he spent considerable time on the ice gleefully pounding the backs and hugging anyone he could find clad in a Bruin uniform. Andy Moog, who made just seven saves—and was luckily helped by the goalpost on one occasion—got credit for the win. The Bruins had somehow levelled the series at 2–2 and were heading back to Boston Garden for Game Five with momentum clearly as an ally.

Leading off the NESN postgame show, studio host Tom Larson claimed, "This is one of those Bruin hockey games that people will be talking about for years to come."[12] Dave Poulin, certainly one of the Bruin heroes, surprisingly said the mood in the Bruins' dressing room was not at all gloomy after the second period. "We weren't as down as you might think," he told Kevin Paul Dupont of the *Boston Globe*. "We had this feeling, what we did in the third period—win or lose—would go a long way toward dictating what would happen in the series."[13]

The unexpected collapse left the Whalers grasping for explanations. Captain Ron Francis offered this one: "[The Bruins] came out firing [in the third period] and got some bounces and some breaks. We kind of dug ourselves a hole out there. I don't know. It's hard to explain things like that."[14] Hartford coach Rick Ley identified "mental mistakes" as the cause for his team's defeat. "[The loss] wasn't from lack of effort, it was from lack of thought. Our old team reared its ugly head. We had players working as individuals instead of as a team."[15]

Hartford goaltender Peter Sidorkiewicz came under fire for allowing the odd winning goal to elude him. Indeed, he certainly looked bad on the play. "It's a tough way to lose it," he admitted to reporters. "Basically, we gave them the game and that's what really hurts."[16] Sidorkiewicz recalled the sixth Boston goal this way: "Burridge had the puck. I saw Poulin coming to the net with one of our defensemen [Ulf Samuelsson]. All of a sudden, Burridge just threw it in their feet. The two of them kept coming and I just couldn't get a grasp of the puck."[17]

Andy Moog was Boston's goalie for the remainder of the series as it returned to Boston for Game Five. April 13 was not an unlucky Friday for the Bruins. Now the more confident of the two teams, they won the pivotal fifth contest, 3–2. (Cam Neely scored twice, once on the power play and the game-winner in the third period while Boston was shorthanded.) Hartford scraped out an overtime win in Game Six by the identical score, but the Bruins won Game Seven at Boston Garden, 3–1. That victory earned them another meeting in their never-ending playoff rivalry versus Montreal. As in 1988, Boston prevailed in five games. Next up, in the conference finals, were the Washington Capitals who barely put up a scuffle in being swept by Mike Milbury's crew in four straight games. In the Stanley Cup finals, the Bruins faced the same Edmonton Oilers club that had gotten the better of them in the championship round two seasons before. Wayne Gretzky was no longer with the team in 1990, but Edmonton was still an extremely solid and talent-laden squad. To some observers, Boston seemed to have exhausted themselves on their tough journey to the deciding round of the postseason. The Bruins only won one contest and scored just eight goals in those five games. As is often the case in Boston history, the 1989–90 team had proven they were the second-best outfit in the NHL.

None of that likely occurs if the Whalers do not fall apart on April 11 at the Hartford Civic Center. One day after it occurred, Kevin Paul Dupont of the *Boston Globe* was quick to perceive Game Four versus Hartford as an enormous one in the club's history. He wrote, "Without a doubt it was the Bruins' biggest postseason victory since they dispatched the Canadiens in the 1988 playoffs. For thrills, it may be unparalleled."[18]

Scoring Summary

First Period
- 1:18 HAR Dean Evason (unassisted)

Second Period
- 2:04 HAR Brad Shaw (unassisted)
- 4:35 BOS Dave Christian (assists: Craig Janney, John Carter)
- 7:02 HAR Kevin Dineen (assists: Dave Babych, Mikael Andersson)
- 8:29 HAR Yvon Corriveau (assists: Jody Hull, Dave Babych)
- 10:24 BOS Glen Wesley (assists: Bob Carpenter, Peter Douris)
- 16:15 HAR Ron Francis (unassisted)

Third Period
- 1:28 BOS Dave Poulin (unassisted)
- 7:00 BOS Bob Beers (assists: Craig Janney, Cam Neely)
- 8:10 BOS Dave Christian (assists: Dave Poulin, Randy Burridge)
- 18:16 BOS Dave Poulin (assists: Randy Burridge, Cam Neely)

24

April 10, 2010

Bruins Score Three Shorthanded Goals on One Penalty

People watch sports to be surprised. Of course, that is not the only reason they do so, but unexpected delights are certainly an allurement. Very occasionally, if you are lucky, when you tune into a game on television or buy a ticket to a sports event, you will see something occur that you have never seen before. That was certainly the case for the Boston Bruins and their fans on the afternoon of April 10, 2010. That Saturday, with a playoff berth up for grabs, their team hosted the Carolina Hurricanes at TD Garden. In the space of 64 seconds at the beginning of the second period, Boston scored three shorthanded goals while killing the same minor penalty! "That has got to be a club record!"[1] television announcer Jack Edwards promptly assumed after the red light signaled Steve Begin's tally to conclude the brief scoring surge. It absolutely was; in fact, at the time of the odd occurrence no other NHL team had ever achieved the feat in the 93-year history of the league.

Power-play and shorthanded goals have been part of hockey ever since the penalty system was instituted in the game's formative years. Minor penalties were once three-minutes in duration—and the entire penalty had to be served regardless of whether the team with the man advantage scored. (The second part of that rule was not changed until the late 1950s.) Fans will never know for certain how many NHL goals have truly been scored by teams playing shorthanded because the league did not start keeping specific track of such goals until the 1933–34 season. During the first 17 years of NHL play, apparently no one considered such esoterica important enough to record as an official statistic. Early NHL game reports leave a lot of details to be desired in the eyes of hockey historians. Well into the 1930s, precise data showing exactly when penalties were assessed in NHL games were not meticulously

24. April 10, 2010

recorded. Thus, it is unlikely that this noticeable gap in the sport's records can ever accurately be filled.

The most prolific team in NHL history when it came to scoring goals while shorthanded was the 1983–84 Edmonton Oilers who attained the feat a spectacular 36 times in an 80-game schedule. (The wave was led by Wayne Gretzky, who has a career high 12 shorthanded tallies that season—a record at the time that stood until 1988–89 when Mario Lemieux of the Pittsburgh penguins would raise the mark by one.) The team record was, at one time, held by the Boston Bruins, who set it during the 1970–71 season in the heyday of Bobby Orr and Phil Esposito. Those Bruins managed to score 26 times while shorthanded that year in their 78 games—nearly doubling the old record of 14. It was a figure that some fans wrongly thought might never be approached.

Three Bruins were largely responsible for the team setting the impressive mark. Don Marcotte and Ed Westfall each scored seven shorthanded goals for Boston. Derek Sanderson was close behind; he got six. All three of those Bruins were defensive specialists who reveled in not only shutting down opponents on the power play but making them concede goals frequently, too. Bobby Orr (three), Dallas Smith (two) and Phil Esposito (one) accounted for the other six goals the Bruins notched that season when their adversaries had superior numbers on the ice. The Bruins were putting up such astronomical offensive records in 1970–71 that few people paid much attention to all their goals that had been subtly marked with an "SH" notation. In all the years since 1971, the Bruins have not scored more than 19 shorthanded goals in a season.

Prior to their clash with the Carolina Hurricanes on April 10, 2010, the Bruins had played 80 games in 2009–10 and had scored just three shorthanded goals. They came from the sticks of Patrice Bergeron, Marco Sturm, and Matt Hunwick who got one each. That statistic made what happened that crazy Saturday afternoon look even more freakish in retrospect.

The Bruins had been a surprising disappointment as the NHL's 2009–10 regular-season wound down. Pegged in October by many observers to be Stanley Cup contenders, the Bruins, at this very late juncture of the campaign, had not even secured a spot in the playoffs. At one dismal point in the campaign, they had fallen to as low as twelfth place in the NHL's Eastern Conference. Overall, Boston ranked a miserable 30th out of 31 NHL teams in goals scored, but they were second in the league in fewest goals allowed—a necessary trait that kept them competitive and in the playoff chase.

Injuries had been a major issue for Boston all season. Milan Lucic, Marc Savard, "and seemingly every defenseman with a spoked B on his chest," according to *Boston Globe* scribe Fluto Shinzawa, "prevented the Bruins from finding any roster regularity."[2] Worse still, some of the Bruins' most lackluster efforts of 2009–10 came on home ice, much to the displeasure of the vocal ticket-buyers who were highly critical of what they were witnessing. Nevertheless, that did not stop a sellout crowd of 17,565 from turning out for the club's last home game on the schedule, on April 10. It was an afternoon tilt versus the Carolina Hurricanes, who were going to miss the playoffs regardless of the outcome of the game at TD Garden. Boston would conclude its regular-season schedule with a game versus the Capitals in Washington the following afternoon.

Boston and Carolina skated through a scoreless first period with goaltenders Cam Ward of the Hurricanes and Tuukka Rask of the Bruins thwarting all shooters. Boston had outshot Carolina by an 18:14 ratio with nothing concrete to show for their efforts. As the TD Garden clock approached zeroes, Matt Hunwick of the Bruins was penalized for a hooking infraction with just 18 seconds left in the opening period. Hunwick felt guilty about putting his team in a shorthanded position. After the game he was almost apologetic about it. "I thought we had outplayed [Carolina] in the first period," he declared. "We had a lot of momentum. To give them an opportunity to go out in the second period for a power play with fresh ice and a chance to take the lead obviously makes you a little nervous."[3] Nevertheless, Boston successfully killed off the dozen-and-a-half seconds left in the opening 20 minutes. Still, the Bruins knew the Hurricanes would have 1:42 remaining on their power play on resurfaced ice when the second stanza began. When the teams returned from the first intermission, Hunwick headed to the home team's penalty box to serve the rest of his minor—and witness some unexpected NHL history unfold indirectly due to his presence there.

Carolina began the period by applying limited pressure on the Bruins, but lost control of the puck about 20 seconds after play resumed. Boston's towering defenseman Zdeno Chara got control of the puck and cleared it into the visitors' end of the ice. Hot in pursuit was Daniel Paille, a 26-year-old Bruin mired in a dreadful scoring slump. Paille whizzed past Carolina's Bryan Rodney and chased down the puck in the right corner. "Paille fished the puck out," wrote Shinzawa, "slashed across the crease and beat Cam Ward 32 seconds into the period to give the Bruins a 1–0 lead."[4] Ward looked bad on the play as the puck slid under his pads and into the goal. Paille seemed a bit stunned, too, that his shot had eluded the Carolina netminder, but the defensive-minded left-winger was happy to have notched his first goal in 22 games. His last one came versus Buffalo, his former team, on February 9. (Paille scored twice in that contest.) His shorthanded goal versus Carolina was his tenth tally of the 2009–10 season.

Following Paille's marker, the Bruins won the subsequent faceoff at center ice and, still shorthanded, fired the puck behind the Carolina net without fear of being called for an icing violation. Ward left his cage to take control of the puck. He fired it along the left-side boards toward a teammate, Brett Carson, a rookie defenseman. Carson may have been unnerved by the sight of an oncoming Bruin, David Krejci, who was fast moving in on him. According to Shinzawa, Carson "alligator-armed the puck and coughed it up."[5] Krejci got control of the disc, settled it, and fired a perfect pass to Blake Wheeler who was positioned in the slot with no Hurricane within checking distance of him. Wheeler fired a low one-timer past Ward to make it 2–0 for the home team at 1:21, just 49 seconds after Paille's marker. Like Paille, Wheeler had also not scored for a while. It was his first goal in 12 games but his 18th for the season. The Bruins had achieved a noteworthy rarity: two shorthand goals while killing the same penalty. They were not quite done, though. Hunwick remained seated in the Boston penalty box, but with his team suddenly two goals to the good, he was considerably happier about the situation than when he was penalized by referee Chris Lee at 19:42 of the first period.

Steve Begin won the next faceoff for Boston. He advanced forward as the puck was passed backward to Dennis Wideman in the Bruins' defensive zone. Wideman alertly spotted Begin in the open and flipped him an accurate pass from a considerable distance. With Daniel Paille also attacking, Boston had a two-on-one situation on Ward as the home crowd began to roar in anticipation. Begin moved in on the shell-shocked Cam Ward. His wrist shot was only partially stopped by the goalie's pads. It possessed enough power to fly between Ward's legs and into the top half of the Carolina net. The time of the goal, Begin's fifth of 2009–10, was 1:36. It had come just 15 seconds after Wheeler's tally. Boston, unbelievably, now led the Hurricanes 3–0. The Bruins' three shorthanded goals had come within a span of 64 seconds—an NHL record. Hunwick still had six seconds to serve in his hooking penalty. "There's been the burst of a dam here!"[6] Jack Edwards happily declared on his NESN broadcast. Carolina coach Paul Maurice immediately took his timeout to settle his rattled troops.

"Nobody's ever seen three [shorthanded] goals that quick," marveled Blake Wheeler after the game. "To have them *bam, bam, bam* on the penalty kill is something everyone knew was special. It's not surprising that it's an NHL record."[7] Hunwick concurred. "I've never seen three shorthanded goals on the same penalty," he said. "That doesn't happen at any level [of hockey], never mind the NHL."[8] Steve Begin, Boston's fourth-string center, was thrilled that he had played a role in creating hockey history. "We made the books!" he amusingly shouted when he learned his team had set an NHL record. "We made the books in a good way!"[9]

As it turned out, Boston required every one of those three goals to win the game. By the time the second period had ended, Carolina had narrowed the Bruins' lead to an uncomfortable 3–2. The comeback began at 14:30. Eric Cole came around the Bruins' net with the puck, and facing little defensive resistance, beat Tuukka Rask with a backhand shot from the slot to give the visitors their first goal of the game. About two and a half minutes later, Patrick Dwyer also beat Rask from the slot—this one was a booming forehand—and the score was suddenly just 3–2 in Boston's favor.

Boston coach Claude Julien was irked by Carolina's quick pair of goals late in the second period that whittled the Boston lead down to a mere one. "We were pretty mad coming in [the dressing room] after the second period. So there was a sense of urgency. As you probably witnessed, we seem to be more comfortable playing in tight games than games [where we have] a little bit of breathing room."[10]

There were no goals in the first 19 minutes of the third period, although late pressure from Carolina had the Bruins reeling at times. The closest the Hurricanes came to adding a third goal was a self-inflicted wound the Bruins almost applied to themselves. Early in the third period, referee Chris Lee called a delayed penalty on Carolina's Jerome Samson for high-sticking. Tuukka Rask alertly realized the situation and vacated the Boston goal for a sixth attacker. This development escaped the attention of Blake Wheeler who sent an errant backwards pass in the general direction of teammate Michael Ryder. Ryder was not expecting it and the puck seemed to be heading directly to the center of the vacant Boston net. Fortunately for the home team, Patrice Bergeron, the man who had stepped onto the ice after Rask had raced to the Boston bench, had enough speed to chase down the puck and just barely stop it from entering the Boston net. (A terrific and dramatic photo in the *Boston Globe* the next day showed Bergeron stopping the puck with his stick on the goal line.) Bergeron later said he was motivated by not wanting to be shown retrieving the puck from his own net on a sports blooper reel. "There are those Not Top Ten plays on ESPN," he said with relief. "I didn't want to be on that."[11]

Wheeler, who was very nearly the goat on the peculiar play, later explained to the media what had occurred. "I didn't even know there was a delayed [penalty] call," he admitted. "I tried to pass [the puck] to

24. April 10, 2010

Ryder—and, all of a sudden, I see it going into an empty net. I started shaking my head. I was like, 'Here we go. This is how the season has gone.'"[12]

Boston did not score with Jerome Samson residing in the penalty box. In fact, they did not score on any of their five power plays versus Carolina in the game. "The Bruins are downright painful, mind-numbing to watch, when working with the man advantage,"[13] wrote Kevin Paul Dupont in his account of the game for the *Boston Globe*. The scribe's comment was a harsh one, but it was justified. Indeed, Boston's power play had been thoroughly dreadful for about a month, having accounted for a score just once in 45 opportunities over a stretch of its prior 15 games. Apparently, the Bruins were only lethal when playing a man short.

The outcome of the game was only settled when Milan Lucic scored an empty-net goal for Boston with precisely one minute showing on the TD Garden clock. After an arduous season, a playoff berth for the Bruins was assured. Dupont eloquently summarized, "More than six months into a motley and muddled season, the Bruins ... tripped, fell, landed face-first in a puddle of mud, and got up with the redolent scent of the most unlikely of hattricks. Now, we wonder, what else might they salvage?"[14]

The three shorthanded goals were cause for levity among Boston's hockey writers. Perhaps the best quip also came from the witty Dupont. He joked in Sunday's *Boston Globe*, "The Bruins are in the playoffs, but we don't know whom they will oppose in the first round. But amid all the uncertainty and excitement, we do hold this one truth to be self-evident: The Bruins absolutely will open the 2010 Stanley Cup playoffs with Matt Hunwick parked in the penalty box."[15]

Scoring Summary

First Period
- No scoring

Second Period
- 0:32 BOS Daniel Paille (assists: Zdeno Chara, Johnny Boychuk) SH
- 1:21 BOS Blake Wheeler (assist: David Krejci) SH
- 1:36 BOS Steve Begin (assists: Dennis Wideman, Daniel Paille) SH
- 14:30 CAR Eric Cole (assists: Patrick Dwyer, Claude Larose)
- 170:06 CAR Patrick Dwyer (assists: Jerome Samson, Bryan Rodney)

Third Period
- 19:00 BOS Milan Lucic (unassisted) EN

25

May 13, 2013

*Bruins Erase a 4–1 Deficit
to Oust Maple Leafs*

"It was only a first-round series against a team that hasn't won a playoff series in nine years," wrote Dan Shaughnessy in the May 14, 2013, edition of the *Boston Globe*. "It was not Bobby Orr scoring to win a Stanley Cup ... or [the 2004 Red Sox] coming back from a 3–0 deficit against the Yankees. But it was one of the great moments in Boston sports history."[1] Any Bruins fan who watched the previous night's Boston-Toronto Game Seven on television or who resolutely stayed the discouraging course at TD for the full 60 minutes of regulation play would undoubtedly agree with that bold assessment. It may have been the most spectacular victory in nearly a century of Boston Bruins hockey.

The final 11 minutes of the third period—particularly the final 90 seconds—will long live in Bruins lore. "We showed some character coming back,"[2] Patrice Bergeron said afterward. The home team certainly did. Their mettle was good enough to nullify a daunting 4–1 lead held by the visiting Toronto Maple Leafs with slightly more than half the third period remaining to play. Few Bruin fans saw it coming. Most of them had sadly but sensibly resigned themselves to a bitter defeat. For the most part it looked like it was going to be another disappointing and exasperating end to a promising Boston season. "To be honest, I kind of thought we were done,"[3] Boston defenseman Dougie Hamilton candidly admitted afterward. Any Bruin fan who was completely honest with himself had to feel that way too. Instead, the Bruins pulled off something that no other NHL team had ever managed to do—erase a three goal-deficit in the final period of a seventh game in Stanley Cup play. It was a remarkable feat as the league had first instituted best-of-seven playoff series back in 1939.

Prior to their memorable 2013 playoff series, the Maple Leafs and

25. May 13, 2013

Bruins had been longtime postseason rivals dating back to 1933. That year, the two teams took their best-of-five get-together to extremes. The climactic fifth game, contested at Maple Leaf Gardens, went into a sixth overtime period deadlocked at 0–0 before the winning goal came from the stick of Toronto's Ken Doraty who scored on a breakaway in the wee hours of the morning. The clubs met four more times in the postseason in the 1930s with Toronto taking the first three and Boston winning in 1939 in the finals to give the Bruins their first Stanley Cup championship. After Boston beat Toronto in four straight quarterfinal games to start the 1974 playoffs, the two teams had to wait 39 years before the hockey gods paired them up in another postseason series. The Leafs had won eight out of the 13 series going into the 2013 Stanley Cup playoffs, but Boston had won the three most recent clashes. Toronto had last ousted the Bruins from Cup play in a tight, seven-game tilt in 1959.

Boston entered the series as minor favorites. They had enjoyed a productive, albeit short, regular season in 2012–13 with a 28–14–6 record for 62 points, a total good enough for the fifth seed in the NHL's Eastern Conference. The Leafs finished five points behind Boston. The puny number of games that season was the result of a nasty labor dispute. A bitter lockout eliminated a huge chunk of games from the NHL slate. Each team's workload was reduced to just 48 games from the typical 82 to decide the usual number of playoff positions. (The last time such a compact schedule had been played was way back in 1941–42 when the NHL was a seven-team league.) There were no interconference games scheduled at all until the Stanley Cup finals. Competitive play did not begin until January 19, resulting in the cancellation of both the annual NHL All-Star Game and the league's New Year's Day outdoor Winter Classic. Hockey's playoffs would start on the first day of May and could (and would) extend into late June and the accompanying summertime.

As is normally the case in a playoff series between the fourth and fifth seeds, the Bruins–Maple Leafs clash was generally perceived by hockey prognosticators as a tossup. No outcome would be too surprising, it was thought. However, the result of Game Seven in Boston turned out to be utterly startling for its unprecedented and wildly dramatic conclusion.

For finishing ahead of the Leafs in regular-season play, Boston was rewarded with home-ice advantage in the best-of-seven affair. The Boston-Toronto series opened with two games at TD Garden. They resulted in a split. Boston took the opener, 4–1, but the Maple Leafs responded with a solid 4–2 victory three days later to send the series to Toronto on level terms. Boston liked the change of venue better than

Toronto, apparently. The Bruins took both of the Maple Leafs' home contests, 5–2 and 4–3, to assume a 3–1 series lead. (Game Four required overtime, with David Krejci providing the winning goal for Boston at 13:06 of the extra frame. Toronto had led the Bruins 2–0 going into the second period.)

If the Maple Leafs were downcast about their overall chances, they did not show it. Two well-played defensive efforts gave the Canadian-based team a pair of 2–1 triumphs in the fifth and sixth games of the series. The Bruins offense had seemingly petered out. Boston never held a lead in either contest. Everything was now up for grabs in Game Seven on Monday, May 13—the very next night—in front of cynical and worried Bruin fans at TD Garden.

The Bruins began Game Seven well. Matt Bartkowski took advantage of a sloppy giveaway in the Toronto zone to score an unassisted goal on a rising wrist shot. It beat Toronto goalie James Reimer about five and a half minutes into the first period to get the home crowd excited. Their optimism did not last very long. Toronto evened the score about four minutes later on a power play. With Zdeno Chara serving a high-sticking penalty, Cody Franson got the Leaf goal, backhanding a loose puck that was enticingly sitting in the goal crease behind Boston goaltender Tuukka Rask. The game remained tied through the rest of the first period, but Franson put Toronto ahead 2–1 with the only goal of the second frame on a delayed-penalty situation. His screen shot found the net just underneath the crossbar. The home crowd began to grumble as they sensed another loss was forthcoming for their Bruins.

Two minutes into the third period, former Bruin Phil Kessel, who scored 66 goals in three seasons for Boston, was standing unguarded at the front of the Boston net. He rammed home a puck that had eluded Rask and gently struck the goal post. Toronto led 3–1. In the Maple Leafs' radio booth, announcer Joe Bowen yelled, "Thank you, Kessel!"[4] It was a mocking reference to the very same chant with which Bruin fans taunted their ex-star player at every opportunity. (Injured and often accused of indifferent play, Kessel had been traded to Toronto in September 2009 for three draft choices. Two of them ended up being high-quality players: Tyler Seguin and Dougie Hamilton. Thus, the thank-yous.) The visitors upped their advantage to 4–1 at the 5:29 mark. The Leafs carried a two-on-one rush into the Boston zone. Rask made the initial stop on Kessel's wrist shot but the rebound went directly to Nazem Kadri. He had most of an open Boston net to shoot at from short range. He did not miss. In the NESN TV booth, Boston announcer Jack Edwards sullenly stated the hard facts to his viewers: "The Toronto Maple Leafs," he said, "unless they suffer a colossal collapse, are going to eliminate the Boston Bruins. Fourteen minutes is a lot of hockey. Boston is going to have to score as many goals in that stretch of time as they have in the last three games."[5] Edwards' off-the-cuff remark proved to be a remarkably prescient one.

It seemed that the Bruins would be the authors of their own demise. According to the recap of the game published on NHL.com,

> [The home team] began well, but soon found themselves short on defensemen, discipline and inspiration. Upset at the officiating as the game wore on, the Boston players seemed preoccupied with a jab here, a punch there. It was as if they were more interested in getting even on the ice than the scoreboard. Boston began to look tired and dispirited. The opportunistic Leafs, in contrast, grew in stature and confidence.[6]

As the seconds resolutely ticked off the TD Garden clock, the Bruins were a discouraged-looking bunch slouching on the home team's bench. "They were going down hard. They were going to be punching bags,"[7] according to Dan Shaughnessy. Milan Lucic admitted he was wondering if what was shaping up to be a Bruins loss would spell the end of the team as he knew it. He commented, "You start thinking to yourself, 'Is this the end of this group here?' Because it probably would have been if we hadn't won this game."[8] Some frustrated Boston supporters were openly jeering the Bruins and what appeared to be their team's startling inability in recent years to finish off opponents in the Stanley Cup playoffs. "It was tough being on the bench, getting booed," declared Brad Marchand. "But after [David Krejci's line] got that first one for us and we started to climb back, you could see the emotion on the bench. Guys started to believe. That's what we needed."[9]

The goal Marchand referred to came at 9:18 of the third period. It was the catalyst that started Boston's improbable rally. Milan Lucic skated a lap around the Toronto net with the puck and fed a perfect pass to Nathan Horton who was waiting in the faceoff circle to the right of James Reimer for such an opening. His shot beat Reimer to narrow the visitors' advantage to 4–2. With more than ten and a half minutes left on the TD Garden clock, the Bruins now had renewed life and hope. Nevertheless, the goal celebration was somewhat muted as it seemed to most of the patrons in the seats and the Boston players that a three-goal comeback was an unlikely scenario.

For more than nine minutes, the Bruins failed to chip away further at Toronto's two-goal edge. They had a couple of good scoring opportunities, but the best chance to score was a wasted one for Toronto. With about three and a half minutes left on the clock, Matt Frattin had a breakaway on Tuukka Rask, but he lofted a high backhand wide of the goal. The Maple Leafs were still leading, 4–2, but a fifth goal would have certainly secured a Game Seven victory for the visitors.

Boston coach Claude Julien, whose job may have been in jeopardy, rolled the proverbial dice and lifted goalie Rask for a sixth Bruin attacker. At 18:38, the desperate move paid dividends. Zdeno Chara ripped a long shot from the blue line. Reimer made the initial save with his right pad, but Boston forward Milan Lucic, positioned in the slot, pounced on the rebound and fired it into the gaping Toronto net. (In trying to corral the rebound, Reimer inadvertently pushed the puck directly onto Lucic's stick.) Suddenly, the Toronto lead, now whittled down to just one goal at 4–3, looked shaky—as did the Leafs themselves. "This is a young, inexperienced playoff team," Boston analyst Andy Brickley said of the Maple Leafs on the NESN telecast. "There is a seed of doubt—perhaps something larger—right now. A-minute-22 is a long time."[10] The TD Garden crowd was now in a frenzied uproar sensing that a memorable and miraculous comeback victory was within reach. Julien called his timeout to formulate a plan for a game-leveling goal to salvage his club's season. It worked almost immediately.

With Rask removed again from the Boston cage, Boston's tying score came. The Bruins again gained control of the puck into the Toronto zone as the Leafs looked disorganized and nervous. As part of Julien's strategy, this time Zdeno Chara planted his huge, 6'9" body in front of Reimer to cause extra havoc. Taking advantage of the traffic in front of the screened Leaf goalie, assistant captain Patrice Bergeron launched a low wrist shot, perhaps from 40 feet out, that somehow found its way past both Chara and Reimer and into the Toronto net. The arena exploded with a cacophony of noise when the red light flashed to signal a fourth Boston tally. The time of the marker was 19:09. Game Seven was now tied, at four goals apiece, but the momentum was clearly on the side of the home team. Incredibly, the Bruins almost won the game in the dying seconds of regulation time. With about 15 ticks left on the clock, Boston's Rich Peverley, standing just a few feet from the Toronto net, had an enticing rebound roll off his stick, and he failed to launch a shot toward the goal being guarded by the faltering Reimer. Regulation time of Game Seven ended with the Bruins and Maple Leafs tied, 4–4, and TD Garden thoroughly abuzz.

"The capacity crowd, which had been disgruntled most of the night, partied as it waited for an overtime period that never seemed in the cards,"[11] wrote an unnamed correspondent for NHL.com. It probably was not necessary, but between the third and fourth periods the person in charge of arena operations at TD Garden played a selection of upbeat, optimistic songs over the public-address system, such as "Livin' on a Prayer," "Don't Stop Believin'" and the always popular local favorite "I'm Shipping Up to Boston" to keep the crowd excited and hopeful.

"Belief is a funny thing," wrote Fluto Shinzawa in his report for the next day's *Boston Globe*. "It can transform a dead-leg team into one than cannot be stopped. The Leafs, winners of Game Five and Six, were in command. But in the span of 9:51 in the third period, the formerly stone-handed Bruins poured three pucks behind James Reimer to send the game into overtime."[12]

For the numerous ticketholders who had given up on the home team's chances and left the premises early, they learned there was no reprieve from their hasty decisions, no chance to return to their seats. Reentries were not permitted at TD Garden once a patron walked out the door onto Causeway Street. Many fans who became aware of the sudden, exciting change in the game's score and momentum tried in vain to return to watch the overtime action but were sternly turned away by the arena's unsympathetic ushers.

The Bruins accurately sensed the Maple Leafs were a psychologically wounded bunch. For all intents and purposes, the two late Boston goals had already done them in. The Bruins wisely proceeded to take the initiative in the overtime period. Sustained pressure produced the winning goal for the home team. Again, it was Patrice Bergeron who did the damage. The decider came at 6:05, after a scramble around the Toronto net. Bergeron, thanks to teammate Tyler Seguin's tenacious work in front of the Leafs goalie, found the loose disc on his stick to the right of a sprawled and helpless Reimer. Bergeron made the glorious opportunity count and calmly drove home the winning tally from short range.

Bedlam engulfed TD Garden. In the NESN booth, play-by-play man Jack Edwards, who never let objectivity get in the way of his calling a hockey game featuring his beloved Bruins, could not contain himself. He excitedly declared, "Bergeron scores! Patrice Bergeron! With the point of the dagger at their throats, they rip it out of Toronto's hands and kill the beast! The Boston Bruins have won it after being three down in the third!"[13]

Amid the celebrations and excitement on most of the ice at TD Garden, Toronto goalie James Reimer was a pitiable figure. He was lying face down on the ice for several moments, obviously distraught about the catastrophe that befell him personally and his Maple Leafs collectively. A poignant photograph of the prostrate, defeated goaltender appeared on the front page of the next morning's *Toronto Sun* along with the unflattering caption, "The Choke's on Us."

The traditional post-series handshake between the two clubs—a laudable custom in pro sports that seems to be unique to hockey—was noticeably slower paced and more personal than the usual series-ending ritual. There were many sincere congratulations offered from the Maple Leafs to the victors, and equally heartfelt condolences from the Bruins to the vanquished Torontonians. Both teams knew they had severely tested each other over seven tough games and the series' outcome could have easily been reversed. "The hands [the Bruins] shook resembled their own from 2007 to 2008 when they took the heavyweight Canadiens to Game Seven in the opening round,"[14] noted the scholarly Dan Shaughnessy.

Frustration was the dominant emotion in the visitors' dressing room. "We played extremely hard for six games. That 55 minutes (in Game 7) we threw everything we had at them. It's just an extremely disappointing loss,"[15] said a muted Dion Phaneuf.

Boston's hockey writers struggled to find superlatives for their reports. Fluto Shinzawa succinctly summarized in his *Globe* commentary, "This was one for the ages."[16] Shaughnessy opted for the slightly hackneyed, "In the end it was [the Bruins'] miracle on ice."[17]

Several minutes later, when Jack Edwards regained something akin to control of himself, he thoughtfully commented about the home team's effort. "It may not have been their finest hour," he concluded, "but for 16 minutes and 47 seconds four unanswered goals will live in Boston Bruins history forever. I doubt we'll ever see the likes of this again."[18]

Statisticians searched to find a game remotely comparable in Bruins history. Twenty-three years earlier something similar had happened. On April 11, 1990, in the opening round of the Stanley Cup playoffs, Boston had rallied from a three-goal disadvantage versus the Whalers in Hartford. [Authors' note: Chapter 23 discusses the game fully.] The visiting Bruins trailed 5–2 entering the third period and remarkably scored four unanswered goals for an improbable 6–5 victory in regulation time. Dave Poulin had banged home the game-winning goal with 1:44 left on the clock. At the time, the Bruins were trailing the series two games to one, so the come-from-behind win was a huge one. In the next day's *Boston Globe*, Kevin Paul Dupont described the dramatic triumph as "one of the most dramatic playoff wins in club history."[19] Impressive as that game was, May 13, 2013, had topped it. On January 19, 2020, it was declared "Game of the Decade" by NHL.com.

With the Bruins next scheduled to face the New York Rangers in an Eastern Conference semifinal series, Dan Shaughnessy also added the following afterthought to conclude his report. "[The Bruins]," he wrote, "may go on to win the Cup or they may fall aside. But we will never forget the comeback against the Leafs."[20] Boston ousted the Rangers in five games. The Bruins bettered that in the Eastern Conference final, drubbing the Pittsburgh Penguins in four straight contests. However, Boston fell to Chicago in six hard-fought games in the Stanley Cup finals.

A joyful Milan Lucic tried to explain his club's late-game heroics versus Toronto to the media. He came up with a gem of a quote that sounded like something Yogi Berra could have uttered. "Anything can happen," he noted. "And that's exactly what happened."[21]

Scoring Summary

First Period
- 5:39 BOS Matt Bartkowski (unassisted)
- 9:35 TOR Cody Franson (assists: James Van Riemsdyk, Dion Phaneuf) PP

Second Period
- 5:48 TOR Cody Franson (assists: Clarke MacArthur, Mikhail Grabovsky)

Third Period
- 2:09 TOR Phil Kessel (assists: Nazem Kadri, James van Riemsdyk)
- 5:29 TOR Nazem Kadri (assists: Phil Kessler, Jake Gardiner)
- 9:18 BOS Nathan Horton (assists: Milan Lucic, David Krejci)
- 18:38 BOS Milan Lucic (assists: Zdeno Chara, Patrice Bergeron)
- 19:09 BOS Patrice Bergeron (assists: David Krejci, Jaromir Jagr)

Overtime
- 6:05 BOS Patrice Bergeron (assists: Tyler Seguin, Brad Marchand)

26

Games That Just Missed the Cut

In selecting the 25 Bruins games for inclusion in this book, a handful of notable games had to be culled. In the opinion of the authors, they just were not up to snuff. Here they are:

April 13, 1927: One of the nastiest incidents in Boston Bruins history unfolds in one of their earliest big games. The best-of-five Stanley Cup final of 1927 pits the upstart Boston Bruins against one of the great teams in the early years of professional hockey: the original Ottawa Senators. The Bruins enter the championship series as decided underdogs—and play that way. After three games, the Senators have won one of them, but two other contests ended in ties when the ice became too rough for play to continue. (Producing high quality artificial ice in springtime is still an inexact science in some NHL arenas in 1927.) A win by the Senators in Canada's capital city would clinch the Cup for Ottawa. The bitterly fought game goes to Ottawa by a 3–1 count. It features a third-period brawl that requires local police to break it up. At the conclusion of the game, the Bruins and their coach Art Ross are not at all happy with the game's officiating—and they let referee Dr. Jerry LaFlamme know it. They are particularly livid that Harry Oliver, who scored Boston's only goal in the final minute of play, is butt-ended in the face shortly thereafter by Ottawa's Hooley Smith. Oliver exits the ice groggily with a broken nose. A report in the next day's *Ottawa Citizen*, accuses Ross of grabbing Laflamme by his sweater in a corridor leading to the referees' dressing room. This act is followed by several Bruins pounding on the hapless ref. The most zealous of the bunch is 34-year-old Billy Coutu, a well-traveled veteran who has a sordid history of nasty incidents with Laflamme and other NHL officials. Laflamme's partner, the much more physically imposing Billy Bell, is also manhandled by Coutu. Within 24 hours, Coutu is suspended for life by the NHL and is also fined $100 for his violent transgressions. The harsh sentence no doubt pleases an unnamed scribe for the *Montreal Gazette*. He editorializes in his postgame summary, "Manhandling referees is a dangerous practice to creep into any sport series ... it might be well if some consideration is given by the authorities to rules which will halt such displays and assaults against officials as were in evidence tonight.... Penalties and small fines are not enough."[1] Coutu is eventually reinstated in 1930 at age 37 when he is too old to latch onto any NHL team, but he does return to play minor professional hockey for a couple of years before retiring at age 40. One lasting impact of the shameful Coutu-Laflamme incident is the NHL's creation of its referee-in-chief position to oversee all matters pertaining to the officiating of league games.

April 3, 1933: Boston loses what is at the time the longest playoff game in NHL history. In Game #5 of the best-of-five semifinal versus Toronto at Maple Leaf Gardens, Ken Doraty of the Maple Leafs intercepts a careless Eddie Shore pass and beats Boston netminder Tiny Thompson on a breakaway at 4:46 of the sixth overtime period. It is the only goal of the epic game—at least it is the only one that counts. Thompson could hardly be faulted. He makes 112 saves—yes, 112— before surrendering Doraty's goal. Often forgotten about the historic battle is that Boston thought they had taken the lead with about five minutes left in the third period, but Alex Smith's tally was controversially disallowed by the refereeing duo of Odie Cleghorn and Eusebe Daigneault. A bleary-eyed Victor O. Jones of the *Boston Globe* writes in the wee hours of the morning, "Everyone is agreed, I think, that Cleghorn and Daigneault are not the best whistle-blowers in the NHL." Jones angrily continued, "Hockey can stand just so much monkey business in its officiating. As far as Boston is concerned, the saturation point has just about been reached. It won't take much more incompetent refereeing to make the Boston hockey followers regard [the sport] in much the same light as wrestling."[2]

December 4, 1938: Twenty-three-year-old Frank Brimsek, in the unenviable position of replacing hugely popular Boston goaltender Tiny Thompson, records his first NHL shutout. Thompson had been a fixture on the Bruins since 1928, but Art Ross liked what he saw in the youthful puck-stopper from Eveleth, Minnesota. Thompson is injured early in the 1938–39 season, so Brimsek is summoned to Boston where he wins the two games he plays—and is promptly returned to the Bruins' farm club in Providence once Thompson returns. According to

Bruin lore, before Brimsek packs his bags, Ross conducts an impromptu test of his two netminders, firing a series of shots at each man. A couple get by Thompson—but none elude Brimsek. Based on a hunch and that small sample of pucks he fired, Ross deals Thompson to Detroit in late November. It is a surprise move to everyone who follows the NHL—and it is widely criticized as foolhardy. However, Victor O. Jones sagely writes in the *Boston Globe*, "If Brimsek is as good as Thompson, [Ross is] also getting an advantage in age because Brimsek is 11 years younger [sic]."[3] [Authors' note: The 35-year-old Thompson was actually more than 12 years older than Brimsek.] On December 1, the newcomer loses his first game as Boston's new permanent goalie, 2–0, in Montreal. However, on Sunday, December 4, Brimsek beats the Blackhawks, 5–0, in Chicago. Dit Clapper and Milt Schmidt tally two goals apiece in the Boston victory; Charlie Sands gets the other. The Bruins score four third-period goals—three in the space of 58 seconds—to put the game out of reach. (The Associated Press scribe covering the game dwells on Boston's scorers and never once mentions Brimsek!) Two nights later in Boston, Brimsek records another whitewash, 2–0, versus the same opposition. He notches four more shutouts in his next five games, setting a record for a scoreless streak by a Boston goalie that even the celebrated Thomson never attained. Suddenly Ross' rash decision about Boston's goaltending future is not as crazy as it had seemed. In recognition of his spotless netminding, the fawning Boston press dubs Brimsek "Mr. Zero." At the end of the 1938–39 season, Brimsek is named a First Team All-Star. He also wins the Vezina Trophy as the NHL's best goaltender and the Calder Trophy as the league's rookie of the year. Tiny Thompson has two disappointing seasons in Detroit and retires in 1940.

November 12, 1942: The curious effects of the Second World War on the NHL are clearly on display this Thursday night at Toronto's Maple Leaf Gardens. The prime exhibit is Armand (Bep) Guidolin, a junior star with the Oshawa Generals, who is making his debut for the Boston Bruins as a left winger. With most of the NHL's regular players now in the Canadian (or American) military, finding capable hockey talent to fill rosters becomes more challenging—especially for the four teams located outside the Dominion of Canada. Some teams opt for players too old to be drafted. In this one glaring instance, Boston goes the other direction and employs Guidolin, who is underage for military conscription. On the night of his first NHL game, Guidolin is 16 years and 11 months old. The Bruins lose 3–1 to Toronto, making it four losses in four games to open the 1942–43 season. Guidolin does not record a point nor get a penalty. Guidolin's presence in the Boston lineup that night attracts barely more than a ripple of attention. In its game coverage, the *Boston Globe* merely notes that Guidolin was teamed with two other youthful Bruins (17-year-old Don Gallinger and 19-year-old Bill Shill) to form a "kid line"—but there is no specific mention of his record-setting age. The threesome would eventually be referred to by Boston hockey scribes as the Sprout Line—an amusing, rhyming allusion to the Bruins' vaunted Kraut line of Woody Dumart, Bobby Bauer and Milt Schmidt who were all now serving in the Royal Canadian Air Force. Twelve days later, Guidolin notches his first NHL goal in Boston's 5–5 tie versus Chicago, making him the youngest person to score a goal in the league's 25-year history. Before the war ends, Guidolin becomes eligible for military service, joins Canada's navy, and misses a year of pro hockey. Guidolin eventually plays four seasons with Boston and then is dealt to Detroit, and then Chicago, retiring as a player in 1952. In February 1973, Guidolin will replace Tom Johnson and take over the coaching duties of the Boston Bruins.

January 18, 1958: Boston's Willie O'Ree, age 22, becomes the first black player to appear in an NHL game. It occurs at the Montreal Forum. That Saturday night the Bruins upset the mighty Habs, 3–0. (The Bruins score a goal in each period; the marksmen are Johnny Bucyk, Larry Regan and Bronco Horvath. Harry Lumley records the shutout.) O'Ree plays sparingly, getting no points nor penalties in the visitor's victory. A *Boston Globe* scribe comments that O'Ree's debut "was undistinguished as Boston coach Milt Schmidt played him only a half turn at a time, alternating him with veteran Johnny Peirson ... to ease the pressure."[4] O'Ree also dresses for the rematch in Boston the next night (won by Montreal, 6–2) and then vanishes from pro hockey's elite ranks for two seasons. A native of Fredericton, New Brunswick, O'Ree's career in the NHL is a marginal one. It consists of just 45 games for Boston: the two aforementioned 1958 contests and 43 played during the 1960–61 season. He ends up with four goals and 10 assists. O'Ree secretly plays under a handicap, having lost the vision in his right eye after being struck in the face with a puck as an amateur. In a 2012 interview O'Ree recalled the mental anguish he underwent after being told his disability was permanent. "When I got out of the hospital," he said, "I told myself I just can't accept the fact that this doctor is telling me I'll never play hockey again. He doesn't know the burning desire I have within myself, and the goals and dreams that I've set for myself of not only playing professional hockey but making it into the National Hockey League. So I started playing again."[5] Throughout his professional hockey career, O'Ree simply keeps his partial blindness a secret from everyone.

December 14, 1980: Doing his best impression of Chris Oddleifson, obscure Boston rookie Doug Morrison scores three goals—all of them coming consecutively in the third period—as the struggling Bruins thump one of the NHL's leading teams, the Los Angeles Kings, with unexpected ease, 7–1. Morrison's first goal gives the home team a comfortable 5–1 lead. (It is more appreciated for its assist, as Rick Middleton fed him a perfect pass while stickhandling on his knees.) Forty-one seconds later, his second goal came on a wrist shot that sailed by the glove of future Boston goalie Doug Keans. Morrison's hattrick goal comes on a late Boston power play, assisted by Jean Ratelle. A 20-year-old Vancouverite, Morrison has one goal to his credit entering the game. He will only score three more in his short-lived NHL career. Its entirety was with Boston, spread over three scattered and brief call-ups to the Bruins from 1980 to 1985.

March 21, 1991: At Boston Garden, the Bruins set a modern regular-season record by firing the stunning sum of 73 shots on goal versus the lowly Quebec Nordiques—yet the game ends in a disappointing 3–3 tie. Disappointing for the home team, that is. Bruin defenseman Raymond Bourque gets 19 of the 73 shots, a figure believed to be an NHL record. Ron Tugnutt is the harried and heroic goalie for the visitors. Kevin Paul Dupont of the *Boston Globe* calls Tugnutt's head-shaking outing, "one part Charlie Chaplin, one part Ken Dryden." Remarkably, the Nordiques thrice held leads. Boston required two third-period goals to escape with a point. The aforementioned Bourque gets the game-tying tally at 10:36 of the final frame. Tugnutt's seventieth stop is his most spectacular, thwarting Bourque with a dazzling glove save from point-blank range with eight seconds left in the game. "We had 70 [sic] shots," marveled Bourque afterward. "I bet 30 to 35 of them were good, quality shots. I'm telling you, it was scary."[6] Quebec launches a mere 26 shots at Boston goaltender Reggie Lemelin.

March 31, 1991: In the Bruins' 7–3 home victory over the Hartford Whalers, Boston's ill-tempered Chris Nilan sets a dubious NHL record that Sunday evening by accruing ten penalties in a single game! It is a meaningless encounter to conclude the 1990–91 regular season as far as the league standings are concerned, but since the same two teams are destined to meet in the first round of the Stanley Cup playoffs three days later, the rough stuff conveniently serves a purpose to send various messages. The Bruins' top messenger, in that aspect, was 33-year-old Chris (Knuckles) Nilan. The veteran enforcer's prominent parade to the sin bin begins at 12:53 of the opening period when he is whistled for a holding infraction. At 10:04 of the second period, Nilan picks up a fighting major for battling Hartford's Jim McKenzie. Shortly after stepping out of the penalty box, the less-than-contrite Nilan gets three further penalties at 15:36: a pair of minors for roughing and elbowing Doug Houda, plus a ten-minute misconduct for not-so-good measure. Nilan tops that act of malice at 13:08 of the third period by collecting five penalties at once. The charges are elbowing, instigating, roughing, fighting, and a game misconduct. The succinct headline in the next day's *Boston Globe* sports section correctly proclaims "Bruins Smack Whalers." Kevin Paul Dupont writes in his report that Nilan came out on the short end of his two fistic encounters, but he fared better in his third bout "clocking Rob Brown in a farewell to arms (and uppercuts). [Nilan] didn't play much hockey, but no one appeared to ask him for that." Altogether, Boston and Hartford combine for the hefty total of 210 penalty minutes. That alarming statistic prompts Dupont to add, "You want a prediction for the upcoming playoff round between these clubs? Try *Ring Magazine*."[7] The 1990–91 campaign was Nilan's only season as a Bruin.

February 14, 2003: Boston notches an exciting 6–5 road victory over the Florida Panthers this Friday night on a goal by Brian Rolston. However, it was the start of the game that people were mostly discussing. Thirty-year-old Mike Knuble of the Bruins sets an impressive NHL record for the fastest two goals by one player to start a game: 27 seconds. Knuble's first goal comes 10 seconds after the opening faceoff. He knocks home a bouncing puck that comes from a Jozef Stumpel pass across the slot. His second tally follows just 17 seconds later when Knuble scores on his own rebound through traffic. Florida goalie Roberto Luongo initially stops Knuble's backhand shot, but the Boston forward fortuitously gets the puck a second time and makes it count, connecting with a forehand. Boston fails to securely hold their two-goal lead for very long, however. The game is level at 2–2 after the first period. Eventually extra time is required for Rolston to settle matters in favor of the visitors. "It was just one of those games," Knuble humbly tells ESPN afterward. "Sometimes when you get ahead like that, you tend to back off a bit. Even personally, when you score two goals like that, you sit back sometimes. But you still have to play 59 more minutes."[8] Upon being informed that he had set an NHL record, Knuble is surprised by his feat. He amusingly tells Nancy Marrapese-Burrell of the *Boston Globe* he feared that if his name ever did make it into the league's record books, it would be for something infamous "like worst plus-minus ever. Nothing positive."[9] Knuble's individual record is just three seconds shy of the NHL's team record for fastest two goals from the start a game, set by Mark Messier and Dave Lumley of the Edmonton Oilers in a game played on March 28, 1982, in Los Angeles.

27

... And 12 Games That Are Best Forgotten

Being a fan of the Boston Bruins is not all unicorns and rainbows. That hard fact is generally well known among those who follow the Black and Gold with any degree of regularity. Along those doleful lines, here are a dozen notably disappointing games that really ought to be expunged from one's memory bank. Consider these examples ... but only briefly.

December 25, 1928: Under normal circumstances, a 2–1 loss to the Chicago Blackhawks would not be especially humiliating, but in the grand scheme of things this particular setback truly was an embarrassment of the first order. The 1928–29 Hawks were among the worst teams ever to take to the ice in NHL competition. In 44 regular-season games, they compiled a dismal record of 7–29–8 to finish dead last in the American Division. (That was actually a slight improvement from the season before when the Blackhawks recorded an even more dreadful mark of 7–34–3 in 1927–28!) However, the 1928–29 Hawks were an offensively challenged bunch: They scored a meagre 33 goals all season—a pathetic average of just 0.75 goals per game, less than half of their total of 68 from the previous season. Vic Ripley, who would later play 37 games for the Bruins, accounted for fully one-third of Chicago's goals with 11. Yet the anemic Hawks managed to get two of those goals in an upset win at Boston Garden against a strong Boston team that would go on to win its first Stanley Cup in the spring. (Perhaps it was just the Bruins' way of spreading cheer and goodwill toward their guests during the Christmas season.) A month earlier the Hawks had played the Bruins to a 1–1 tie in Chicago. According to various game reports, Boston dominated play on that Christmas Day, but Charlie Gardiner was excellent in the Chicago goal. "The Blackhawks looked better than anyone anticipated,"[1] declared John J. Hallahan of the *Boston Globe*. Dick Irvin opened the scoring for the visitors in the first period. Dutch Gainor equalized for Boston in the second, but Alex McKinnon got the winner for Chicago at 14:12 of the third period. "If the Bruins are going to be in the thick of the fight for National Hockey League honors, they will surely have to pick up their goal-getting,"[2] warned Hallahan. The Bruins must have been thoroughly chastised. In the clubs' final meeting of the season, on March 12, 1929, at Boston Garden, the Bruins routed the Blackhawks, 11–1.

January 18, 1973: In what was quite likely the most humiliating defeat in the long history of the Bruins, Boston was upended 9–7 at home by the expansion New York Islanders. The Isles were a pitiful team that won just 12 of their 78 games in 1972–73. They had lost their previous dozen games before that stunning Thursday night at Boston Garden. The Bruins were the defending Stanley Cup champions at the time. "Good Grief! Islanders, 9 Bruins 7" roared the large headline atop the *Boston Globe's* sports section the following day. In his report on the game, Tom Fitzgerald figured the shocking result "must be raising skeptical eyebrows over the length and breadth of the NHL. This has to be practically incomprehensible to anyone who pays even casual attention to pro hockey."[3] How bad was it? The Islanders jumped out to a huge 5–0 lead after just 18 minutes. With the score 5–1, goaltender John Adams was yanked from the game at the end of the first 20 minutes by Boston coach Tom Johnson and replaced by Ed Johnston. (One falsehood about this game that has persisted over the years is that Johnston was so bad in his relief role that Adams was returned to the ice. This is not true. Johnston played the remaining 40 minutes, albeit not especially well.) Boston tried to fight back. Thanks mostly to four goals by Johnny Bucyk, the home team narrowed the score to within 7–6 and 8–7 to excite Boston Garden's 15,003 gobsmacked fans, but they got no closer. Billy Harris' goal with about two and a half minutes left in the third period was the final dagger. Ex-Bruin Ed Westfall, who was selected by the Islanders from Boston in the NHL's expansion draft, scored twice for the winners. The delighted Westfall said he was inspired by a bit of sage philosophy once uttered by former Bruin coach Harry Sinden: "When things aren't going well, if you let up, they surely won't get any better."[4]

May 9, 1974: After winning the first game of the Stanley Cup finals versus the Philadelphia Flyers two nights earlier on a dramatic, last-minute goal by Bobby Orr, the Bruins sought to make it two straight victories in two home games. The Bruins jumped out to a two-goal lead in the first period on goals by Wayne Cashman and Phil Esposito and appeared to be on their way, but Philadelphia goalie Bernie Parent was unbeatable after that. His biggest save came halfway through the third period when he thwarted Gregg Sheppard on a partial breakaway, rushing out of his net to stifle the Boston center's room to maneuver. The Bruins held a shaky 2–1 edge over the Flyers entering the last minute of the third period. This time Orr made a rare defensive miscue, failing to utilize an opportunity to corral a loose puck behind the Bruins' net and clear it out of the Boston zone. Instead, Bobby Clarke won the puck from Orr and fed a pass to teammate Rick MacLeish. He spotted André (Moose) Dupont alone in the slot. Dupont ("hardly famous for his scoring power,"[5] bitterly wrote Francis Rosa in the next day's *Boston Globe*) tied the game with a quick, low shot through traffic that eluded Boston goaltender Gilles Gilbert. Bobby Clarke won it at 12:01 of overtime for Philadelphia on a play that had four Bruins scattered and sprawled in disarray around the Boston net. It was the turning point in the series. "Now that we've won on their ice, I believe we're going to do it,"[6] said Flyers coach Fred Shero afterward. He was absolutely correct. Philadelphia won all three of their home games in the finals to capture the franchise's first Stanley Cup, and the first earned by one of the 1967 expansion teams.

April 11, 1975: The Bruins recorded a 94-point season in 1974–75, but they did not finish first in the newly formed Adams Division. (Buffalo did; the Sabres accordingly received a first-round bye in the postseason.) Under the NHL's revised playoff system, as a mere also-ran, Boston had to meet the mediocre Chicago Blackhawks in a best-of-three series to start their quest for the Stanley Cup where there was not much room for error. The confrontation was supposed to be a laugher for Boston, as the Hawks finished the regular season just two games above .500 amid heavy criticism from the Chicago media. Things began fully according to expectations as the Bruins cruised in the opener at Boston Garden, winning 8–2. Chicago goalie Tony Esposito looked very shaky and was mocked by the Boston media. Two nights later, Game Two in Chicago was won by the Blackhawks in overtime, 4–3, on an Ivan Boldirev goal that may have been offside. (Referee Bruce Hood angered the Bruins by refusing to call several flagrant offenses committed by the Hawks in the extra period.) That result forced a winner-take-all game back in Boston the very next night. Boston dominated play, but somehow ended up losing, 6–4. This time Tony Esposito was the hero of the game, facing 56 shots from the home team and stopping 52 of them. "He kept us in there in the first period, the second period and the third period," remarked Chicago's John Marks about his goalie. "Had the game gone into overtime, he would have won it for us. [There's] no way he could have been beaten tonight."[7] Conversely, Boston goaltender Gilles Gilbert faced only 19 Chicago shots and stopped just 13 of them. His alibi that most of the goals he allowed came on tough shots did not endear him to first-year coach Don Cherry. No one knew it, but the Bruins' upset loss that night was the final playoff appearance for Bobby Orr and the last one for Phil Esposito in a Boston uniform.

February 7, 1976: Entering that Saturday night's game at Maple Leaf Gardens, the Bruins had compiled an impressive seven-game winning streak. It certainly didn't seem that way once the game began. Boston's skein of victories came to an abrupt and embarrassing end in a godawful 11–4 loss to the Toronto Maple Leafs. The ghastly debacle was broadcast to a large *Hockey Night in Canada* television audience. "It must have been like sitting at the bottom of a hill watching a snowball gather momentum and size as it comes at you. Complete helplessness,"[8] surmised longtime *Boston Globe* hockey writer Francis Rosa. Darryl Sittler famously had the best night ever enjoyed by any player in NHL history, a record-setting 10-point game (six goals and four assists) for the victors. The last one was a goal that encapsulated the dismal night for the visitors: He scored from behind the Boston net on a centering pass that deflected off defenseman Brad Park's skate and past startled and disheartened goaltender Dave Reece. The hapless Reece played the entire 60 minutes of the fiasco without hope of relief because the Bruins supposedly had no healthy backup goalie available. It was Reece's NHL swansong. Six of Toronto's goals came in the second period. "It was 20 minutes of hockey (I use the word loosely)," quipped Rosa, "in which the Bruins cleansed their systems of more poor hockey than they've played in two months."[9] Rosa was right about the horrid setback having a positive cleansing effect on the team. The next night, with steady Gerry Cheevers in goal, Boston regained their old form and won comfortably, 7–0, at home versus Detroit. It was the start of an 11-game undefeated streak for the Bruins, making the horrible loss to Toronto—the team's only defeat in a span of 19 games—an egregious outlier.

May 7, 1983: In 1982–83, the Bruins accrued 110 points—the best record in the NHL. Playoff victories over the Quebec Nordiques and Buffalo Sabres put them in a promising position to earn their first berth in the Stanley Cup finals in five years. All the Bruins had to do was defeat the three-time defending Cup champion New York Islanders in the conference finals. It was not as daunting a task as it seemed—at least on paper. The Isles appeared wholly beatable, having finished 16 points in arrears of Boston during the regular season. Inexplicably, the Bruins' goaltending, which had been reliable all season, swiftly fell apart. Showing their championship mettle, New York scored 30 goals in six games. In their three home contests, the Isles twice netted eight scores and seven once. The last game—a horrid 8–4 Boston loss on Long Island—featured especially terrible defense and shoddy goaltending by the Bruins. Pete Peeters, a heroic figure in the Boston net all season, mysteriously turned into a sieve when facing the onslaught of the reigning champs. He was taunted by the Islander fans with mocking, derisive chants of his surname throughout the contest. Leigh Montville wrote in the *Boston Globe*, "On the night the Bruins needed invincibility from their invincible man, they didn't receive it. Goalie Pete Peeters was definitely a human being."[10] Mike Bossy was the offensive star of the game, scoring four goals for the deserving winners. The *Globe*'s Francis Rosa accurately commented, "The better team won the game, won the series."[11] Near the end of the one-sided game, Boston coach Gerry Cheevers made an extraordinary gesture with his hand toward the Bruins' conquerors. He held up four fingers, apparently predicting the outcome of the next round of the playoffs for the dominant Prince of Wales Conference champions—a fourth consecutive Stanley Cup. Indeed, the Islanders went on to defeat the up-and-coming Edmonton Oilers in the finals to fulfill what Cheevers had indicated on May 7.

April 5, 1989: After having reached the Stanley Cup finals in 1988, the Bruins entered the 1989 Stanley Cup playoffs with optimism and home-ice advantage. Their opponents in the first-round of postseason play (formally known as the Adams Division semifinals) were the Buffalo Sabres, a team Boston had successfully vanquished in all three of the clubs' previous playoff series. One of those triumphs happened the previous spring. In Game One, however, Buffalo did not follow the script. They came into Boston Garden and thoroughly blasted the Bruins by an embarrassing 6–0 score. Even worse, all six goals were scored by the Sabres' special teams. Four occurred with the Bruins a man down while the other two came with Buffalo playing shorthanded! Mike Foligno started the rout with a power-play goal at 5:54 with Ray Neufeld sitting in Boston's penalty box for roughing. About eight minutes later, Rob Cimetta hurt the Bruins' chances by drawing a major penalty for high sticking and an automatic game misconduct. Buffalo's Rick Vaive capitalized on the situation by adding the Sabres' second goal. With the Bruins down 2–0 early in the second period and Benoit Hogue of the Sabres sitting out an interference penalty, Buffalo stunned the Boston Garden faithful with a shorthanded tally scored by Scott Arniel. The game was probably lost at that point. It was certainly lost when Buffalo scored twice more on the power play to lead 5–0 after 40 awful minutes of action. To pile on the humiliation, the Sabres' sixth marker was another shorthanded goal, notched about 13 minutes into the third period, by Foligno. Goaltender Jacques Cloutier got the well-earned Buffalo shutout, recording 29 saves. At the other end of the ice, Boston goalie Reggie Lemelin was less than stellar, having stopped only 13 of Buffalo's paltry 19 shots. In the next day's *Boston Globe*, Kevin Paul Dupont tersely wrote, "What happened to the Bruins last night at the Garden, a 6–0 humbling at the hands of the Buffalo Sabres, was one of the worst pastings the Bruins have ever taken in the playoffs."[12] Boston coach Terry O'Reilly was almost at a loss for words to describe the debacle. "A reasonable explanation?" he said with incredulity. "This was a complete no-show by the Boston Bruins."[13] His harsh words seemed to have the desired positive effect on O'Reilly's charges, however: The Bruins promptly steamrolled the Sabres in the next four games to take the series.

October 14, 1995: "For more than 59 minutes, the Boston Bruins thoroughly outplayed the Dallas Stars," declared the October 15, 1995, edition of the *Washington Post*. "It was the final minute that killed them."[14] That was the abridged version of what oddly transpired that dreadful Saturday night in Texas. "You play so well, then to lose like that, it's hard to take," said discouraged defenseman Ray Bourque. "But it just goes to show that you've got to keep playing the entire 60 minutes no matter how big your lead is."[15] Bourque was referring to an epic, head-shaking, late-game collapse in which the Dallas Stars *scored three times within 44.4 seconds in the final minute of the third period* To turn a 5–3 deficit into a thoroughly stunning 6–5 win over the visiting Bruins at Reunion Arena. The Stars' three late goals came in rapid succession courtesy of Kevin Hatcher, Mike Modano and Guy Carbonneau. Modano's tally came with Dallas goaltender Andy Moog, an ex-Bruin, pulled for a sixth attacker—and with just 16 seconds left in the final period. Ridiculously, the Bruins' crumbling defense could not run out the clock to force overtime. Instead, they failed to prevent Carbonneau's game-winner with fewer than five ticks remaining on the clock. On the other side of the coin, the atrocious Boston collapse provided a new club record for the home team: It marked the fastest three goals in the history of the Dallas franchise that began its existence in Minnesota in 1967 as the North Stars. "This is, without a doubt, the worst defeat I've ever been associated with," remarked Boston's cheerful and philosophical first-year coach Steve Kasper in the Monday edition of the *Boston Globe*. "But the sun came up the next day; I knew it would."[16]

May 14, 2010: Game Seven of an Eastern Conference semifinal witnessed the Bruins race out to a 3–0 lead by the 14:10 mark of the first period at TD Garden—and then catastrophically fritter it away. The final score was 4–3 for the visiting Philadelphia Flyers. Especially galling was that Boston had led the playoff series three games to zero. The Bruins thus became the third club in NHL history to fail to win a best-of-seven series after taking the first three games, and the first one to stumble in such a manner in 35 years since the 1975 Pittsburgh Penguins fell apart before the onrushing New York Islanders. By the end of the first period the Flyers had narrowed the score to 3–1. Boston's three-goal lead was completely gone eight and a half minutes into the second period—and so was any momentum possessed by the home team. Philadelphia's winning goal came at 12:52 of the third period. Cruelly, Simon Gagne scored late on a Flyer power play while the Bruins were attempting to kill a bench penalty for having too many men on the ice, incredibly duplicating the same infamous circumstance that befell Boston during Game Seven of their heartbreaking 1979 semifinal at the Montreal Forum. The spectacular playoff choke nearly cost Boston coach Claude Julien his job. After the game, Julien candidly summarized, "We had a 3–0 lead in the series and a 3–0 lead tonight—and we blew both. There are no excuses."[17] The ice at TD Garden was littered with all sorts of debris and Bruins paraphernalia at the end of the game—including several expensive team jerseys discarded in disgust by angry fans. The club learned well from their gut-wrenching defeat, however: The Bruins won the Stanley Cup the following season with Julien still behind the bench. Along the way they blew away the favored Flyers in four straight games, winning the fourth contest easily, 5–1, at home. There was no Boston choke in 2011.

June 24, 2013: It looked like a certainty that there would be a Game Seven in the 2013 Stanley Cup finals. The Bruins, trailing the Chicago Blackhawks three games to two in a highly competitive topsy-turvy series, held a 2–1 lead on home ice late in the third period of Game Six and were playing well. With about 90 seconds left in the third period, Chicago coach Joel Quenneville pulled his goaltender, Corey Crawford, for a sixth attacker. The ploy worked. The Hawks' tying goal came on a scrambly play with 1:16 left on the clock from the stick of Bryan Bickell after the Bruins had whiffed on a chance to safely clear the puck from their zone. Overtime was looming, but there would be no extra session. In slightly less than 18 seconds after play resumed, Chicago potted the Cup-winning goal, scored by Dave Bolland, on a similar sloppy play in front of goaltender Tuukka Rask. "This place is stunned," said one

Chicago radio announcer about the teams' sudden change of momentum and fortunes and the crowd's reaction at TD Garden, "and so am I."[18] Dan Shaughnessy commented in the *Boston Globe*, "The greatest puck series of a generation was going to play out in a seventh game on Wednesday night. Then it melted like a snow cone on Causeway Street on the hottest day of the new summer. Two goals in 17.7 seconds. That's all it took to go from ecstasy to agony. It was hard to believe. It will always be hard to believe."[19] In the same publication, scribe Kevin Paul Dupont bluntly wrote that the Bruins "botched Game Six of the Stanley Cup final in epic fashion."[20] Never in the 120-year history of the Stanley Cup had a team gone from trailing a finals game in the third period to leading it with so little time remaining on the clock. The happy Bolland had high praise for the vanquished. "They're a great team," he graciously said of the defeated Bruins. "They battled to the end. We always battle to the end, too."[21] When asked about the lingering effect such a defeat might have, Boston's Johnny Boychuk sadly said, "Forever. You'll remember that forever."[22]

April 9, 2016: The Bruins' final regular-season game of the 2015–16 season was a Saturday matinee versus the Ottawa Senators at TD Garden. It was a must-win affair for the Bruins if they wanted to retain any chance of qualifying for the Stanley Cup playoffs. A seemingly ideal, uninterested opponent was waiting for them. The Senators, in contrast, were a moribund lot, 10 points in arrears of Boston in the standings with no hope for Stanley Cup competition that spring. Boston's David Pastrnak got the game's important first goal 5:04 into the opening frame to give the Bruins an early edge, but thereafter the home team perplexingly played without discernable passion for the rest of the contest. Ottawa scored four times in the second period on shaky backup goalie Jonas Gustavsson. (Scheduled starter Tuukka Rask took pregame warmups, but he opted not to play due to illness.) The Senators tacked on two empty net goals—both shorthanded!—in the third period to win handily, 6–1. It was a game where the Bruins "cratered,"[23] according to *Boston Globe* reporter Fluto Shinzawa. "It's unacceptable, the way we showed up,"[24] commented Patrice Bergeron. The disgruntled fans agreed with that assessment. The Bruins were roundly booed as they departed the ice and headed to their early start on their summer vacations. Adding to the embarrassment of the overwhelming defeat, Boston had held first place in the NHL's Atlantic Division as late as March 14.

June 12, 2019: Despite being in the Stanley Cup finals plenty of times, remarkably the Boston Bruins have only played one seventh game in the championship round. That lone instance was a match that most Bruins fans do not relish discussing or reliving. Game Seven versus the St. Louis Blues to conclude the 2018–19 NHL season was an absolute stinker for the Black and Gold. The Blues entered the finals, a rematch of the 1970 championship series, as underdogs as the Bruins were widely perceived to be the more skillful club. The momentum of the series had shifted in the Bruins' favor after a huge road win in Game Six, with the deciding seventh game to be played at TD Garden before an electrified home crowd. Still, St Louis won it handily, 4–1. The Bruins got the better offensive chances during the first dozen minutes of play but were largely an ineffective bunch thereafter. Tuukka Rask had a mediocre performance in the Boston goal, providing more ammunition to a vocal segment of Boston fans who often criticized him for substandard outings in important contests. Dan Shaughnessy of the *Boston Globe* quipped, "The Finnish Flash could not finish."[25] Overall, the Blues seemed to be the more relaxed and poised squad. St. Louis, against the run of play, opened the scoring on a shot launched from the Boston blue line by Jay Bouwmeester that was subtly deflected past Rask by Ryan O'Reilly. The second goal by the visitors was the game's most important, scored with just 7.9 seconds left in the opening frame. A St. Louis rush began when Brad Marchand misread the situation when the Bruins had the puck in the St. Louis zone; he went to the Bruins' bench instead of remaining on the ice. That error in judgment allowed for an easy odd-man breakout for the Blues. It culminated with a goal backhanded over Rask's shoulder by Alex Pietrangelo. There was no scoring in the second period, but the Blues put the home team away with two more tallies in the third period to assume an unreachable 4–0 lead. A late goal by Boston's Matt Grzelcyk at 17:50 only served to break the shutout bid by St. Louis netminder Jordan Binnington, who had been superb. "[Boston's 2018–19 season] ended in abject disappointment," penned a doleful Shaughnessy. "It was a stunning defeat in an era when we have become accustomed to only good things happening to Boston sports teams. And it feels like a lost opportunity."[26]

28

A Brief History of the Boston Bruins, Decade by Decade

"Hockey is a game for aficionados. It's not for everyone, but for those who embrace it, the sport is a passion. Nowhere in the United States is it more loved than it is in Boston"[1]—Mike Milbury

1920s

Vermont-born grocery-store magnate Charles Adams is granted a franchise by the National Hockey League for the city of Boston, the first American-based team in the circuit. The club wins its debut game, played at cozy Boston Arena, 2–1, over the Montreal Maroons, another expansion club, on December 1, 1924. However, the Bruins finish their inaugural campaign mired in last place with a dismal 6–24 record. When the NHL enters its modern era in 1926–27, Boston steadily becomes a daunting opponent, thanks in a huge part to Adams buying the contracts of seven star players from the defunct Western Hockey League for $50,000. Eddie Shore is the most noteworthy of the bunch. The Bruins advance to the Stanley Cup finals that season (losing to Ottawa). Three days after hosting a boxing card as its first public event, Boston Garden opens for hockey on November 20, 1928. The Montreal Canadiens spoil the first NHL game contested there, inflicting a 1–0 loss on the Bruins before an overflow crowd estimated at 16,000. John J. Hallahan of the *Boston Globe* advises local hockey fans not to take the setback as a bad omen. His hunch is a correct one. Slightly more than four months later, the club captures its first Stanley Cup at the end of that 1928–29 season, beating the New York Rangers in two straight games in a best-of-three final.

28. Brief History of Boston Bruins by Decade

Three noteworthy players from the early days of the Boston franchise are shown in this photograph (from left): Eddie Shore, George Owen and Lionel Hitchman. Shore and Hitchman both have their jerseys retired by the Bruins, but George Owen was a reliable blueliner too. Before playing five seasons with the Bruins, Owen had been a three-sport star at Harvard University (courtesy Boston Public Library, Leslie Jones Collection).

Cecil (Tiny) Thompson takes over the team's goalkeeping duties from Hal Winkler in 1928. Remarkably playing in all but five of Boston's games for the next decade, Thompson sets numerous Bruin netminding marks, many of which still stand today.

Star Players: Dit Clapper, Dutch Gainor, Lionel Hitchman, Harry Oliver, George Owen, Eddie Shore, Tiny Thompson, Cooney Weiland, Hal Winkler

A typical cross-section of Bruin personnel during the war years: (from left) the old (Dit Clapper), the underqualified (Vic Damore), and the young (Jack Shill). Clapper had been with Boston since 1927. Goaltender Damore played just one NHL game. Shill was elevated to the NHL at age 17. The lofty Bruins were especially hard hit by the war's manpower demands. It took 30 years for them to regain their former powerhouse status (courtesy Boston Public Library, Leslie Jones Collection).

1930s

For most of the decade the Bruins have championship-caliber lineups, but seemingly every spring they routinely fail to live up to their potential and underperform in the league's playoffs. The club's only Stanley Cup of the 1930s comes in 1938–39 with a victory over Toronto in the first best-of-seven finals in modern NHL history. The decade sees the color scheme of the Bruins' uniforms switched from brown and gold to black and gold in 1936. It also sees the debut of American-born goaltender Frank Brimsek in 1938 who quickly earns the nickname "Mr. Zero" for his frequent shutout netminding, spectacularly accruing six clean sheets in his first eight games as a Bruin. The famous Kraut Line, comprised of three boyhood pals of German descent from Kitchener, Ontario—Milt Schmidt, Bobby Bauer and Woody Dumart—is formed and quickly becomes the best offensive unit in the NHL.

28. Brief History of Boston Bruins by Decade

William (Flash) Hollett began his career with Ottawa and Toronto before Boston splurged to purchase his contract for $16,000. He was a Bruin from 1936 until 1944 when he was traded to Detroit. As a Red Wing, he scored 20 goals in 1944–45, an NHL record for a defenseman that stood until Bobby Orr came along (courtesy Boston Public Library, Leslie Jones Collection).

Star Players: Bobby Bauer, Frank Brimsek, Dit Clapper, Roy Conacher, Bill Cowley, Woody Dumart, Mel Hill, Flash Hollett, Harry Oliver, Milt Schmidt, Eddie Shore, Tiny Thompson

1940s

The Bruins begin the decade well, continuing their trend as a powerhouse club from the late 1930s. In a season where they compile a remarkable unbeaten streak of 23 games, Boston's third Stanley Cup comes to fruition in 1940–41. However, world events conspire to

Two of Boston's lethal "Krauts"—Bobby Bauer (#17) and Milt Schmidt (#15)—attempt to score on Toronto goaltender Turk Broda during Stanley Cup action in the late 1940s (courtesy Boston Public Library, Leslie Jones Collection).

wreck the team. The manpower demands of the Second World War send most of Boston's star players into military service through 1945, gutting the heart of the club. Despite financial difficulties on occasion, Boston advances to Cup finals in both 1943 and 1946, but they come up short both times. In 1945–46 Dit Clapper becomes a player-coach for Boston, replacing Art Ross. Clapper concludes his 20-season playing career in 1947 and has his #5 retired alongside Eddie Shore's #2 that same year.

Star Players: Bobby Bauer, Frank Brimsek, Dit Clapper, Bill Cowley, Don Gallinger, Flash Hollett, Art Jackson, Milt Schmidt

1950s

Boston advances to three Stanley Cup finals in the decade (1953, 1957, 1958) without winning any of them. The NHL's new territorial rules regarding teams' rights to amateur players works strongly for Montreal, Toronto and Detroit, but decidedly against Boston, New

York, and Chicago. The latter three teams struggle to remain competitive. Milt Schmidt becomes Boston's coach. The Bruins are ousted from the Cup playoffs by Montreal six times in seven springs, including four years in a row from 1952 through 1955. Boston's famed Uke Line, featuring Johnny Bucyk, Vic Stasiuk and Bronco Horvath, debuts in 1957. Coming to the Bruins in a trade which sent goalie Terry Sawchuk back to Detroit, Bucyk became a popular and enduring figure within the club. Over the years he has had three separate special nights to honor him: In 1968 when a back injury threatened to end his career; in 1980 when his #9 was retired by the club; and finally in 2007 to recognize his half-century of service to the Bruins.

Famous for being part of Boston's "Uke Line" with fellow Ukrainian-Canadians Johnny Bucyk and Vic Stasiuk, Bronco Horvath spent four productive seasons in Boston from 1957 to 1961. He came within one point of winning the NHL scoring title in 1959–60. Bronco was not a nickname; it really was Horvath's first name (Jaques, Louis/Library and Archives Canada/ e002343733).

Star Players: Johnny Bucyk, Réal Chevrefils, Dave Creighton, Bronco Horvath, Fleming Mackell, Don McKenney, Johnny Peirson, Bill Quackenbush, Milt Schmidt, Don Simmons, Vic Stasiuk, Jerry Toppazzini

1960s

The 1960s begin as the most dismal decade of Boston hockey but endless optimism abounds by its end. The outclassed Bruins embarrassingly fail to qualify for the playoffs in the six-team NHL for eight consecutive seasons (1959–60 through 1966–67) to set a league record for futility that has since been surpassed by several teams. (As of 2022, Buffalo presently holds the dubious record at 11 straight seasons without a postseason sniff.) Six of those eight times Boston finishes in last place. The debut of much-heralded 18-year-old rookie defenseman Bobby Orr in 1966 and a key trade with the Chicago Blackhawks the following summer (in which the club acquires Phil Esposito, Ken Hodge and Fred Stanfield) swiftly put the Bruins onto the path to dominance. Absolutely turning their fortunes around, the 1967–68 season—the beginning of the league's Expansion Era—marks the beginning of an NHL record 29 straight campaigns in which Boston gains a Stanley Cup playoff berth.

Star Players: Johnny Bucyk, Gerry Cheevers, Phil Esposito, Jean-Guy Gendron, Ken Hodge, Ed Johnston, John McKenzie, Murray Oliver, Bobby Orr, Dean Prentice, Derek Sanderson, Jerry Toppazzini, Ed Westfall

1970s

The 1970s showcase the Bruins as a perennial Stanley Cup threat. The club wins Lord Stanley's silver trophy twice (1969–70 and 1971–72) but, considering the team's depth, probably should have won as many as five over the course of the decade. Former child prodigy Bep Guidolin takes over the team's coaching duties partway through the 1972–73 season when Tom Johnson unexpectedly resigns. (Guidolin himself quits almost as suddenly in a contract dispute after Boston loses in the 1974 Stanley Cup finals to Philadelphia.) Over the course of the decade the Bruins slowly morph from a high-scoring outfit led by Bobby Orr, Phil Esposito and a superb cast of helpers to the beloved "lunch pail" squad coached by colorful Don Cherry that wins its games by combining

28. Brief History of Boston Bruins by Decade

talent with sheer grit and hard work. Bad knees force Orr's somewhat rancorous departure from the Bruins in 1976 and his eventual retirement from hockey at age 30. In 1975, Phil Esposito is sent to the New York Rangers in a swap that brings both Jean Ratelle and Brad Park to Boston. Another trade with the Rangers in 1976 brings youthful sniper Rick Middleton to the team in exchange for fading Ken Hodge. Johnny Bucyk retires with 545 regular-season goals as a Bruin—still the club record. Cherry's squad wins no Stanley Cups, but it but does capture four Adams Division titles in five years and thrice tests the dynastic Montreal Canadiens in the playoffs. Bobby Orr's uniform number is retired by the Bruins in a memorable ceremony on January 9, 1979. He receives a thunderous, 11-minute standing ovation from the Boston Garden faithful.

Star Players: Johnny Bucyk, Wayne Cashman, Gerry Cheevers, Phil Esposito, Ken Hodge, Don Marcotte, Peter McNab, Rick Middleton, Terry O'Reilly, Bobby Orr, Brad Park, Jean Ratelle, Gregg Sheppard

1980s

In 1980 Milt Schmidt's #15 jersey is retired by the Bruins. The 1980s Bruins continue routinely as a strong outfit, twice finishing with the best regular-season record of any NHL club. They are unable to hoist the Stanley Cup, however. Rick Middleton annually dazzles as an offensive threat and a superb penalty killer. Forward Cam Neely, acquired from Vancouver in a June 1986 trade for Barry Pederson, becomes a force both physically and on the scoresheet. Raymond Bourque steadily becomes the best defenseman in the NHL, continuing the long tradition of solid blueliners for Boston going back to the heyday of Eddie Shore. The Bruins' maddening bugaboo of being unable to oust Montreal in playoff competition finally ends in the 1988 Adams Division final with a four-games-to-one series triumph. Prior to that uncharacteristic Bruin triumph, Montreal had remarkably beaten Boston in 18 consecutive playoff series. That same season, Boston advances to their first Stanley Cup finals since 1977–78 where they lose to Edmonton in five games.

Star Players: Raymond Bourque, Randy Burridge, Bruce Crowder, Craig Janney, Ken Linseman, Peter McNab, Rick Middleton, Andy Moog, Cam Neely, Terry O'Reilly, Barry Pederson, Pete Peeters

1990s

The Bruins produce competitive teams in the first few seasons in the 1990s, advancing to the Stanley Cup finals in 1990 (losing to Edmonton in five games) and dropping playoff series to the emerging powerhouse Pittsburgh Penguins the following two seasons. An excellent 1992–93 campaign ends in an unexpected and disappointing playoff loss to Buffalo. This setback heralds a troublesome remainder of the decade which sees the team's long playoff-appearance streak of 29 consecutive seasons come to an end in 1996–97 when the Bruins finish 21 games under .500. Similar to Bobby Orr, injuries terminate Cam Neely's career well before it should have ended. Raymond Bourque surpasses the 1,000-point mark, becoming only the second Bruin to do so. (He ends up with 1,506 regular-season points in a Boston uniform, well ahead of second-place Johnny Bucyk's 1,339.) After 2,247 regular-season contests, Boston Garden hosts its last game on September 26, 1995. Billed as "The Last Hurrah," it is a special 50-minute exhibition—divided into two 25-minute halves—versus the Montreal Canadiens. The game is won by the Bruins, 3–0, but it is mostly remembered for its thoroughly classy and emotional closing ceremonies. To conclude the grand night of nostalgia, many Bruin alumni take one final, optional skate as "Auld Lang Syne" wafts through the old building. Fittingly, Bobby Orr is the last Bruin to exit the Garden's ice surface.

Star Players: Raymond Bourque, Anson Carter, Ted Donato, Steve Heinze, Stephen Leach, Glen Murray, Cam Neely, Adam Oates, Don Sweeney

2000s

The first ten years of the twenty-first-century comprise a hugely disappointing decade for Boston hockey followers. The Bruins are unusually absent from the postseason on four occasions and remarkably do not win a single Stanley Cup playoff series until the spring of 2009 when they oust Montreal in the opening round. Cynics might argue that the 2004–05 season is the team's best of the decade. (That is the year the NHL is wholly shut down due to a labor dispute. No league games are played that season and no Stanley Cup champion is crowned for the first time since 1919.) As the 2010s approach, however, there are signs of hope on the horizon for the beleaguered Bruins and their loyal supporters.

Star Players: Jason Allison, Patrice Bergeron, Zdeno Chara, Sergei Samsonov, Marc Savard, Joe Thornton

2010s

After a long 39-year drought, Boston wins its sixth Stanley Cup in 2010–11—one year after embarrassingly squandering a 3–0 advantage in a second-round playoff series versus Philadelphia. The Cup does not come easily, though. Three of the four playoff series Boston wins require dramatic seventh games to settle matters. The last one is played in Vancouver in the finals. It highlights the club's young stars as Patrice Bergeron and Brad Marchand combine to score all the goals in Boston's 4–0 victory over the Canucks. Goaltender Tim Thomas, a late bloomer, deservedly captures the Conn Smythe Trophy as the playoff MVP at age 37. Other years in this decade can be classified as could-have-beens and should-have-beens, particularly 2013 and 2019. The former sees the Bruins abruptly collapse in Game Six of the finals versus Chicago. The latter has the Bruins again advancing to the Stanley Cup finals and end their run by playing quite badly in a 4–1 Game Seven loss at home versus St. Louis. During the generally successful decade, Claude Julien surpasses Don Cherry as the winningest coach in Boston history.

Star Players: Patrice Bergeron, Zdeno Chara, David Krejci, Torey Krug, Milan Lucic, Brad Marchand, David Pastrnak, Tuukka Rask, Tim Thomas

2020s

The three members of the Bruins' Perfection Line (Patrice Bergeron, Brad Marchand and David Pasternak) continue to individually ascend the club's list in all-time scoring. The mercurial Marchand surpasses Rick Middleton to become the team's career leader in short-handed goals. Before abruptly retiring in 2022, Finnish-born Tuukka Rask overtakes Tiny Thompson to become Boston's winningest goaltender. Over 15 seasons, Rask records 308 wins for the Bruins.

Star Players: Patrice Bergeron, Brad Marchand, Charlie McAvoy, David Pastrnak

Chapter Notes

Chapter 1

1. "Senators Score Decisive Win," *Ottawa Citizen*, April 14, 1927, 10.
2. "Rangers Win Group Honors from Bruins," *Ottawa Citizen*, April 4, 1928, 11.
3. John J. Hallahan, "Bruins Defeat Rangers in Stanley Cup Game 2–0," *Boston Globe*, March 29, 1929, 30.
4. Ibid.
5. Ibid.
6. John J. Hallahan, "Bruins Clinch World Title," *Boston Globe*, March 30, 1929, 9.
7. Ibid.
8. John Devaney and Burt Goldblatt, *The Stanley Cup: A Complete Pictorial History* (Chicago: Rand McNally, 1975), 24.
9. John J. Hallahan, "Bruins Clinch World Title," *Boston Globe*, March 30, 1929, 9.
10. Ibid.
11. Ibid.
12. Ibid.
13. "Boston Conquers Rangers, 2–1, to Win Stanley Cup," *Montreal Gazette*, March 30, 1929, 18.
14. Matt Kalman, 100 Things Bruins Fans Should Know & Do Before They Die (Chicago: Triumph, 2011), 63.

Chapter 2

1. "Chicago Forfeits Game to Bruins," *Boston Globe*, March 15, 1933, 7.
2. Ibid.
3. "Gorman Withdraws Hawks in Overtime," *Ottawa Citizen*, March 15, 1933, 11.
4. "Chicago Forfeits Game to Bruins," *Boston Globe*, March 15, 1933, 7.
5. "Gorman Withdraws Hawks in Overtime," *Ottawa Citizen*, March 15, 1933, 11.
6. Ibid.
7. "Chicago Forfeits Game to Bruins," *Boston Globe*, March 15, 1933, 7.
8. Ibid.

Chapter 3

1. John Robertson, "The Eddie Shore-Ace Bailey Incident," *Kitchener-Waterloo Record*, December 15, 1994.
2. Joanne Madden, "Number 16: The Ace Bailey-Eddie Shore Incident," Joanne16.com, December 12, 2011.
3. John Robertson, "The Eddie Shore-Ace Bailey Incident," *Kitchener-Waterloo Record*, December 15, 1994.
4. Joanne Madden, "Number 16: The Ace Bailey-Eddie Shore Incident," Joanne16.com, December 12, 2011.
5. Ibid.
6. John Robertson, "The Eddie Shore-Ace Bailey Incident," *Kitchener-Waterloo Record*, December 15, 1994.
7. Melville E. Webb, Jr., "Hockey Stars Fight, Two Knocked Cold," *Boston Globe*, December 13, 1933, 1.
8. Victor O. Jones, "Ace Bailey Calls Flood City Hospital," *Boston Globe*, December 15, 1933, 1.
9. Ibid.
10. Brendan Kennedy, "Maple Leafs: Ace Bailey and the Birth of Leafs Nation," *Toronto Star*, December 11, 2013.
11. David Wencer, "Historicist: The Greatest Hockey Match Ever Staged," *Torontoist*, January 28, 2017.
12. Ibid.
13. John Robertson, "The Eddie Shore-Ace Bailey Incident," *Kitchener-Waterloo Record*, December 15, 1994.
14. Victor O. Jones, "Ace Bailey Calls

Flood City Hospital," *Boston Globe*, December 15, 1933, 15.

15. Stan Fischler, "First NHL All-Star Game in 1934 Played to Benefit Ace Bailey," NHL.com, February 2, 2022.

16. Joanne Madden, "Number 16: The Ace Bailey-Eddie Shore Incident," Joanne16.com, December 12, 2011.

17. David Wencer, "Historicist: The Greatest Hockey Match Ever Staged," *Torontoist*, January 28, 2017.

Chapter 4

1. Victor O. Jones, "Bruins Off to Three-Goal Lead," *Boston Globe*, March 25, 1936, 1.

2. *Ibid.*

3. D.A.L. MacDonald, "Sports on Parade," *Montreal Gazette*, March 25, 1936, 14.

4. Victor O. Jones, "Bruins Off to Three-Goal Lead," *Boston Globe*, March 25, 1936, 1.

5. Victor O. Jones, "Toronto Smothers Bruins By 8 to 3," *Boston Globe* (main edition), March 27, 1936, 29.

6. Brian McFarlane, *The Lively World of Hockey* (New York: Signet, 1968), 61.

7. Victor O. Jones, "Bruins Off to Three-Goal Lead," *Boston Globe*, March 25, 1936, 1.

8. Victor O. Jones, "Toronto Smothers Bruins By 8 to 3," *Boston Globe* (main edition), March 27, 1936, 29.

9. Victor O. Jones, "Incompetent Officiating Ruins the Bruins," *Boston Globe* (evening edition), March 27, 1936, 28.

10. *Ibid.*

11. *Ibid.*

12. *Ibid.*

13. "Leafs Oust Bruins with Surprise Win as Conacher Stars," *Montreal Gazette*, March 27, 1936, 14.

14. *Ibid.*

15. Victor O. Jones, "Incompetent Officiating Ruins the Bruins," *Boston Globe* (evening edition), March 27, 1936, 28.

Chapter 5

1. Stan Fischler, "Mel 'Sudden Death' Hill of Bruins Scored Three OT Goals in Series," NHL.com, May 31, 2017.

2. "Mel 'Sudden Death' Hill Boston Bruins 1941," Hockeygods.com.

3. Victor O. Jones, "All 3 Bruins Lines Share 4–1 Victory," *Boston Globe*, March 27, 1939, 4.

4. Victor O. Jones, "Cracked Ice," *Boston Globe*, April 3, 1939, 5.

5. *Ibid.*

6. *Ibid.*

7. *Ibid.*

8. *Ibid.*

9. Stan Fischler, "Mel 'Sudden Death' Hill of Bruins Scored Three OT Goals in Series," NHL.com, May 31, 2017.

10. "Mel 'Sudden Death' Hill Boston Bruins 1941," Hockeygods.com.

11. Victor O. Jones, "Bruins Take Playoff Final, 2–1," *Boston Globe*, April 3, 1939, 1.

12. *Ibid.*

13. *Ibid.*

14. *Ibid.*

15. Victor O. Jones, "Bruins Take Stanley Cup, Winning, 3–1." *Boston Globe*, April 17, 1939, 1.

Chapter 6

1. Cassidy Chisholm, "'Zombies' of WWII: Poem Reveals How Volunteer Soldier Felt About the Conscripted," CBCNews.ca, July 17, 2019.

2. Jerry Nason, "B's Trip Hawks, 6–4, as Cain Sets Record," *Boston Globe*, March 15, 1944, 15.

3. "Detroit Wins, 10–9, Eliminate Bruins," *Montreal Gazette*, March 17, 1944, 16.

4. "Bruins Crushed, 10–2, by Leafs in Curtain Tilt," *Boston Globe*, March 19, 1944, 20.

5. Dink Carroll, "Canadiens Win Cup Title Game, 5–4, Overtime," *Montreal Gazette*, April 14, 1944, 1.

Chapter 7

1. Roger Birtwell, "B's Rout Rangers, 14–3," *Boston Globe*, January 22, 1945, 4.

2. Brian McFarlane, *The Lively World of Hockey* (New York: Signet, 1968), 86.

3. "Bruins Play Rangers on Garden Ice," *Boston Globe*, January 21, 1945, 25.

4. Roger Birtwell, "B's Rout Rangers, 14–3," *Boston Globe*, January 22, 1945, 4.
5. *Ibid.*
6. *Ibid.*
7. "Canadiens Boost Lead by Two Wins," *Calgary Herald*, January 22, 1945, 11.
8. "Canadiens Widen Gap; Toe Blake Suspended," *Saskatoon Star-Phoenix*, January 22, 1945, 11.
9. Harold Kaese, "Stalingrad Stand by Bruins Makes Playoff Berth Seem Certain," *Boston Globe*, January 22, 1945, 6.
10. *Ibid.*
11. "Bruins Roll Up Huge Total Off NY Rangers," *Nashua Telegraph*, January 22, 1945, 9.

Chapter 8

1. "Gifts Worth $15,000 Given to Schmidt, Dumart," *Boston Globe*, March 19, 1952, 10.
2. Herb Ralby, "'Unforgettable!' Agree Kraut Mates—and It Was Mrs. Schmidt's Birthday!" *Boston Globe*, March 19, 1952, 16.
3. Matt Kalman, *100 Things Bruins Fans Should Know & Do Before They Die* (Chicago: Triumph, 2011), 166.
4. Herb Ralby, "Throng Expected Tonight at Kraut Line Reunion," *Boston Globe*, March 18, 1952, 30.
5. *Ibid.*
6. *Ibid.*
7. Tom Fitzgerald, "Boston Grabs Playoff Spot, Henry Gets 7th Shutout," *Boston Globe*, March 19, 1952, 10.
8. *Ibid.*
9. Herb Ralby, "'Unforgettable!' Agree Kraut Mates—and It Was Mrs. Schmidt's Birthday!" *Boston Globe*, March 19, 1952, 16.
10. Stan Fischler, "Bauer Made Splash in One-Night Comeback with the Bruins," NHL.com, August, 5, 2020.
11. Tom Fitzgerald, "Boston Grabs Playoff Spot, Henry Gets 7th Shutout," *Boston Globe*, March 19, 1952, 10.
12. "Milt Schmidt, 1918–2017," *Toronto Star*, January 4, 2017.

Chapter 9

1. Tom Fitzgerald, "Canadiens Score 2 in Third Period, Oust Bruins 3–1," *Boston Globe*, April 9, 1952, 11.
2. Tom Fitzgerald, "Bruins Beat Montreal, 3–2, to Even Cup Playoff Series," *Boston Globe*, April 2, 1952, 1.
3. Tom Fitzgerald, "Bruins Lose, 3–2, in Second Overtime," *Boston Globe*, April 7, 1952, 1.
4. Jennifer Conway, "Greatest Playoff Moments: Rocket's Most Heroic Goal," BleacherReport.com, May 1, 2008.
5. Kevin van Steendelaar, "Recalling the Rocket's Greatest Goal," Habseyeontheprize.com, April 8, 2012.
6. *Ibid.*
7. *Ibid.*
8. Stan Fischler, "From the Archives: Maurice Richard's Greatest Goal," Thehockeynews.com, January 12, 2022.
9. Kevin van Steendelaar, "Recalling the Rocket's Greatest Goal," Habseyeontheprize.com, April 8, 2012.
10. Stan Fischler, "From the Archives: Maurice Richard's Greatest Goal," Thehockeynews.com, January 12, 2022.
11. *Ibid.*
12. *Ibid.*
13. Leigh Montville, "No Gain, Just Pain," *Sports Illustrated*, April 25, 1988, 27.
14. Kevin van Steendelaar, "Recalling the Rocket's Greatest Goal," Habseyeontheprize.com, April 8, 2012.
15. Brian McFarlane, *The Lively World of Hockey* (New York: Signet, 1968), 111.

Chapter 10

1. "Grounded Plane Keeps Goalie Simmons in NHL," *Ottawa Citizen*, January 20, 1964, 11.
2. "Bruins Explode, Rip Leafs, 11–0," *Boston Globe*, January 19, 1964, 61–62.
3. "Grounded Plane Keeps Goalie Simmons in NHL," *Ottawa Citizen*, January 20, 1964, 11.
4. "Bruins Explode, Rip Leafs, 11–0," *Boston Globe*, January 19, 1964, 61–62.
5. "January 18, 1964: Boston 11 Toronto 0," *HF Boards*, June 17, 2011.
6. "Leafs Show to Extremes," *Calgary Herald*, January 20, 1964, 10.

Chapter 11

1. "Road Jinx No Worry to Bruins," *Montreal Gazette*, April 2, 1969, 8.
2. Dink Carroll, "Playing the Field," *Montreal Gazette*, April 2, 1969, 8.
3. "Bruins Belt Leafs Between Brawls," *Montreal Gazette*, April 3, 1969, 27.
4. Ray Fitzgerald, "Quinn Defends Check on Orr: 'It Was Clean,'" *Boston Globe*, April 3, 1969, 25.
5. "Bruins Belt Leafs Between Brawls," *Montreal Gazette*, April 3, 1969, 27.
6. "Pat Quinn Elbows Bobby Orr," YouTube, April 30, 2012.
7. "Bruins Belt Leafs Between Brawls," *Montreal Gazette*, April 3, 1969, 27.
8. Tom Fitzgerald, "Espo (4), Bruins Crush Toronto in Wild Opener, 10–0; Orr Hurt," *Boston Globe*, April 3, 1969, 49.
9. *Ibid.*
10. Francis Rosa, "Espo Puts an End to Rumors," *Boston Globe*, April 3, 1969, 50.
11. *Ibid.*
12. *Ibid.*
13. Tom Fitzgerald, "Espo (4), Bruins Crush Toronto in Wild Opener, 10–0; Orr Hurt," *Boston Globe*, April 3, 1969, 49.
14. "Punch Fired as Leafs Ousted," *Montreal Gazette*, April 7, 1969, 21.
15. Tom Fitzgerald, "Bruins in 3–2 Sweep, Toronto Fires Coach," *Boston Globe*, April 7, 1969, 1.

Chapter 12

1. Tom Fitzgerald, "Future Belongs to the Bruins," *Boston Globe* (main edition), April 27, 1969, 83.
2. Pat Curran, "Cheevers Seeks Revenge Against Habs," *Montreal Gazette*, April 10, 1969, 14.
3. *Ibid.*
4. *Ibid.*
5. John Ahern, "Bruins Didn't Play 60 Minutes, Moans Sinden," *Boston Globe* (evening edition), April 11, 1969, 25.
6. *Ibid.*
7. *Ibid.*
8. *Ibid.*
9. Tom Fitzgerald, "Bruins Fall 2-Down on 4–3 OT Loss," *Boston Globe* (main edition), April 14, 1969, 27.
10. *Ibid.*
11. *Ibid.*
12. Tom Fitzgerald, "Bruins Back Boasts, 5–0," *Boston Globe* (main edition), April 18, 1969, 47.
13. Tom Fitzgerald, "Orr's First Playoff Goal Clinches 3–2 Win Over Canadiens as Bruins Tie Series, at 2-All," *Boston Globe* (main edition), April 21, 1969, 19.
14. Bud Collins, "Bruins to Have a Tomorrow," *Boston Globe* (main edition), April 25, 1969, 45.
15. Tom Fitzgerald, "Bruins Thwarted After Quick Score by Murphy," *Boston Globe* (main edition), April 25, 1969, 45.
16. *Ibid.*
17. John Ahern, "They Were So Vigorous, Then Death Struck—Suddenly," *Boston Globe* (evening edition), April 25, 1969, 29.
18. *Ibid.*
19. *Ibid.*
20. *Ibid.*
21. *Ibid.*
22. *Ibid.*
23. *Ibid.*
24. Kevin Walsh, "Beliveau Had Cheevers at His Mercy," *Boston Globe* (main edition), April 25, 1969, 45.
25. *Ibid.*
26. John Ahern, "They Were So Vigorous, Then Death Struck—Suddenly," *Boston Globe* (evening edition), April 25, 1969, 29.
27. *Ibid.*
28. *Ibid.*
29. *Ibid.*
30. Pat Curran, "Béliveau Scores in Overtime," *Montreal Gazette*, April 25, 1969, 29.
31. Tom Fitzgerald, "Future Belongs to the Bruins," *Boston Globe* (main edition), April 27, 1969, 83.

Chapter 13

1. Johnny Bucyk, *Hockey in My Blood* (Richmond Hill, ON: Scholastic-TAB Publications Limited, 1972), 72.
2. John Ahern, "There's a 3-Letter Word for It ... Orr!" *Boston Globe*, April 17, 1970, 27.
3. *Ibid.*
4. *Ibid.*
5. Gary Ronberg, "Tea Party for

Bobby's Bruins," *Sports Illustrated* online archives, May 4, 1970.
  6. Pat Curran, "McKenzie Scores on Order," *Montreal Gazette*, April 27, 1970, 17.
  7. *Ibid.*
  8. Tom Fitzgerald, "'Other Guy Fantastic'—Cheevers," *Boston Globe*, April 27, 1970, 22.
  9. *Ibid.*
  10. Pat Curran, "McKenzie Scores on Order," *Montreal Gazette*, April 27, 1970, 17.
  11. Tom Fitzgerald, "'Other Guy Fantastic'—Cheevers," *Boston Globe*, April 27, 1970, 22.
  12. Pat Curran, "McKenzie Scores on Order," *Montreal Gazette*, April 27, 1970, 17.

Chapter 14

  1. "Bruins Romp—Espo Ties Record," *Boston Globe*, March 11, 1971, 29.
  2. *Ibid.*
  3. John Robertson, "Espo Set New Scoring Standard in '71," *Kitchener-Waterloo Record*, November 28, 1998.
  4. "Espo's 59th, 60th shatter record in 7–2 win," *Boston Globe*, March 12, 1971, 29.
  5. John Robertson, "Espo Set New Scoring Standard in '71," *Kitchener-Waterloo Record*, November 28, 1998.
  6. *Ibid.*
  7. *Ibid.*
  8. *Ibid.*
  9. Francis Rosa, "Standing Ovation Embarrasses Esposito," *Boston Globe*, April 5, 1971, 19.
  10. *Ibid.*
  11. *Ibid.*
  12. *Ibid.*
  13. *Ibid.*
  14. *Ibid.*

Chapter 15

  1. Ray Fitzgerald, "For Rick, Reggie, an Unkind Cut," *Boston Globe*, February 24, 1972, 29.
  2. Francis Rosa, "Seals Do Quick Fade, Bruins Decide to Play," *Boston Globe*, February 24, 1972, 29.
  3. *Ibid.*
  4. *Ibid.*
  5. *Ibid.*
  6. *Ibid.*
  7. Kevin Walsh, "Bruins Get Seal All-Star Vadnais," *Boston Globe*, February 24, 1972, 51.
  8. Harold Kaese, "Guys Prefer Carol While Girls Hate to See Rick Go," *Boston Globe*, February 24, 1972, 51.

Chapter 16

  1. Ted Blackman, "Francis Defied 'Hot Hand' on a Day Orr Wasn't Ablaze," *Montreal Gazette*, May 1, 1972, 13.
  2. Tim Burke, "Rangers Down One, But They're Happy," *Montreal Gazette*, May 1, 1972, 13.
  3. *Ibid.*
  4. Ted Blackman, "Francis defied 'Hot Hand' on a Day Orr Wasn't Ablaze," *Montreal Gazette*, May 1, 1972, 13.
  5. Tim Burke, "Rangers Down One, But They're Happy," *Montreal Gazette*, May 1, 1972, 13.
  6. Harold Kaese, "Sagging Bruins Needed Hero—Bailey Obliged," *Boston Globe*, May 1, 1972, 1.
  7. *Ibid.*
  8. Tim Burke, "Rangers Down One, But They're Happy," *Montreal Gazette*, May 1, 1972, 13.
  9. *Ibid.*
  10. Ted Blackman, "Francis defied 'Hot Hand' on a Day Orr Wasn't Ablaze," *Montreal Gazette*, May 1, 1972, 13.
  11. Tim Burke, "Rangers Down One, But They're Happy," *Montreal Gazette*, May 1, 1972, 13.
  12. *Ibid.*
  13. *Ibid.*
  14. Ted Blackman, "Francis defied 'Hot Hand' on a Day Orr Wasn't Ablaze," *Montreal Gazette*, May 1, 1972, 13.
  15. *Ibid.*
  16. Tim Burke, "Rangers Down One, But They're Happy," *Montreal Gazette*, May 1, 1972, 13.

Chapter 17

  1. John Powers, "Oddleifson Gets Four Goals in a Row, So Guidolin Experiment

Looks Good," *Boston Globe*, December 31, 1973, 15.
  2. *Ibid.*
  3. *Ibid.*
  4. *Ibid.*
  5. "Reshuffled Bruins Erupt 8–1; Oddleifson Scores Four Goals," *Boston Globe*, December 31, 1973, 17.
  6. John Powers, "Oddleifson Gets Four Goals in a Row, So Guidolin experiment looks good," *Boston Globe*, December 31, 1973, 15.
  7. "Reshuffled Bruins Erupt 8–1; Oddleifson Scores Four Goals," *Boston Globe*, December 31, 1973, 17.
  8. *Ibid.*
  9. Tom Fitzgerald, "Sinden Gets His Man: Enter Bob Schmautz," *Boston Globe*, February 8, 1974, 25.
  10. "Chris Oddleifson," CanucksLegends.Blogspot.com, March 2007.

Chapter 18

  1. Ray Fitzgerald, "First Rumor was in 1917," *Boston Globe*, May 27, 1976, 81.
  2. Tom Fitzgerald, "'Terrific,' says Hodge, Sent to Rangers for Middleton," *Boston Globe*, May 27, 1976, 81.
  3. *Ibid.*
  4. *Ibid.*
  5. *Ibid.*
  6. *Ibid.*
  7. Francis Rosa, "Middleton's Three Get Bruins Going, 6–2," *Boston Globe*, October 8, 1976, 35.
  8. *Ibid.*
  9. *Ibid.*
  10. *Ibid.*
  11. *Ibid.*
  12. *Ibid.*
  13. Tom Fitzgerald, "Bruins, Fans Slow to Warm Up," *Boston Globe*, October 8, 1976, 38.
  14. *Ibid.*
  15. George Grimm, "Retro Rangers: The Worst Trade in Ranger History," Insidehockey.com, November 13, 2018.
  16. Ibid.

Chapter 19

  1. Emily Sweeney, "Remembering the Craziest Boston Bruins Fight Ever: When Mike Milbury Hit a Fan with His Own Shoe," BostonGlobe.com, December 22, 2021.
  2. Francis Rosa, "Bruins Take 4–3 Win, Then Take on Fans," *Boston Globe*, December 24, 1979, 21.
  3. *Ibid.*
  4. "This Day in Hockey History—December 23, 1979—Bruins, Rangers, Stick and Shoe," ThePinkPuck.com, December 23, 2018.
  5. *Ibid.*
  6. *Ibid.*
  7. *Ibid.*
  8. Dave Seminara, "Over the Glass and into Hockey Lore," NewYorkTimes.com, December 23, 2009.
  9. "This Day in Hockey History—December 23, 1979—Bruins, Rangers, Stick and Shoe," ThePinkPuck.com, December 23, 2018.
  10. Francis Rosa, "Bruins take 4–3 Win, Then Take on Fans," *Boston Globe*, December 24, 1979, 23.
  11. Dave Seminara, "Over the Glass and into Hockey Lore," NewYorkTimes.com, December 23, 2009.
  12. *Ibid.*
  13. Emily Sweeney, "Remembering the Craziest Boston Bruins Fight Ever: When Mike Milbury Hit a Fan with His Own Shoe," BostonGlobe.com, December 22, 2021.
  14. *Ibid.*
  15. Dave Seminara, "Over the Glass and into Hockey Lore," NewYorkTimes.com, December 23, 2009.
  16. "This Day in Hockey History—December 23, 1979—Bruins, Rangers, Stick and Shoe," ThePinkPuck.com, December 23, 2018.
  17. *Ibid.*
  18. Ibid.

Chapter 20

  1. Jerry Kirshenbaum (editor), "Scorecard," *Sports Illustrated*, November 17, 1980, 26.
  2. Ryan Kennedy, "The Biggest: Bench Brawl," Thehockeynews.com, November 3, 2013.
  3. *Ibid.*
  4. *Ibid.*
  5. *Ibid.*

6. Jeff Day, "40 Years Ago Today, the Meek, Mild Minnesota North Stars Started the Greatest Brawl in NHL History," StarTribune.com, February 26, 2021.
7. Francis Rosa, "Bruins Win a Record War, 5–1," *Boston Globe*, February 27, 1981, 23.
8. *Ibid.*
9. Francis Rosa, "Bruins win a Record War, 5–1," *Boston Globe*, February 27, 1981, 23.
10. Ryan Kennedy, "The Biggest: Bench Brawl," TheHockeyNews.com, November 3, 2013.
11. Francis Rosa, "Bruins Win a Record War, 5–1," *Boston Globe*, February 27, 1981, 23.
12. Jeff Day, "40 Years Ago Today, the Meek, Mild Minnesota North Stars Started the Greatest Brawl in NHL History," StarTribune.com, February 26, 2021.

Chapter 21

1. Larry Brooks, "'Have Another Donut' Clash Still Lives in Infamy 30 Years Later," Nypost.com, May 8, 2018.
2. John Robertson, "Doughnut-Gate," *Kitchener-Waterloo Record*, May 8, 1997.
3. *Ibid.*
4. Kevin Paul Dupont, "Crew from NHL Refuses to Work," *Boston Globe*, March 9, 1988, 45.
5. *Ibid.*
6. *Ibid.*
7. John Robertson, "Doughnut-Gate," *Kitchener-Waterloo Record*, May 8, 1997.
8. *Ibid.*
9. *Ibid.*
10. Francis Rosa, "Devils win 3–1; Tie Series," *Boston Globe*, May 9, 1988, 45.
11. John Robertson, "Doughnut-Gate," *Kitchener-Waterloo Record*, May 8, 1997.
12. Michael Madden, "Some Puckish Humor," *Boston Globe*, May 9, 1988, 45.
13. John Robertson, "Doughnut-Gate," *Kitchener-Waterloo Record*, May 8, 1997.
14. *Ibid.*
15. *Ibid.*

Chapter 22

1. Francis Rosa, "Bruins' Opening a Smash, 2–1," *Boston Globe*, October 7, 1988, 109.
2. Francis Rosa, "Gretzky, Kings Blast Bruins," *Boston Globe*, October 13, 1988, 41.
3. Francis Rosa, "Erratic Bruins Fall, 5–1," *Boston Globe*, October 16, 1988, 57.
4. *Ibid.*
5. Francis Rosa, "Neely, Bruins Trample Black Hawks, 10–3," *Boston Globe*, October 17, 1988, 43.
6. *Ibid.*
7. *Ibid.*
8. *Ibid.*
9. *Ibid.*
10. *Ibid.*

Chapter 23

1. "Hockey: Stanley Cup Playoffs," *Pittsburgh Press*, April 6, 1990, C2.
2. Kevin Paul Dupont, "Whalers Get the Jump on Bruins," *Boston Globe*, April 6, 1990, 25.
3. Kevin Paul Dupont, "Bruins Power past Whalers," *Boston Globe*, April 8, 1990, 41.
4. Dave Molinari, "Orr Gives Whalers Lift Against Bruins," *Pittsburgh Press*, April 10, 1990, C3.
5. Kevin Paul Dupont, "Bruins Battered by Whalers," *Boston Globe*, April 10, 1990, 25.
6. Fred Cusick, NESN broadcast of Boston-Hartford NHL game, April 11, 1990.
7. Derek Sanderson, NESN broadcast of Boston-Hartford NHL game, April 11, 1990.
8. Fred Cusick, NESN broadcast of Boston-Hartford NHL game, April 11, 1990.
9. Derek Sanderson, NESN broadcast of Boston-Hartford NHL game, April 11, 1990.
10. *Ibid.*
11. Kevin Paul Dupont, "Bruins Turn Flop into Hit Revival," *Boston Globe*, April 12, 1990, 49.
12. Tom Larson, NESN broadcast of Boston-Hartford NHL game, April 11, 1990.
13. Kevin Paul Dupont, "Bruins Turn Flop into Hit Revival," *Boston Globe*, April 12, 1990, 49.
14. Nancy L. Marrapese, "Hartford is

Left at a Loss," *Boston Globe*, April 12, 1990, 49.
15. *Ibid.*
16. *Ibid.*
17. *Ibid.*
18. Kevin Paul Dupont, "Bruins Turn Flop into Hit Revival," *Boston Globe*, April 12, 1990, 49.

Chapter 24

1. Jack Edwards, NESN broadcast of Carolina-Boston NHL game, April 10, 2010.
2. Fluto Shinzawa, "Shortcut to Playoffs for Bruins," *Boston Globe*, April 11, 2010, D1.
3. *Ibid.*
4. *Ibid.*
5. *Ibid.*
6. Jack Edwards, NESN broadcast of Carolina-Boston NHL game, April 10, 2010.
7. Fluto Shinzawa, "Shortcut to Playoffs for Bruins," *Boston Globe*, April 11, 2010, D1.
8. Kevin Paul Dupont, "They Must Do Even More with Less," *Boston Globe*, April 11, 2010, D7.
9. *Ibid.*
10. Fluto Shinzawa, "Shortcut to Playoffs for Bruins," *Boston Globe*, April 11, 2010, D1.
11. *Ibid.*
12. *Ibid.*
13. Kevin Paul Dupont, "They Must Do Even More with Less," *Boston Globe*, April 11, 2010, D7.
14. *Ibid.*
15. Ibid.

Chapter 25

1. Dan Shaughnessy, "It Was Their Miracle on Ice," *Boston Globe*, May 14, 2013, C1.
2. *Ibid.*
3. Fluto Shinzawa, "Bergeron's Goal in OT Caps Boston Comeback for the Ages," *Boston Globe*, May 14, 2013, C1.
4. Joe Bowen, Toronto Maple Leafs Radio Network broadcast, May 13, 2013.
5. Jack Edwards, NESN broadcast of Toronto-Boston NHL playoff game, May 13, 2013.
6. "Leafs Eliminated from Playoffs in Stunning OT loss," NHL.com, May 13, 2013.
7. Dan Shaughnessy, "It Was Their Miracle on Ice," *Boston Globe*, May 14, 2013, C1.
8. Fluto Shinzawa, "Bergeron's Goal in OT Caps Boston Comeback for the Ages," *Boston Globe*, May 14, 2013, C1.
9. *Ibid.*
10. Andy Brickley, NESN broadcast of Toronto-Boston NHL playoff game, May 13, 2013.
11. "Leafs Eliminated from Playoffs in Stunning OT Loss," NHL.com, May 13, 2013.
12. Fluto Shinzawa, "Bergeron's Goal in OT Caps Boston Comeback for the Ages," *Boston Globe*, May 14, 2013, C1.
13. Jack Edwards, NESN broadcast of Toronto-Boston NHL playoff game, May 13, 2013.
14. Dan Shaughnessy, "It Was Their Miracle on Ice," *Boston Globe*, May 14, 2013, C1.
15. "Leafs Eliminated from Playoffs in Stunning OT loss," NHL.com, May 13, 2013.
16. Fluto Shinzawa, "Bergeron's Goal in OT Caps Boston Comeback for the Ages," *Boston Globe*, May 14, 2013, C1.
17. Dan Shaughnessy, "It Was Their Miracle on Ice," *Boston Globe*, May 14, 2013, C1.
18. Jack Edwards, NESN broadcast of Toronto-Boston NHL playoff game, May 13, 2013.
19. Kevin Paul Dupont, "Bruins Turn Flop into hit Revival," *Boston Globe*, April 12, 1990, 49.
20. Dan Shaughnessy, "It Was Their Miracle on Ice," *Boston Globe*, May 14, 2013, C1.
21. Fluto Shinzawa, "Bergeron's Goal in OT Caps Boston Comeback for the Ages," *Boston Globe*, May 14, 2013, C1.

Chapter 26

1. "Wild Scenes When Ottawa Trounced Boston Bruins, 3–1," *Montreal Gazette*, April 14, 1927, 16.
2. Victor O. Jones, "Referee Who

Doesn't Know Rules Robbed Bruins," *Boston Globe*, April 4, 1933, 21.
3. Victor O. Jones, "What About It?" *Boston Globe*, November 28, 1938, 10.
4. "Bruins Trounce Canadiens, 3–0," *Boston Globe*, January 19, 1958, 57.
5. Luke Fox, "The Remarkable Secret of Willie O'Ree," Sportnet.ca, February 29, 2012.
6. Kevin Paul Dupont, "Tugnutt Stops 70; Bruins Tie," *Boston Globe*, March 22, 1991, 29.
7. Kevin Paul Dupont, "Bruins Smack Whalers," *Boston Globe*, April 1, 1991, 25.
8. "Knuble Sets Record for Fastest Two Goals to Start Game," ESPN.com, February 15, 2003.
9. Nancy Marrapese-Burrell, "Rolston Key in Florida," *Boston Globe*, February 15, 2003, D1.

Chapter 27

1. John J. Hallahan, "Bruins Apparently Still in Quest of Goal-Scoring Punch," *Boston Globe*, December 26, 1928, 27.
2. *Ibid.*
3. Tom Fitzgerald, "Good Grief! Islanders 9, Bruins 7," *Boston Globe*, January 19, 1973, 29.
4. Tom Fitzgerald, "How Sweet it Was for Capt. Westfall," *Boston Globe*, January 19, 1973, 30.
5. Francis Rosa, "Clarke Fires, Bruins Die Sudden-ly, 3–2," *Boston Globe*, May 10, 1974, 49.
6. *Ibid.*
7. John Ahern, "Esposito Redeems the Black Hawks' Year," *Boston Globe*, April 12, 1975, 20.
8. Francis Rosa, "Sittler's Record 10-Point Explosion Buries Bruins," *Boston Globe*, February 8, 1976,
9. *Ibid.*
10. Leigh Montville, "Bad Goals, Grand Year," *Boston Globe*, May 8, 1983, 39.

11. Francis Rosa, "Bossy, Islanders Deliver Four-Gone Conclusion, 8–4," *Boston Globe*, May 8, 1983, 39.
12. Kevin Paul Dupont, "Buffalo Humbles Bruins, 6–0," *Boston Globe*, April 6, 1989, 49.
13. *Ibid.*
14. "Stars Score 3 in Final Seconds," WashingtonPost.com, October 15, 1995.
15. *Ibid.*
16. Nancy L. Marrapese, "Loss Cuts to the Quick," *Boston Globe*, October 16, 1995, 42.
17. Kevin Paul Dupont, "Infamy Revisited One Too Many Times," *Boston Globe*, May 15, 2010, C6.
18. WGN Radio coverage of Game Six of the 2013 Stanley Cup finals, June 24, 2013.
19. Dan Shaughnessy, "Visitors' Sudden Burst Ends a Magical Two-Month run," *Boston Globe*, June 25, 2013, A1.
20. Kevin Paul Dupont, "Passivity Led to Unrest," *Boston Globe*, June 25, 2013, D6.
21. Nancy Marrapese-Burrell, "Bolland Ends It on a High Note," *Boston Globe*, June 25, 2013, D2.
22. Kevin Paul Dupont, "Passivity Led to Unrest," *Boston Globe*, June 25, 2013, D6.
23. Fluto Shinzawa, "Must-Win Finale a Dud; Season Over," *Boston Globe*, April 10, 2016, C1.
24. Dan Shaughnessy, "Collapse Complete," *Boston Globe*, April 10, 2016, C1.
25. Dan Shaughnessy, "No Third Title for City, as Bruins Fall Flat in Game 7," *Boston Globe*, June 13, 2019, 1.
26. *Ibid.*

Chapter 28

1. Matt Kalman, *100 Things Bruins Fans Should Know & Do Before They Die* (Chicago: Triumph, 2011), ix.

Bibliography

Books

Brunt, Stephen. *Searching for Bobby Orr.* Toronto: Knopf Canada, 2006.

Bucyk, Johnny. *Hockey in My Blood.* Richmond Hill, ON: Scholastic-TAB, 1972.

Devaney, John, and Burt Goldblatt. *The Stanley Cup: A Complete Pictorial History.* Chicago: Rand McNally, 1975.

Diamond, Dan. *The Ultimate Prize: The Stanley Cup.* Kansas City: Andrews McMeel, 2003.

Esposito, Phil, and Peter Golenbock. *Phil Esposito: Thunder and Lightning.* New York: Triumph, 2003.

Kalman, Matt. *100 Things Bruins Fans Should Know & Do Before They Die.* Chicago: Triumph, 2011.

Keene, Kerry. *Tales from the Boston Bruins Locker Room.* New York: Sports Publishing, 2011.

McFarlane, Brian. *The Lively World of Hockey.* New York: Signet, 1968.

Orr, Bobby. *Bobby: My Story in Pictures.* New York: Viking, 2018.

Zweig, Eric. *Stanley Cup: The Complete History.* Richmond Hill, ON: Firefly, 2018.

Newspaper Archives

Boston Globe
Boston Post
Calgary Herald
Edmonton Journal
Kitchener-Waterloo Record
Minneapolis Star Tribune
Montreal Gazette
Montreal Star
New York Daily News
New York Post
New York Times
Oakland Tribune
Ottawa Citizen
Ottawa Journal
Pittsburgh Post-Gazette
Pittsburgh Press
Regina Leader-Post
Toronto Empire & Mail
Toronto Globe
Toronto Star
Toronto Sun
Washington Post

Online Resources

BleacherReport.com
CanucksLegends.Blogspot.com
CBCnews.ca
Encyclopedia.com
Habseyeontheprize.com
Hockeydb.com
Hockeygods.com
Hockey-reference.com
Icehockey.fandom.com
Insidehockey.com
NHL.com
SI.com
StadiumTalk.com
TheHockeyNews.com
ThePinkPuck.com
Youtube.com

Index

Abel, Sid 78, 108
Abel, Taffy 9
Adams, Charles 5–6, 214
Adams, John 206
Adams, Weston 90
Adams, Weston, Jr. 58, 90, 105
Ahern, John 99, 103, 105
Allison, Jason 223
Armstrong, Bob 76
Armstrong, George 84
Arniel, Scott 209
Ashley, John 91
"Auld Lang Syne" (song) 222
Awrey, Don 102, 129, 130

Babych, Dave 177
Backstrom, Ralph 99, 100
Bailey, (Ace) Garnet 131–132
Bailey, (Ace) Irvine 19–27, 131
Bailey, Joanne 22
Baillie, Harold 25
Bak, Richard 56
Baltimore Clippers (hockey club) 86
Barry, Marty 15
Bartkowski, Matt 192
Bauer, Bobby 42, 63–68, 201, 218
Beers, Bob 179, 180, 181
Begin, Steve 184, 187, 188
Béliveau, Jean 99, 102, 103, 105
Bell, Billy 31, 32, 198
Berra, Yogi 197
Bibeault, Paul 59, 61
Bickell, Bryan 211
Binnington, Jordan 213
Birtwell, Roger 55, 58, 59
Blackman, Ted 129, 130, 132, 133
Blake, Toe 53, 76
Boivin, Leo 84
Boldirev, Ivan 136, 207
Boll, Buzz 22, 34
Bolland, Dave 211, 212
Bonvie, Dennis 82
Bossy, Mike 209
Boston Celtics (NBA team) 163
Bouchard, Butch 76

Boucher, Frank 56, 57, 60, 61
Bouwmeester, Jay 213
Boychuk, Johnny 212
Brickley, Andy 194
Brière, Michel 113
Brooks, Ross 139
Broseker, Gord 157, 158, 159, 161, 166
Brown, Doug 165
Bruneteau, Mud 51
Burke, Tim 129
Burman, Emmanuel 43
Burridge, Randy 181, 182, 221
Byers, Mike 118

Cain, Herb 51
Calder, Frank 14, 16, 21, 22–23
Campbell, Bryan 112
Campbell, Clarence 17, 63, 133, 169
Carbonneau, Guy 210
Carleton, Wayne 124
Carlson, Jack 157, 158
Carpenter, Bobby 177–178
Carr, Gene 129
Carrier, Roch 75
Carroll, Dink 54
Carson, Bill 10, 12
Carson, Brett 187
Carter, Anson 222
Chapman, Art 16
Chamberlain, Murph 65–66
Champoux, Bob 137, 139
Chaplin, Charlie 202
Chara, Zdeno 186, 192, 194, 223
Chevrefils, Réal 68, 72, 220
Christian, Dave 179, 181
Christoff, Steve 158, 160, 161
Ciccarelli, Dino 160
Cimetta, Rob 209
Clancy, King 19, 22, 33, 34
Clarke, Bobby 207
Cleghorn, Odie 19, 20, 23, 31–32, 33–34, 35, 36, 199
Cloutier, Jacques 210
Cole, Eric 188
Collins, Bud 102

Collins, Kevin 157, 158
Colville, Neil 42
Conacher, Charlie 31, 33, 34
Conacher, Roy 43, 44, 217
Corriveau, Yvon 179
Courteau, Maurice 51, 52
Coutu, Billy 198–199
Crawford, Corey 211
Crawford, Jack 43, 51, 58
Creighton, Dave 67, 74, 220
Creighton, Fred 148, 149, 151
Croteau, Gary 123, 124
Crowder, Bruce 221
Crowder, Keith 157, 158, 173
Cupolo, Bill 58
Curran, Pat 98, 99, 105, 113
Cusick, Fred 179

Daigneault, Eusebe 19, 199
Davidson, John 149, 150
Day, Hap 22
DeJordy, Denis 118
Delvecchio, Alex 78, 108
DeMarco, Ab 60
DeMerchant, Gerald 49
Denver Invaders (hockey club) 85
Dineen, Kevin 177, 178, 179
Dion, Connie 51
Domi, Tie 71
Donato, Ted 222
"Don't Stop Believin'" (song) 195
Doraty, Ken 18, 191, 199
Dornhoefer, Gary 82, 84
Dryden, Ken 202
Dubois, Hector 75
Duguid, Lorne 30, 35
Dunnell, Milt 25
Dupont, André 207
Dwyer, Patrick 188

Eagles, Mike 173
Edestrand, Darryl 137
Edmonton Eskimos (hockey club) 7
Edwards, Jack 184, 187, 192–93, 195, 196
Egan, Pat 52
Ellis, Ron 24–25
Evason, Dean 178, 179

Feller, Bob 17
Ferguson, John 98, 99, 101, 102, 142, 146
Fischler, Stan 38, 43–44, 68, 77
Fitzgerald, Ray 90, 121–122, 142
Fogolin, Lee 67
Foligno, Mike 209, 210
Foster, Dwight 160
Francis, Emile 109, 130, 132
Francis, Ron 177, 182
Franson, Cody 192
Fraser, Kerry 167, 179, 180, 181
Frattin, Matt 193–194
Friday, Bill 111, 130

Gadsby, Bill 108
Gagne, Simon 211
Gainor, Dutch 9, 28, 206, 215
Galley, Garry 170, 177
Gallinger, Don 201, 218
Gamble, Bruce 92, 93
Gardiner, Bert 39, 44
Gardiner, Charlie 15–16, 205
Gendron, Jean-Guy 84, 220
Getliffe, Ray 42
Giacomin, Ed 109, 129–130, 131, 132
Gilbert, Gilles 207, 208
Gilbert, Rod 129, 130
Gilhooley, Walter 24
Gillis, Mike 158
Glover, Fred 138
Godleski, Vin 167
Gorman, Tommy 14, 15, 16
Gottselig, Johnny 15
Grant, Benny 53
Gravel, George 72
Green, Ted 84, 99, 118
Green Bay Packers (NFL football club) 104
Greschner, Ron 150
Gretzky, Wayne 119, 169, 170, 171, 183, 185
Grimm, George 146
Grosso, Don 51
Grzelcyk, Matt 216
Gustavsson, Jonas 212

Hadfield, Vic 130, 132
Hall, Bob 173
Hamilton, Dougie 190, 192
Harris, Billy 206
Hartsburg, Craig 158
Harvey, Doug 26, 74
Hatcher, Kevin 210
Head, Bill 75
Hebenton, Andy 82, 83, 84
Hedberg, Anders 149
Heinze, Steve 222
Hershey Bears (hockey club) 114
Hewitt, Foster 19
Hextall, Bryan 56
Hill, Mel 38–47
Hitchman, Lionel 28, 215
Hogue, Benoit 209
Hollett, Flash 217, 218
Hood, Bruce 207
Horner, Red, 19, 20, 21, 23, 27, 32, 33–34, 35
Horton, Nathan 193
Horton, Tim 84
Horvath, Bronco 201, 219, 220
Houda, Doug 203
Howe, Gordie 78, 108, 109, 129
Howe, Syd 51
Hudson, Mike 173
Hull, Bobby 85, 108, 109, 116, 117, 118

Index

Hull, Dennis 111
Hunt, Jim 169
Hunwick, Matt 185, 186, 187, 188, 189

"I'm Shipping Up to Boston" (song) 195
Imlach, Punch 82–83, 94
Irvin, Dick 19, 32, 73, 76, 205–206
Irvine, Ted 131

Jackson, Art 30–31, 218
Jackson, Busher 52
Janney, Craig 221
Jennings, Bill 51
Johnson, Tom 122, 124, 125, 201, 206, 220
Jonathan, Stan 149, 150, 151, 152, 157
Joyce, Bob 171, 173
Julien, Claude 188, 194, 211, 223

Kadri, Nazem 192
Kaese, Harold 59, 60, 125, 131
Kaptain, Catherine 153
Kaptain, John 148, 150, 151, 152, 153, 154
Kaptain, Manny 154
Kasper, Steve 157, 159, 160, 174, 210
Keans, Doug 202
Keeling, Butch 9–10
Keenan, Mike 172, 173
Kennedy, Forbes 91, 92
Kenworthy, Leonard 20
Keon, Dave 84
Kerr, Davey 39
Kessel, Phil 192
Kilrea, Hec 21
Knuble, Mike 203–204
Koharski, Don 165–166
Koroll, Cliff 112
Krejci, David 187, 192, 193, 223
Krug, Torey 223
Kryzanowski, Ed 67, 68
Kurtenbach, Orland 83
Kurvers, Tom 167

Labine, Leo 75, 78
Lach, Elmer 76
Laflamme, Dr. Jerry 198–199
Lalonde, Bobby 140, 160–161
Lamoriello, Lou 166
Laperrière Jacques 101
Larmer, Steve 172
Larson, Tom 182
Laycoe, Hal 75, 76, 77–78
Leach, Reggie 121–122
Leach, Steven 222
Leary, Denis 153
Leduc, Albert 65
LeDuc, Rich 136
Lee, Chris 187, 188
Leiter, Bobby 83
Lewis, Bryan 167
Ley, Rick 182
Linseman, Ken 172, 181, 221

Liscombe, Carl 51, 52
"Livin' on a Prayer" (song) 194–195
LoPresti, Pete 144, 145
Lucic, Milan 185, 189, 193, 194, 197, 223
Lumley, Dave 204
Lumley, Harry 56, 67, 201
Luongo, Roberto 204

MacDonald, D.A.L. 31
MacDonald, Kilby 68
MacGregor, Bruce 131
Mackell, Fleming 72, 91, 220
MacKenzie, Bill 15
MacLeish, Rick 207
MacTavish, Craig 25, 149
Madden, J.F. 166
Madden, Michael 168
Madill, Gregg 149, 152
Magnuson, Keith 111
Mahovlich, Frank 108
Maley, David 167
Maloney, Dave 152
Maloney, Don 149
Maluta, Ray 144
Marchand, Brad 46–47, 161, 193, 213, 223
Mario, Frank 58
Marks, John 207–208
Marois, Mario 149
Marotte, Gilles 115
Marrapese-Burrell, Nancy 204
Marsh, Lou 19, 22
Martin, Pit 115
Masi, Phil 17
Masnick, Paul 74
Masterton, Bill 25
Maurice, Paul 187
Maxwell, Brad 159
Mazur, Eddie 74
McAuley, Ken 56, 58, 59
McAvoy, Charlie 223
McCauley, John 166–167
McCrimmon, Brad 158
McDonald, Bucko 60–61
McFarlane, Brian 33–34
McHale, Kevin 163
McInnis, Paul 167–168
McIntyre, Jack 73
McKechnie, Walt 137, 139
McKenney, Don 91, 220
McKenzie, Jim 203
McKenzie, Johnny
McKinnon, Alex 206
McNab, Peter 151, 152, 153, 221
Meloche, Gilles 123, 125, 158–159
Messier, Mark 204
Mikita, Stan 112
Millar, Al 85
Modano, Mike 210
Montville, Leigh 209
Mooney, J.W. 19
Mooney, Paul 154

Morenz, Howie 5
Morgan, Joe 174
Morrison, Doug 202
Muller, Kirk 165
Munro, Donald 22
Murdoch, Don 149
Murphy, Austin 167–168
Murphy, Ron 101, 104

Nanton Palominos (hockey club) 114
Nason, Jerry 51
Neilson, Jim 129, 131
Neufeld, Ray 209
New York Yankees (baseball club) 104
Newell, Dave 158, 159, 160, 166
Nilan, Chris 202–203
Nilsson, Ulf 149, 150
Norris, Jack 118

Oates, Adam 222
O'Connell, Mike 159, 160, 161, 162
Oddleifson, Chris 136–140
O'Donnell, Fred 139
O'Donoghue, Don 122
Oliver, Harry 10, 12
Oliver, Murray 82, 83, 220
Olmstead, Bert 75, 76
O'Meara, Baz 76, 77
O'Neil, Jim 30
O'Neill, Brian 165
O'Ree, Willie 201–202
O'Reilly, Ryan 216
Owen, George 215

Paille, Daniel 186, 187
Pang, Darren 173
Parent, Bernie 207
Pastrnak, David 93, 212, 223
Patrick, Craig 124
Patrick, Lester 10, 43
Patrick, Lynn 67, 77, 79
Patrick, Muzz 43
Payne, Steve 157
Pederson, Barry 171–172, 174, 223
"Peggy O'Neil" (song) 30
Peeters, Pete 209, 221
Peirson, Johnny 201, 220
Perry, Bert 22
Perry, Corey 46
Pettinger, Gordie 42
Peverley, Rich 194
Phaneuf, Dion 196
Pietrangelo, Alex 216
Plante, Jacques 130
Polich, Mike 159–160
Poulin, Dave 177, 181, 182
Powers, John 137, 138
Prentice, Dean 81–84, 87, 220
Primeau, Joe 30–31
Providence Reds (hockey club) 141, 142, 199

Provost, Claude 102, 103, 105
Pulford, Bob 118

Quackenbush, Bill 76, 77
Quenneville, Joel 211
Quinn, Pat 90–91, 92

Ralby, Herb 64
Reay, Billy 76, 77, 108, 112
Redmond, Dick 123, 160, 162
Redmond, Mickey 99, 100
Reece, Dave 208
Regan, Larry 118, 201
Reid, Lefty 119
Reimer, James 192, 193, 194, 195
Revcroft, Louis 15
Richard, Henri 101
Richard, Maurice 70–79
Richard, Onesime 78
Ripley, Vic 205
Roach, John Ross 9, 10
Roberts, Gordie 158
Rodney, Bryan 186
Rolfe, Dale 129, 132
Rolston, Brian 203
Ronberg, Gary 110–111
Rousseau, Bobby 129, 131, 133
Ruel, Claude 100
Russo, Fred 59
Ryder, Michael 188–189

Samson, Jerome 188, 189
Samsonov, Sergei 223
Samuelsson, Ulf 181, 182
Sandford, Ed 74, 77–78
Sands, Charlie 200
Savard, Denis 173
Savard, Marc 185, 223
Savard, Serge 100, 102
Sawchuk, Terry 72, 78, 219
Scapinello, Ray 166
Schmautz, Bobby 139, 145
Schmidt, Marie 63
Schoenfeld, Jim 165, 166, 168
Secord, Al 150
Seguin, Tyler 192, 195
Selby, Brit 92
Selke, Frank J. 35
Shack, Eddie 83, 99
Shaughnessy, Dan 190. 193, 196, 212, 213
Shaw, Brad 179
Sheppard, Gregg 137, 145, 207
Shero, Fred 149–150, 207
Shill, Bill 201
Shinzawa, Fluto 185, 186, 187, 195
Shmyr, Paul 160
Shore, Aubrey, 18
Sidorkiewicz, Peter 177, 180, 181, 182
Simmons, Don 82, 83, 84, 85, 220
Sittler, Darryl 208

Index

Skov, Art 101, 102, 133
Smith, Alex 15, 32, 199
Smith, Bobby 157, 160
Smith, Clint 41
Smith, Dallas 93, 99, 112, 118, 124, 195
Smith, Gary 117
Smith, Greg 158
Smith, Hooley 198
Smith, Ken 58
Smith, Rick 121, 144, 149
Smythe, Conn 94
Smythe, Stafford 94
Sonmor, Glen 157, 161, 162
Stanfield, Fred 84
Stanley, Allan 84
Stasiuk, Vic 220
Stemkowski, Peter 84
Stewart, Bill 13–17
Stewart, Bob 122
Stubbs, Dave 71
Stumpel, Jozef 203
Sturm, Marco 185
Sullivan, Jim 167
Sweeney, Don 222
Swift, E.M. 168

Talafous, Dean 145
Thelvén, Michael 173
Thomas, Tim 223
Thompson, Paul 9
Thomson, Bill 51
Thornton, Joe 223
Thurrier, Fred 61
Tkaczuk, Walt 130, 133
Toppazzini, Jerry 91, 109, 220
Tremblay, J.C. 101

Tugnutt, Ron 202
Tulsa Oilers (hockey club) 86

Vachon, Rogie 100, 102, 103, 105, 158–159
Vadnais, Carol 121, 122, 123, 125, 132
Vail, Sparky 9
Vaive, Rick 172, 209
Verbeek, Pat 165
Villemure, Gilles 129, 130, 133

Waite, Jimmy 172, 173
Walsh, Kevin 125
Walton, Mike 125, 131
Ward, Cam 186, 187
Warwick, Grant 56
Watt, Tom 172
Webb, Melville K. 21
Weiland, Cooney 28, 34, 136, 215
Wells, John 169
Wensink, John 150
Wesley, Glen 167, 172, 180
Wheeler, Blake 187, 188
Wicks, Ron 117
Wideman, Dennis 187
Wiemer, Jim 179, 180
Winkler, Hal 215
Wirtz, William W. 167
Worsley, Gump 99, 100, 105

Young, Gerry 122
Young, Gordon 75
Young, Tim 144, 145
Younghans, Tom 157, 158

Zanussi, Ron 159, 160
Ziegler, John 153, 154, 166, 168, 169

www.ingramcontent.com/pod-product-compliance
Ingram Content Group UK Ltd.
Pitfield, Milton Keynes, MK11 3LW, UK
UKHW041940140426
5217IPUK00014B/581